T&P BOOKS

ARABIC
VOCABULARY

FOR ENGLISH SPEAKERS

ENGLISH-
ARABIC

The most useful words
To expand your lexicon and sharpen
your language skills

7000 words

Arabic vocabulary for English speakers - 7000 words

By Andrey Taranov

T&P Books vocabularies are intended for helping you learn, memorize and review foreign words. The dictionary is divided into themes, covering all major spheres of everyday activities, business, science, culture, etc.

The process of learning words using T&P Books' theme-based dictionaries gives you the following advantages:

- Correctly grouped source information predetermines success at subsequent stages of word memorization
- Availability of words derived from the same root allowing memorization of word units (rather than separate words)
- Small units of words facilitate the process of establishing associative links needed for consolidation of vocabulary
- Level of language knowledge can be estimated by the number of learned words

T&P Books Publishing
www.tpbooks.com

ISBN: 978-1-78716-701-8

This book is also available in E-book formats.
Please visit www.tpbooks.com or the major online bookstores.

ARABIC VOCABULARY
for English speakers

T&P Books vocabularies are intended to help you learn, memorize, and review foreign words. The vocabulary contains over 7000 commonly used words arranged thematically.

- Vocabulary contains the most commonly used words
- Recommended as an addition to any language course
- Meets the needs of beginners and advanced learners of foreign languages
- Convenient for daily use, revision sessions, and self-testing activities
- Allows you to assess your vocabulary

Special features of the vocabulary

- Words are organized according to their meaning, not alphabetically
- Words are presented in three columns to facilitate the reviewing and self-testing processes
- Words in groups are divided into small blocks to facilitate the learning process
- The vocabulary offers a convenient and simple transcription of each foreign word

The vocabulary has 198 topics including:

Basic Concepts, Numbers, Colors, Months, Seasons, Units of Measurement, Clothing & Accessories, Food & Nutrition, Restaurant, Family Members, Relatives, Character, Feelings, Emotions, Diseases, City, Town, Sightseeing, Shopping, Money, House, Home, Office, Working in the Office, Import & Export, Marketing, Job Search, Sports, Education, Computer, Internet, Tools, Nature, Countries, Nationalities and more ...

T&P BOOKS' THEME-BASED DICTIONARIES

The Correct System for Memorizing Foreign Words

Acquiring vocabulary is one of the most important elements of learning a foreign language, because words allow us to express our thoughts, ask questions, and provide answers. An inadequate vocabulary can impede communication with a foreigner and make it difficult to understand a book or movie well.

The pace of activity in all spheres of modern life, including the learning of modern languages, has increased. Today, we need to memorize large amounts of information (grammar rules, foreign words, etc.) within a short period. However, this does not need to be difficult. All you need to do is to choose the right training materials, learn a few special techniques, and develop your individual training system.

Having a system is critical to the process of language learning. Many people fail to succeed in this regard; they cannot master a foreign language because they fail to follow a system comprised of selecting materials, organizing lessons, arranging new words to be learned, and so on. The lack of a system causes confusion and eventually, lowers self-confidence.

T&P Books' theme-based dictionaries can be included in the list of elements needed for creating an effective system for learning foreign words. These dictionaries were specially developed for learning purposes and are meant to help students effectively memorize words and expand their vocabulary.

Generally speaking, the process of learning words consists of three main elements:

- Reception (creation or acquisition) of a training material, such as a word list
- Work aimed at memorizing new words
- Work aimed at reviewing the learned words, such as self-testing

All three elements are equally important since they determine the quality of work and the final result. All three processes require certain skills and a well-thought-out approach.

New words are often encountered quite randomly when learning a foreign language and it may be difficult to include them all in a unified list. As a result, these words remain written on scraps of paper, in book margins, textbooks, and so on. In order to systematize such words, we have to create and continually update a "book of new words." A paper notebook, a netbook, or a tablet PC can be used for these purposes.

This "book of new words" will be your personal, unique list of words. However, it will only contain the words that you came across during the learning process. For example, you might have written down the words "Sunday," "Tuesday," and "Friday." However, there are additional words for days of the week, for example, "Saturday," that are missing, and your list of words would be incomplete. Using a theme dictionary, in addition to the "book of new words," is a reasonable solution to this problem.

The theme-based dictionary may serve as the basis for expanding your vocabulary.

It will be your big "book of new words" containing the most frequently used words of a foreign language already included. There are quite a few theme-based dictionaries available, and you should ensure that you make the right choice in order to get the maximum benefit from your purchase.

Therefore, we suggest using theme-based dictionaries from T&P Books Publishing as an aid to learning foreign words. Our books are specially developed for effective use in the sphere of vocabulary systematization, expansion and review.

Theme-based dictionaries are not a magical solution to learning new words. However, they can serve as your main database to aid foreign-language acquisition. Apart from theme dictionaries, you can have copybooks for writing down new words, flash cards, glossaries for various texts, as well as other resources; however, a good theme dictionary will always remain your primary collection of words.

T&P Books' theme-based dictionaries are specialty books that contain the most frequently used words in a language.

The main characteristic of such dictionaries is the division of words into themes. For example, the *City* theme contains the words "street," "crossroads," "square," "fountain," and so on. The *Talking* theme might contain words like "to talk," "to ask," "question," and "answer".

All the words in a theme are divided into smaller units, each comprising 3–5 words. Such an arrangement improves the perception of words and makes the learning process less tiresome. Each unit contains a selection of words with similar meanings or identical roots. This allows you to learn words in small groups and establish other associative links that have a positive effect on memorization.

The words on each page are placed in three columns: a word in your native language, its translation, and its transcription. Such positioning allows for the use of techniques for effective memorization. After closing the translation column, you can flip through and review foreign words, and vice versa. "This is an easy and convenient method of review – one that we recommend you do often."

Our theme-based dictionaries contain transcriptions for all the foreign words. Unfortunately, none of the existing transcriptions are able to convey the exact nuances of foreign pronunciation. That is why we recommend using the transcriptions only as a supplementary learning aid. Correct pronunciation can only be acquired with the help of sound. Therefore our collection includes audio theme-based dictionaries.

The process of learning words using T&P Books' theme-based dictionaries gives you the following advantages:

- You have correctly grouped source information, which predetermines your success at subsequent stages of word memorization
- Availability of words derived from the same root (lazy, lazily, lazybones), allowing you to memorize word units instead of separate words
- Small units of words facilitate the process of establishing associative links needed for consolidation of vocabulary
- You can estimate the number of learned words and hence your level of language knowledge
- The dictionary allows for the creation of an effective and high-quality revision process
- You can revise certain themes several times, modifying the revision methods and techniques
- Audio versions of the dictionaries help you to work out the pronunciation of words and develop your skills of auditory word perception

The T&P Books' theme-based dictionaries are offered in several variants differing in the number of words: 1.500, 3.000, 5.000, 7.000, and 9.000 words. There are also dictionaries containing 15,000 words for some language combinations. Your choice of dictionary will depend on your knowledge level and goals.

We sincerely believe that our dictionaries will become your trusty assistant in learning foreign languages and will allow you to easily acquire the necessary vocabulary.

TABLE OF CONTENTS

PRONUNCIATION GUIDE

T&P phonetic alphabet	Arabic example	English example
[a]	طَفَّى [ṭaffa]	shorter than in ask
[ā]	إِخْتَار [iχtār]	calf, palm
[e]	هامبورجر [hamburger]	elm, medal
[i]	زِفاف [zifāf]	shorter than in feet
[ī]	أبريل [abrīl]	feet, meter
[u]	كلكتا [kalkutta]	book
[ū]	جاموس [ʒāmūs]	fuel, tuna
[b]	بِداية [bidāya]	baby, book
[d]	سَعادة [saʿāda]	day, doctor
[ḍ]	وضع [waḍʾ]	[d] pharyngeal
[ʒ]	الأرجنتين [arʒantīn]	forge, pleasure
[ð]	تذكار [tiðkār]	pharyngealized th
[ẓ]	ظَهر [ẓahar]	[z] pharyngeal
[f]	خفيف [χafīf]	face, food
[g]	جولف [gūlf]	game, gold
[h]	إتّجاه [ittiʒāh]	home, have
[ḥ]	أَحبّ [aḥabb]	[h] pharyngeal
[y]	ذهبيّ [ðahabiy]	yes, New York
[k]	كرسيّ [kursiy]	clock, kiss
[l]	لمح [lamaḥ]	lace, people
[m]	مرصد [marṣad]	magic, milk
[n]	جنوب [ʒanūb]	sang, thing
[p]	كابتشينو [kaputʃīnu]	pencil, private
[q]	وثق [waθiq]	king, club
[r]	روح [rūḥ]	rice, radio
[s]	سخريّة [suχriyya]	city, boss
[ṣ]	معصم [miʿṣam]	[s] pharyngeal
[ʃ]	عشاء [ʿaʃāʾ]	machine, shark
[t]	تنّوب [tannūb]	tourist, trip
[ṭ]	خريطة [χarīṭa]	[t] pharyngeal
[θ]	ماموث [mamūθ]	month, tooth
[v]	فيتنام [vitnām]	very, river
[w]	ودّع [waddaʾ]	vase, winter
[χ]	بخيل [baχīl]	as in Scots 'loch'
[ɣ]	تغدَى [taɣadda]	between [g] and [h]
[z]	ماعز [māʿiz]	zebra, please

T&P phonetic alphabet	Arabic example	English example
['] (ayn)	سبعة [sab'a]	voiced pharyngeal fricative
['] (hamza)	سأل [sa'al]	glottal stop

ABBREVIATIONS
used in the vocabulary

Arabic abbreviations

du	-	plural noun (double)
f	-	feminine noun
m	-	masculine noun
pl	-	plural

English abbreviations

ab.	-	about
adj	-	adjective
adv	-	adverb
anim.	-	animate
as adj	-	attributive noun used as adjective
e.g.	-	for example
etc.	-	et cetera
fam.	-	familiar
fem.	-	feminine
form.	-	formal
inanim.	-	inanimate
masc.	-	masculine
math	-	mathematics
mil.	-	military
n	-	noun
pl	-	plural
pron.	-	pronoun
sb	-	somebody
sing.	-	singular
sth	-	something
v aux	-	auxiliary verb
vi	-	intransitive verb
vi, vt	-	intransitive, transitive verb
vt	-	transitive verb

BASIC CONCEPTS

Basic concepts. Part 1

1. Pronouns

I, me	ana	أنا
you (masc.)	anta	أنت
you (fem.)	anti	أنت
he	huwa	هو
she	hiya	هي
we	naḥnu	نحن
you (to a group)	antum	أنتم
they	hum	هم

2. Greetings. Salutations. Farewells

Hello! (form.)	as salāmu 'alaykum!	السلام عليكم!
Good morning!	ṣabāḥ al ҳayr!	صباح الخير!
Good afternoon!	nahārak sa'īd!	نهارك سعيد!
Good evening!	masā' al ҳayr!	مساء الخير!
to say hello	sallam	سلّم
Hi! (hello)	salām!	سلام!
greeting (n)	salām (m)	سلام
to greet (vt)	sallam 'ala	سلّم على
How are you?	kayfa ḥāluka?	كيف حالك؟
What's new?	ma aҳbārak?	ما أخبارك؟
Bye-Bye! Goodbye!	ma' as salāma!	مع السلامة!
See you soon!	ilal liqā'!	إلى اللقاء!
Farewell!	ma' as salāma!	مع السلامة!
to say goodbye	wadda'	ودّع
So long!	bay bay!	باي باي!
Thank you!	ʃukran!	شكرًا!
Thank you very much!	ʃukran ʒazīlan!	شكرًا جزيلًا!
You're welcome	'afwan	عفوا
Don't mention it!	la ʃukr 'ala wāʒib	لا شكر على واجب
It was nothing	al 'afw	العفو
Excuse me! (fam.)	'an iðnak!	عن أذنك!
Excuse me! (form.)	'afwan!	عفوًا!

to excuse (forgive)	ʻaðar	عذر
to apologize (vi)	iʻtaðar	إعتذر
My apologies	ana ʼāsif	أنا آسف
I'm sorry!	la tuʼāҳiðni!	لا تؤاخذني!
to forgive (vt)	ʻafa	عفا
please (adv)	min faḍlak	من فضلك

Don't forget!	la tansa!	لا تنس!
Certainly!	ṭabʻan!	طبعاً!
Of course not!	abadan!	أبداً!
Okay! (I agree)	ittafaqna!	إتّفقنا!
That's enough!	kifāya!	كفاية!

3. Cardinal numbers. Part 1

0 zero	ṣifr	صفر
1 one	wāḥid	واحد
1 one (fem.)	wāḥida	واحدة
2 two	iθnān	إثنان
3 three	θalāθa	ثلاثة
4 four	arbaʻa	أربعة

5 five	ҳamsa	خمسة
6 six	sitta	ستّة
7 seven	sabʻa	سبعة
8 eight	θamāniya	ثمانية
9 nine	tisʻa	تسعة

10 ten	ʻaʃara	عشرة
11 eleven	aḥad ʻaʃar	أحد عشر
12 twelve	iθnā ʻaʃar	إثنا عشر
13 thirteen	θalāθat ʻaʃar	ثلاثة عشر
14 fourteen	arbaʻat ʻaʃar	أربعة عشر

15 fifteen	ҳamsat ʻaʃar	خمسة عشر
16 sixteen	sittat ʻaʃar	ستّة عشر
17 seventeen	sabʻat ʻaʃar	سبعة عشر
18 eighteen	θamāniyat ʻaʃar	ثمانية عشر
19 nineteen	tisʻat ʻaʃar	تسعة عشر

20 twenty	ʻiʃrūn	عشرون
21 twenty-one	wāḥid wa ʻiʃrūn	واحد وعشرون
22 twenty-two	iθnān wa ʻiʃrūn	إثنان وعشرون
23 twenty-three	θalāθa wa ʻiʃrūn	ثلاثة وعشرون

30 thirty	θalāθīn	ثلاثون
31 thirty-one	wāḥid wa θalāθūn	واحد وثلاثون
32 thirty-two	iθnān wa θalāθūn	إثنان وثلاثون
33 thirty-three	θalāθa wa θalāθūn	ثلاثة وثلاثون
40 forty	arbaʻūn	أربعون

41 forty-one	wāḥid wa arba'ūn	واحد وأربعون
42 forty-two	iθnān wa arba'ūn	إثنان وأربعون
43 forty-three	θalāθa wa arba'ūn	ثلاثة وأربعون

50 fifty	χamsūn	خمسون
51 fifty-one	wāḥid wa χamsūn	واحد وخمسون
52 fifty-two	iθnān wa χamsūn	إثنان وخمسون
53 fifty-three	θalāθa wa χamsūn	ثلاثة وخمسون

60 sixty	sittūn	ستّون
61 sixty-one	wāḥid wa sittūn	واحد وستّون
62 sixty-two	iθnān wa sittūn	إثنان وستّون
63 sixty-three	θalāθa wa sittūn	ثلاثة وستّون

70 seventy	sab'ūn	سبعون
71 seventy-one	wāḥid wa sab'ūn	واحد وسبعون
72 seventy-two	iθnān wa sab'ūn	إثنان وسبعون
73 seventy-three	θalāθa wa sab'ūn	ثلاثة وسبعون

80 eighty	θamānūn	ثمانون
81 eighty-one	wāḥid wa θamānūn	واحد وثمانون
82 eighty-two	iθnān wa θamānūn	إثنان وثمانون
83 eighty-three	θalāθa wa θamānūn	ثلاثة وثمانون

90 ninety	tis'ūn	تسعون
91 ninety-one	wāḥid wa tis'ūn	واحد وتسعون
92 ninety-two	iθnān wa tis'ūn	إثنان وتسعون
93 ninety-three	θalāθa wa tis'ūn	ثلاثة وتسعون

4. Cardinal numbers. Part 2

100 one hundred	mi'a	مائة
200 two hundred	mi'atān	مائتان
300 three hundred	θalāθumi'a	ثلاثمائة
400 four hundred	rub'umi'a	أربعمائة
500 five hundred	χamsumi'a	خمسمائة

600 six hundred	sittumi'a	ستّمائة
700 seven hundred	sab'umi'a	سبعمائة
800 eight hundred	θamānimi'a	ثمانمائة
900 nine hundred	tis'umi'a	تسعمائة

1000 one thousand	alf	ألف
2000 two thousand	alfān	ألفان
3000 three thousand	θalāθat 'ālāf	ثلاثة آلاف
10000 ten thousand	'aʃarat 'ālāf	عشرة آلاف
one hundred thousand	mi'at alf	مائة ألف

| million | milyūn (m) | مليون |
| billion | milyār (m) | مليار |

5. Numbers. Fractions

fraction	kasr (m)	كسر
one half	niṣf	نصف
one third	θulθ	ثلث
one quarter	rub'	ربع
one eighth	θumn	ثمن
one tenth	'uʃr	عشر
two thirds	θulθān	ثلثان
three quarters	talātit arbā'	ثلاثة أرباع

6. Numbers. Basic operations

subtraction	ṭarḥ (m)	طرح
to subtract (vi, vt)	ṭaraḥ	طرح
division	qisma (f)	قسمة
to divide (vt)	qasam	قسم
addition	ʒam' (m)	جمع
to add up (vt)	ʒama'	جمع
to add (vi, vt)	ʒama'	جمع
multiplication	ḍarb (m)	ضرب
to multiply (vt)	ḍarab	ضرب

7. Numbers. Miscellaneous

digit, figure	raqm (m)	رقم
number	'adad (m)	عدد
numeral	ism al 'adad (m)	إسم العدد
minus sign	nāqiṣ (m)	ناقص
plus sign	zā'id (m)	زائد
formula	ṣīɣa (f)	صيغة
calculation	ḥisāb (m)	حساب
to count (vi, vt)	'add	عدّ
to count up	ḥasab	حسب
to compare (vt)	qāran	قارن
How much?	kam?	كم؟
sum, total	maʒmū' (m)	مجموع
result	natīʒa (f)	نتيجة
remainder	al bāqi (m)	الباقي
a few (e.g., ~ years ago)	'iddat	عدّة
little (I had ~ time)	qalīl	قليل
the rest	al bāqi (m)	الباقي

| one and a half | wāḥid wa niṣf (m) | واحد ونصف |
| dozen | iθnā 'aʃar (f) | إثنا عشر |

in half (adv)	ila ʃaṭrayn	إلى شطرين
equally (evenly)	bit tasāwi	بالتساوى
half	niṣf (m)	نصف
time (three ~s)	marra (f)	مرَّة

8. The most important verbs. Part 1

to advise (vt)	naṣaḥ	نصح
to agree (say yes)	ittafaq	إتَفق
to answer (vi, vt)	aʒāb	أجاب
to apologize (vi)	i'taðar	إعتذر
to arrive (vi)	waṣal	وصل

to ask (~ oneself)	sa'al	سأل
to ask (~ sb to do sth)	ṭalab	طلب
to be (vi)	kān	كان

to be afraid	χāf	خاف
to be hungry	arād an ya'kul	أراد أن يأكل
to be interested in …	ihtamm	إهتمَ
to be needed	kān maṭlūb	كان مطلوبا
to be surprised	indahaʃ	إندهش
to be thirsty	arād an yaʃrab	أراد أن يشرب
to begin (vt)	bada'	بدأ
to belong to …	χaṣṣ	خصَ
to boast (vi)	tabāha	تباهى
to break (split into pieces)	kasar	كسر

to call (~ for help)	istaɣāθ	إستغاث
can (v aux)	istaṭā'	إستطاع
to catch (vt)	amsak	أمسك
to change (vt)	ɣayyar	غيَر
to choose (select)	iχtār	إختار

to come down (the stairs)	nazil	نزل
to compare (vt)	qāran	قارن
to complain (vi, vt)	ʃaka	شكا
to confuse (mix up)	iχtalaṭ	إختلط
to continue (vt)	istamarr	إستمرَ
to control (vt)	taḥakkam	تحكَم

to cook (dinner)	ḥaḍḍar	حضَر
to cost (vt)	kallaf	كلَف
to count (add up)	'add	عدَ
to count on …	i'tamad 'ala …	إعتمد على…
to create (vt)	χalaq	خلق
to cry (weep)	baka	بكى

9. The most important verbs. Part 2

to deceive (vi, vt)	χadaʿ	خدع
to decorate (tree, street)	zayyan	زيّن
to defend (a country, etc.)	dāfaʿ	دافع
to demand (request firmly)	ṭālib	طالب
to dig (vt)	ḥafar	حفر
to discuss (vt)	nāqaʃ	ناقش
to do (vt)	ʿamal	عمل
to doubt (have doubts)	ʃakk fi	شكّ في
to drop (let fall)	awqaʿ	أوقع
to enter (room, house, etc.)	daχal	دخل
to exist (vi)	kān mawʒūd	كان موجودًا
to expect (foresee)	tanabba'	تنبّأ
to explain (vt)	ʃaraḥ	شرح
to fall (vi)	saqaṭ	سقط
to find (vt)	waʒad	وجد
to finish (vt)	atamm	أتمّ
to fly (vi)	ṭār	طار
to follow ... (come after)	tabaʿ	تبع
to forget (vi, vt)	nasiy	نسي
to forgive (vt)	ʿafa	عفا
to give (vt)	aʿṭa	أعطى
to give a hint	aʿṭa talmīḥ	أعطى تلميحًا
to go (on foot)	maʃa	مشى
to go for a swim	sabaḥ	سبح
to go out (for dinner, etc.)	χaraʒ	خرج
to guess (the answer)	χamman	خمّن
to have (vt)	malak	ملك
to have breakfast	afṭar	أفطر
to have dinner	taʿaʃʃa	تعشّى
to have lunch	taɣadda	تغدّى
to hear (vt)	samiʿ	سمع
to help (vt)	sāʿad	ساعد
to hide (vt)	χaba'	خبّأ
to hope (vi, vt)	tamanna	تمنّى
to hunt (vi, vt)	iṣṭād	إصطاد
to hurry (vi)	istaʿʒal	إستعجل

10. The most important verbs. Part 3

to inform (vt)	aχbar	أخبر
to insist (vi, vt)	aṣarr	أصرّ

to insult (vt)	ahān	أهان
to invite (vt)	da'a	دعا
to joke (vi)	mazaḥ	مزح
to keep (vt)	ḥafaẓ	حفظ
to keep silent	sakat	سكت
to kill (vt)	qatal	قتل
to know (sb)	'araf	عرف
to know (sth)	'araf	عرف
to laugh (vi)	ḍaḥik	ضحك
to liberate (city, etc.)	ḥarrar	حرّر
to like (I like …)	a'ʒab	أعجب
to look for … (search)	baḥaθ	بحث
to love (sb)	aḥabb	أحبّ
to make a mistake	axṭa'	أخطأ
to manage, to run	adār	أدار
to mean (signify)	'ana	عنى
to mention (talk about)	ðakar	ذكر
to miss (school, etc.)	ɣāb	غاب
to notice (see)	lāḥaẓ	لاحظ
to object (vi, vt)	i'taraḍ	إعترض
to observe (see)	rāqab	راقب
to open (vt)	fataḥ	فتح
to order (meal, etc.)	ṭalab	طلب
to order (mil.)	amar	أمر
to own (possess)	malak	ملك
to participate (vi)	iʃtarak	إشترك
to pay (vi, vt)	dafa'	دفع
to permit (vt)	raxxaṣ	رخّص
to plan (vt)	xaṭṭaṭ	خطّط
to play (children)	la'ib	لعب
to pray (vi, vt)	ṣalla	صلّى
to prefer (vt)	faḍḍal	فضّل
to promise (vt)	wa'ad	وعد
to pronounce (vt)	naṭaq	نطق
to propose (vt)	iqtaraḥ	إقترح
to punish (vt)	'āqab	عاقب

11. The most important verbs. Part 4

to read (vi, vt)	qara'	قرأ
to recommend (vt)	naṣaḥ	نصح
to refuse (vi, vt)	rafaḍ	رفض
to regret (be sorry)	nadim	ندم
to rent (sth from sb)	ista'ʒar	إستأجر

to repeat (say again)	karrar	كرّر
to reserve, to book	ḥaʒaz	حجز
to run (vi)	ʒara	جرى
to save (rescue)	anqað	أنقذ
to say (~ thank you)	qāl	قال

to scold (vt)	wabbaχ	وبّخ
to see (vt)	ra'a	رأى
to sell (vt)	bāʿ	باع
to send (vt)	arsal	أرسل
to shoot (vi)	aṭlaq an nār	أطلق النار

to shout (vi)	ṣaraχ	صرخ
to show (vt)	ʿaraḍ	عرض
to sign (document)	waqqaʿ	وقّع
to sit down (vi)	ʒalas	جلس

to smile (vi)	ibtasam	إبتسم
to speak (vi, vt)	takallam	تكلّم
to steal (money, etc.)	saraq	سرق
to stop (for pause, etc.)	waqaf	وقف
to stop (please ~ calling me)	tawaqqaf	توقّف

to study (vt)	daras	درس
to swim (vi)	sabaḥ	سبح
to take (vt)	aχað	أخذ
to think (vi, vt)	ẓann	ظنّ
to threaten (vt)	haddad	هدّد

to touch (with hands)	lamas	لمس
to translate (vt)	tarʒam	ترجم
to trust (vt)	waθiq	وثق
to try (attempt)	ḥāwal	حاول
to turn (e.g., ~ left)	in'aṭaf	إنعطف

to underestimate (vt)	istaχaff	إستخفّ
to understand (vt)	fahim	فهم
to unite (vt)	waḥḥad	وحّد
to wait (vt)	intaẓar	إنتظر

to want (wish, desire)	arād	أراد
to warn (vt)	ḥaððar	حذّر
to work (vi)	ʿamal	عمل
to write (vt)	katab	كتب
to write down	katab	كتب

12. Colors

| color | lawn (m) | لون |
| shade (tint) | daraʒat al lawn (m) | درجة اللون |

| hue | ṣabɣit lūn (f) | لون |
| rainbow | qaws quzaḥ (m) | قوس قزح |

white (adj)	abyaḍ	أبيض
black (adj)	aswad	أسود
gray (adj)	ramādiy	رماديَ

green (adj)	aχdar	أخضر
yellow (adj)	aṣfar	أصفر
red (adj)	aḥmar	أحمر

blue (adj)	azraq	أزرق
light blue (adj)	azraq fātiḥ	أزرق فاتح
pink (adj)	wardiy	ورديَ
orange (adj)	burtuqāliy	برتقاليَ
violet (adj)	banafsaʒiy	بنفسجيَ
brown (adj)	bunniy	بنّيَ

| golden (adj) | ðahabiy | ذهبيَ |
| silvery (adj) | fiḍḍiy | فضيَ |

beige (adj)	bɛ:ʒ	بيج
cream (adj)	ʿāʒiy	عاجيَ
turquoise (adj)	fayrūziy	فيروزيَ
cherry red (adj)	karaziy	كرزيَ
lilac (adj)	laylakiy	ليلكيَ
crimson (adj)	qirmiziy	قرمزيَ

light (adj)	fātiḥ	فاتح
dark (adj)	ɣāmiq	غامق
bright, vivid (adj)	zāhi	زاه

colored (pencils)	mulawwan	ملوَن
color (e.g., ~ film)	mulawwan	ملوَن
black-and-white (adj)	abyaḍ wa aswad	أبيض وأسود
plain (one-colored)	waḥīd al lawn, sāda	وحيد اللون, سادة
multicolored (adj)	mutaʿaddid al alwān	متعدَد الألوان

13. Questions

Who?	man?	من؟
What?	māða?	ماذا؟
Where? (at, in)	ayna?	أين؟
Where (to)?	ila ayna?	إلى أين؟
From where?	min ayna?	من أين؟
When?	mata?	متى؟
Why? (What for?)	li māða?	لماذا؟
Why? (~ are you crying?)	li māða?	لماذا؟
What for?	li māða?	لماذا؟
How? (in what way)	kayfa?	كيف؟

What? (What kind of ...?)	ay?	أي؟
Which?	ay?	أي؟
To whom?	li man?	لمن؟
About whom?	'amman?	عمن؟
About what?	'amma?	عمّا؟
With whom?	ma' man?	مع من؟
How many? How much?	kam?	كم؟
Whose?	li man?	لمن؟

14. Function words. Adverbs. Part 1

Where? (at, in)	ayna?	أين؟
here (adv)	huna	هنا
there (adv)	hunāk	هناك
somewhere (to be)	fi makānin ma	في مكان ما
nowhere (not anywhere)	la fi ay makān	لا في أي مكان
by (near, beside)	bi ʒānib	بجانب
by the window	bi ʒānib aʃ ʃubbāk	بجانب الشبّاك
Where (to)?	ila ayna?	إلى أين؟
here (e.g., come ~!)	huna	هنا
there (e.g., to go ~)	hunāk	هناك
from here (adv)	min huna	من هنا
from there (adv)	min hunāk	من هناك
close (adv)	qarīban	قريبًا
far (adv)	ba'īdan	بعيدًا
near (e.g., ~ Paris)	'ind	عند
nearby (adv)	qarīban	قريبًا
not far (adv)	ɣayr ba'īd	غير بعيد
left (adj)	al yasār	اليسار
on the left	'alaʃ ʃimāl	على الشمال
to the left	ilaʃ ʃimāl	إلى الشمال
right (adj)	al yamīn	اليمين
on the right	'alal yamīn	على اليمين
to the right	llal yamīn	إلى اليمين
in front (adv)	min al amām	من الأمام
front (as adj)	amāmiy	أمامي
ahead (the kids ran ~)	ilal amām	إلى الأمام
behind (adv)	warā'	وراء
from behind	min al warā'	من الوراء

back (towards the rear)	ilal warā'	إلى الوراء
middle	wasaṭ (m)	وسط
in the middle	fil wasat	في الوسط
at the side	bi ʒānib	بجانب
everywhere (adv)	fi kull makān	في كل مكان
around (in all directions)	ḥawl	حَول
from inside	min ad dāχil	من الداخل
somewhere (to go)	ila ayy makān	إلى أيَّ مكان
straight (directly)	bi aqsar ṭarīq	بأقصر طريق
back (e.g., come ~)	īyāban	إيابًا
from anywhere	min ayy makān	من أي مكان
from somewhere	min makānin ma	من مكان ما
firstly (adv)	awwalan	أوَّلَا
secondly (adv)	θāniyan	ثانيًا
thirdly (adv)	θāliθan	ثالثًا
suddenly (adv)	faʒ'a	فجأة
at first (in the beginning)	fil bidāya	في البداية
for the first time	li 'awwal marra	لأوَّل مرَّة
long before ...	qabl ... bi mudda ṭawīla	قبل...بمدَّة طويلة
anew (over again)	min ʒadīd	من جديد
for good (adv)	ilal abad	إلى الأبد
never (adv)	abadan	أبدًا
again (adv)	min ʒadīd	من جديد
now (adv)	al 'ān	الآن
often (adv)	kaθīran	كثيرًا
then (adv)	fi ðalika al waqt	في ذلك الوقت
urgently (quickly)	'āʒilan	عاجلَا
usually (adv)	kal 'āda	كالعادة
by the way, ...	'ala fikra ...	على فكرة...
possible (that is ~)	min al mumkin	من الممكن
probably (adv)	la'alla	لعلَّ
maybe (adv)	min al mumkin	من الممكن
besides ...	bil iḍāfa ila ðalik ...	بالإضافة إلى...
that's why ...	li ðalik	لذلك
in spite of ...	bir raγm min ...	بالرغم من...
thanks to ...	bi faḍl ...	بفضل...
what (pron.)	allaði	الذي
that (conj.)	anna	أنَّ
something	ʃay' (m)	شيء
anything (something)	ʃay' (m)	شيء
nothing	la ʃay'	لا شيء
who (pron.)	allaði	الذي
someone	aḥad	أحد

somebody	aḥad	أحد
nobody	la aḥad	لا أحد
nowhere (a voyage to ~)	la ila ay makān	لا إلى أي مكان
nobody's	la yaχuṣṣ aḥad	لا يخص أحداً
somebody's	li aḥad	لأحد

so (I'm ~ glad)	hakaða	هكذا
also (as well)	kaðalika	كذلك
too (as well)	ayḍan	أيضًا

15. Function words. Adverbs. Part 2

Why?	li māða?	لماذا؟
for some reason	li sababin ma	لسبب ما
because ...	li'anna ...	لأنّ...
for some purpose	li amr mā	لأمر ما

and	wa	و
or	aw	أو
but	lakin	لكن
for (e.g., ~ me)	li	لِ

too (~ many people)	kaθīran ʒiddan	كثير جدًا
only (exclusively)	faqaṭ	فقط
exactly (adv)	biḍ ḍabṭ	بالضبط
about (more or less)	naḥw	نحو

approximately (adv)	taqrīban	تقريبًا
approximate (adj)	taqrībiy	تقريبي
almost (adv)	taqrīban	تقريبًا
the rest	al bāqi (m)	الباقي

each (adj)	kull	كلّ
any (no matter which)	ayy	أيّ
many, much (a lot of)	kaθīr	كثير
many people	kaθīr min an nās	كثير من الناس
all (everyone)	kull an nās	كل الناس

in return for ...	muqābil ...	مقابل...
in exchange (adv)	muqābil	مقابل
by hand (made)	bil yad	باليد
hardly (negative opinion)	hayhāt	هيهات

probably (adv)	la'alla	لعلّ
on purpose (intentionally)	qaṣdan	قصدا
by accident (adv)	ṣudfa	صدفة

very (adv)	ʒiddan	جدًا
for example (adv)	maθalan	مثلا
between	bayn	بين

among	bayn	بين
so much (such a lot)	haðihi al kammiyya	هذه الكمية
especially (adv)	χāṣṣa	خاصّة

Basic concepts. Part 2

16. Weekdays

Monday	yawm al iθnayn (m)	يوم الإثنين
Tuesday	yawm aθ θulāθā' (m)	يوم الثلاثاء
Wednesday	yawm al arbi'ā' (m)	يوم الأربعاء
Thursday	yawm al χamīs (m)	يوم الخميس
Friday	yawm al ʒum'a (m)	يوم الجمعة
Saturday	yawm as sabt (m)	يوم السبت
Sunday	yawm al aḥad (m)	يوم الأحد
today (adv)	al yawm	اليوم
tomorrow (adv)	γadan	غدًا
the day after tomorrow	ba'd γad	بعد غد
yesterday (adv)	ams	أمس
the day before yesterday	awwal ams	أوّل أمس
day	yawm (m)	يوم
working day	yawm 'amal (m)	يوم عمل
public holiday	yawm al 'uṭla ar rasmiyya (m)	يوم العطلة الرسمية
day off	yawm 'uṭla (m)	يوم عطلة
weekend	ayyām al 'uṭla (pl)	أيام العطلة
all day long	ṭūl al yawm	طول اليوم
the next day (adv)	fil yawm at tāli	في اليوم التالي
two days ago	min yawmayn	قبل يومين
the day before	fil yawm as sābiq	في اليوم السابق
daily (adj)	yawmiy	يومي
every day (adv)	yawmiyyan	يوميًا
week	usbū' (m)	أسبوع
last week (adv)	fil isbū' al māḍi	في الأسبوع الماضي
next week (adv)	fil isbū' al qādim	في الأسبوع القادم
weekly (adj)	usbū'iy	أسبوعي
every week (adv)	usbū'iyyan	أسبوعيًا
twice a week	marratayn fil usbū'	مرّتين في الأسبوع
every Tuesday	kull yawm aθ θulaθā'	كل يوم الثلاثاء

17. Hours. Day and night

morning	ṣabāḥ (m)	صباح
in the morning	fiṣ ṣabāḥ	في الصباح

| noon, midday | ẓuhr (m) | ظهر |
| in the afternoon | ba'd aẓ ẓuhr | بعد الظهر |

evening	masā' (m)	مساء
in the evening	fil masā'	في المساء
night	layl (m)	ليل
at night	bil layl	بالليل
midnight	muntaṣif al layl (m)	منتصف الليل

second	θāniya (f)	ثانية
minute	daqīqa (f)	دقيقة
hour	sā'a (f)	ساعة
half an hour	niṣf sā'a (m)	نصف ساعة
a quarter-hour	rub' sā'a (f)	ربع ساعة
fifteen minutes	xamsat 'aʃar daqīqa	خمس عشرة دقيقة
24 hours	yawm kāmil (m)	يوم كامل

sunrise	ʃurūq aʃ ʃams (m)	شروق الشمس
dawn	faʒr (m)	فجر
early morning	ṣabāḥ bākir (m)	صباح باكر
sunset	ɣurūb aʃ ʃams (m)	غروب الشمس

early in the morning	fis ṣabāḥ al bākir	في الصباح الباكر
this morning	al yawm fiṣ ṣabāḥ	اليوم في الصباح
tomorrow morning	ɣadan fiṣ ṣabāḥ	غدًا في الصباح

this afternoon	al yawm ba'd aẓ ẓuhr	اليوم بعد الظهر
in the afternoon	ba'd aẓ ẓuhr	بعد الظهر
tomorrow afternoon	ɣadan ba'd aẓ ẓuhr	غدًا بعد الظهر

| tonight (this evening) | al yawm fil masā' | اليوم في المساء |
| tomorrow night | ɣadan fil masā' | غدًا في المساء |

at 3 o'clock sharp	fis sā'a aθ θāliθa tamāman	في الساعة الثالثة تماما
about 4 o'clock	fis sā'a ar rābi'a taqrīban	في الساعة الرابعة تقريبا
by 12 o'clock	ḥattas sā'a aθ θāniya 'aʃara	حتى الساعة الثانية عشرة

in 20 minutes	ba'd 'iʃrīn daqīqa	بعد عشرين دقيقة
in an hour	ba'd sā'a	بعد ساعة
on time (adv)	fi maw'idih	في موعده

a quarter of ...	illa rub'	إلا ربع
within an hour	ṭiwāl sā'a	طوال الساعة
every 15 minutes	kull rub' sā'a	كل ربع ساعة
round the clock	layl nahār	ليل نهار

18. Months. Seasons

| January | yanāyir (m) | يناير |
| February | fibrāyir (m) | فبراير |

March	māris (m)	مارس
April	abrīl (m)	أبريل
May	māyu (m)	مايو
June	yūnyu (m)	يونيو

July	yūlyu (m)	يوليو
August	aɣusṭus (m)	أغسطس
September	sibtambar (m)	سبتمبر
October	uktūbir (m)	أكتوبر
November	nuvimbar (m)	نوفمبر
December	disimbar (m)	ديسمبر

spring	rabīʿ (m)	ربيع
in spring	fir rabīʿ	في الربيع
spring (as adj)	rabīʿiy	ربيعي

summer	ṣayf (m)	صيف
in summer	fiṣ ṣayf	في الصيف
summer (as adj)	ṣayfiy	صيفي

fall	xarīf (m)	خريف
in fall	fil xarīf	في الخريف
fall (as adj)	xarīfiy	خريفي

winter	ʃitāʾ (m)	شتاء
in winter	fiʃ ʃitāʾ	في الشتاء
winter (as adj)	ʃitawiy	شتويّ

month	ʃahr (m)	شهر
this month	fi haða aʃ ʃahr	في هذا الشهر
next month	fiʃ ʃahr al qādim	في الشهر القادم
last month	fiʃ ʃahr al māḍi	في الشهر الماضي

a month ago	qabl ʃahr	قبل شهر
in a month (a month later)	baʿd ʃahr	بعد شهر
in 2 months (2 months later)	baʿd ʃahrayn	بعد شهرين
the whole month	ṭūl aʃ ʃahr	طول الشهر
all month long	ʃahr kāmil	شهر كامل

monthly (~ magazine)	ʃahriy	شهريّ
monthly (adv)	kull ʃahr	كل شهر
every month	kull ʃahr	كل شهر
twice a month	marratayn fiʃ ʃahr	مرّتين في الشهر

year	sana (f)	سنة
this year	fi haðihi as sana	في هذه السنة
next year	fis sana al qādima	في السنة القادمة
last year	fis sana al māḍiya	في السنة الماضية

| a year ago | qabla sana | قبل سنة |
| in a year | baʿd sana | بعد سنة |

in two years	ba'd sanatayn	بعد سنتين
the whole year	ṭūl as sana	طول السنة
all year long	sana kāmila	سنة كاملة

every year	kull sana	كل سنة
annual (adj)	sanawiy	سنويّ
annually (adv)	kull sana	كل سنة
4 times a year	arba' marrāt fis sana	أربع مرّات في السنة

date (e.g., today's ~)	tarīχ (m)	تاريخ
date (e.g., ~ of birth)	tarīχ (m)	تاريخ
calendar	taqwīm (m)	تقويم

half a year	niṣf sana (m)	نصف سنة
six months	niṣf sana (m)	نصف سنة
season (summer, etc.)	faṣl (m)	فصل
century	qarn (m)	قرن

19. Time. Miscellaneous

time	waqt (m)	وقت
moment	laḥza (f)	لحظة
instant (n)	laḥza (f)	لحظة
instant (adj)	χāṭif	خاطف
lapse (of time)	fatra (f)	فترة
life	ḥayāt (f)	حياة
eternity	abadiyya (f)	أبديّة

epoch	'ahd (m)	عهد
era	'aṣr (m)	عصر
cycle	dawra (f)	دورة
period	fatra (f)	فترة
term (short-~)	fatra (f)	فترة

the future	al mustaqbal (m)	المستقبل
future (as adj)	qādim	قادم
next time	fil marra al qādima	في المرّة القادمة
the past	al māḍi (m)	الماضي
past (recent)	māḍi	ماض
last time	fil marra al māḍiya	في المرّة الماضية

later (adv)	fima ba'd	فيما بعد
after (prep.)	ba'd	بعد
nowadays (adv)	fi haðihi al ayyām	في هذه الأيام
now (adv)	al 'ān	الآن
immediately (adv)	ḥālan	حالًا
soon (adv)	qarīban	قريبًا
in advance (beforehand)	muqaddaman	مقدّمًا
a long time ago	min zamān	من زمان
recently (adv)	min zaman qarīb	من زمان قريب

destiny	maṣīr (m)	مصير
memories (childhood ~)	ðikra (f)	ذكرى
archives	arʃīf (m)	أرشيف

during ...	aθnā'...	...أثناء
long, a long time (adv)	li mudda ṭawīla	لمدّة طويلة
not long (adv)	li mudda qaṣīra	لمدّة قصيرة
early (in the morning)	bākiran	باكرًا
late (not early)	muta'aχχiran	متأخّرًا

forever (for good)	lil abad	للأبد
to start (begin)	bada'	بدأ
to postpone (vt)	aʒʒal	أجّل

at the same time	fi nafs al waqt	في نفس الوقت
permanently (adv)	dā'iman	دائمًا
constant (noise, pain)	mustamirr	مستمرّ
temporary (adj)	mu'aqqat	مؤقّت

sometimes (adv)	min ḥīn li 'āχar	من حين لآخر
rarely (adv)	nādiran	نادرًا
often (adv)	kaθīran	كثيرًا

20. Opposites

| rich (adj) | ɣaniy | غنيّ |
| poor (adj) | faqīr | فقير |

| ill, sick (adj) | marīḍ | مريض |
| well (not sick) | salīm | سليم |

| big (adj) | kabīr | كبير |
| small (adj) | ṣaɣīr | صغير |

| quickly (adv) | bi sur'a | بسرعة |
| slowly (adv) | bi buṭ' | ببطء |

| fast (adj) | sarī' | سريع |
| slow (adj) | baṭī' | بطيء |

| glad (adj) | farḥān | فرحان |
| sad (adj) | ḥazīn | حزين |

| together (adv) | ma'an | معًا |
| separately (adv) | bi mufradih | بمفرده |

aloud (to read)	bi ṣawt 'āli	بصوت عال
silently (to oneself)	sirran	سرًا
tall (adj)	'āli	عال
low (adj)	munχafiḍ	منخفض

deep (adj)	ʿamīq	عميق
shallow (adj)	ḍaḥl	ضحل
yes	naʿam	نعم
no	la	لا
distant (in space)	baʿīd	بعيد
nearby (adj)	qarīb	قريب
far (adv)	baʿīdan	بعيدًا
nearby (adv)	qarīban	قريبًا
long (adj)	ṭawīl	طويل
short (adj)	qaṣīr	قصير
good (kindhearted)	ṭayyib	طيّب
evil (adj)	ʃarīr	شرير
married (adj)	mutazawwiʒ	متزوّج
single (adj)	aʿzab	أعزب
to forbid (vt)	manaʿ	منع
to permit (vt)	samaḥ	سمح
end	nihāya (f)	نهاية
beginning	bidāya (f)	بداية
left (adj)	al yasār	اليسار
right (adj)	al yamīn	اليمين
first (adj)	awwal	أوّل
last (adj)	ʼāχir	آخر
crime	ʒarīma (f)	جريمة
punishment	ʿuqūba (f), ʿiqāb (m)	عقوبة, عقاب
to order (vt)	amar	أمر
to obey (vi, vt)	ṭāʿ	طاع
straight (adj)	mustaqīm	مستقيم
curved (adj)	munḥani	منحن
paradise	al ʒanna (f)	الجنّة
hell	al ʒaḥīm (f)	الجحيم
to be born	wulid	وُلد
to die (vi)	māt	مات
strong (adj)	qawiy	قويّ
weak (adj)	ḍaʿīf	ضعيف
old (adj)	ʿaʒūz	عجوز
young (adj)	ʃābb	شابّ

| old (adj) | qadīm | قديم |
| new (adj) | ʒadīd | جديد |

| hard (adj) | ṣalb | صلب |
| soft (adj) | ṭariy | طري |

| warm (tepid) | dāfiʾ | دافئ |
| cold (adj) | bārid | بارد |

| fat (adj) | θaxīn | ثخين |
| thin (adj) | naḥīf | نحيف |

| narrow (adj) | ḍayyiq | ضيّق |
| wide (adj) | wāsiʿ | واسع |

| good (adj) | ʒayyid | جيّد |
| bad (adj) | sayyiʾ | سيئ |

| brave (adj) | ʃuʒāʿ | شجاع |
| cowardly (adj) | ʒabān | جبان |

21. Lines and shapes

square	murabbaʿ (m)	مربّع
square (as adj)	murabbaʿ	مربّع
circle	dāʾira (f)	دائرة
round (adj)	mudawwar	مدوّر
triangle	muθallaθ (m)	مثلّث
triangular (adj)	muθallaθ	مثلّث

oval	bayḍawiy (m)	بيضويّ
oval (as adj)	bayḍawiy	بيضويّ
rectangle	mustaṭīl (m)	مستطيل
rectangular (adj)	mustaṭīliy	مستطيليّ

pyramid	haram (m)	هرم
rhombus	muʿayyan (m)	معيّن
trapezoid	murabbaʿ munḥarif (m)	مربّع منحرف
cube	mukaʿʿab (m)	مكعّب
prism	manʃūr (m)	منشور

circumference	muḥīṭ munḥanan muɣlaq (m)	محيط منحنى مغلق
sphere	kura (f)	كرة
ball (solid sphere)	kura (f)	كرة
diameter	quṭr (m)	قطر
radius	niṣf qaṭr (m)	نصف قطر
perimeter (circle's ~)	muḥīṭ (m)	محيط
center	wasaṭ (m)	وسط
horizontal (adj)	ufuqiy	أفقيّ

vertical (adj)	ʿamūdiy	عَمُودِيّ
parallel (n)	χaṭṭ mutawāzi (m)	خَطّ مُتَوَازٍ
parallel (as adj)	mutawāzi	مُتَوَازٍ
line	χaṭṭ (m)	خَطّ
stroke	ḥaraka (m)	حَرَكَة
straight line	χaṭṭ mustaqīm (m)	خَطّ مُسْتَقِيم
curve (curved line)	χaṭṭ munḥani (m)	خَطّ مُنْحَنٍ
thin (line, etc.)	rafīʿ	رَقِيع
contour (outline)	kuntūr (m)	كِنْتُور
intersection	taqāṭuʿ (m)	تَقَاطُع
right angle	zāwya mustaqīma (f)	زَاوِيَة مُسْتَقِيمَة
segment	qiṭʿa (f)	قِطْعَة
sector	qiṭāʿ (m)	قِطَاع
side (of triangle)	ḍilʿ (m)	ضِلْع
angle	zāwiya (f)	زَاوِيَة

22. Units of measurement

weight	wazn (m)	وَزْن
length	ṭūl (m)	طُول
width	ʿarḍ (m)	عَرْض
height	irtifāʿ (m)	إرْتِفَاع
depth	ʿumq (m)	عُمْق
volume	ḥaʒm (m)	حَجْم
area	misāḥa (f)	مِسَاحَة
gram	grām (m)	جِرَام
milligram	milliɣrām (m)	مِلِّيغْرَام
kilogram	kiluɣrām (m)	كِيلُوغْرَام
ton	ṭunn (m)	طُنّ
pound	raṭl (m)	رَطْل
ounce	ūnṣa (f)	أُونْصَة
meter	mitr (m)	مِتْر
millimeter	millimitr (m)	مِلِّيمِتْر
centimeter	santimitr (m)	سِنْتِيمِتْر
kilometer	kilumitr (m)	كِيلُومِتْر
mile	mīl (m)	مِيل
inch	būṣa (f)	بُوصَة
foot	qadam (f)	قَدَم
yard	yārda (f)	يَارْدَة
square meter	mitr murabbaʿ (m)	مِتْر مُرَبَّع
hectare	hiktār (m)	هِكْتَار
liter	litr (m)	لِتْر
degree	daraʒa (f)	دَرَجَة

volt	vūlt (m)	فولت
ampere	ambīr (m)	أمبير
horsepower	ḥiṣān (m)	حصان
quantity	kammiyya (f)	كمِّيَة
a little bit of ...	qalīl ...	قليل...
half	niṣf (m)	نصف
dozen	iθnā 'aʃar (f)	إثنا عشر
piece (item)	waḥda (f)	وحدة
size	ḥaჳm (m)	حجم
scale (map ~)	miqyās (m)	مقياس
minimal (adj)	al adna	الأدنى
the smallest (adj)	al aṣɣar	الأصغر
medium (adj)	mutawassiṭ	متوسَّط
maximal (adj)	al aqṣa	الأقصى
the largest (adj)	al akbar	الأكبر

23. Containers

canning jar (glass ~)	barṭamān (m)	برطمان
can	tanaka (f)	تنكة
bucket	ჳardal (m)	جردل
barrel	barmīl (m)	برميل
wash basin (e.g., plastic ~)	ḥawḍ lil ɣasīl (m)	حوض للغسيل
tank (100L water ~)	χazzān (m)	خزّان
hip flask	zamzamiyya (f)	زمزمِيَة
jerrycan	ჳirikan (m)	جركن
tank (e.g., tank car)	χazzān (m)	خزّان
mug	māgg (m)	ماجَ
cup (of coffee, etc.)	finჳān (m)	فنجان
saucer	ṭabaq finჳān (m)	طبق فنجان
glass (tumbler)	kubbāya (f)	كبّاية
wine glass	ka's (f)	كأس
stock pot (soup pot)	kassirūlla (f)	كاسرولة
bottle (~ of wine)	zuჳāჳa (f)	زجاجة
neck (of the bottle, etc.)	'unq (m)	عنق
carafe (decanter)	dawraq zuჳāჳiy (m)	دورق زجاجيّ
pitcher	ibrīq (m)	إبريق
vessel (container)	inā' (m)	إناء
pot (crock, stoneware ~)	aṣīṣ (m)	أصيص
vase	vāza (f)	فازة
bottle (perfume ~)	zuჳāჳa (f)	زجاجة

vial, small bottle	zuʒāʒa (f)	زجاجة
tube (of toothpaste)	umbūba (f)	أنبوبة
sack (bag)	kīs (m)	كيس

| bag (paper ~, plastic ~) | kīs (m) | كيس |
| pack (of cigarettes, etc.) | 'ulba (f) | علبة |

box (e.g., shoebox)	'ulba (f)	علبة
crate	ṣundū' (m)	صندوق
basket	salla (f)	سلّة

24. Materials

material	mādda (f)	مادّة
wood (n)	χaʃab (m)	خشب
wood-, wooden (adj)	χaʃabiy	خشبيّ

| glass (n) | zuʒāʒ (m) | زجاج |
| glass (as adj) | zuʒāʒiy | زجاجيّ |

| stone (n) | haʒar (m) | حجر |
| stone (as adj) | haʒariy | حجريّ |

| plastic (n) | blastīk (m) | بلاستيك |
| plastic (as adj) | min al blastīk | من البلاستيك |

| rubber (n) | maṭṭāṭ (m) | مطّاط |
| rubber (as adj) | maṭṭāṭiy | مطّاطيّ |

| cloth, fabric (n) | qumāʃ (m) | قماش |
| fabric (as adj) | min al qumāʃ | من القماش |

| paper (n) | waraq (m) | ورق |
| paper (as adj) | waraqiy | ورقيّ |

| cardboard (n) | kartūn (m) | كرتون |
| cardboard (as adj) | kartūniy | كرتونيّ |

polyethylene	buli iθilīn (m)	بولي إثيلين
cellophane	silufān (m)	سيلوفان
plywood	ablakāʃ (m)	أبلكاش

| porcelain (n) | bursilān (m) | بورسلان |
| porcelain (as adj) | min il bursilān | من البورسلان |

| clay (n) | ṭīn (m) | طين |
| clay (as adj) | faχχāry | فخّاري |

| ceramic (n) | siramīk (m) | سيراميك |
| ceramic (as adj) | siramīkiy | سيراميكيّ |

25. Metals

metal (n)	ma'dan (m)	معدن
metal (as adj)	ma'daniy	معدنيّ
alloy (n)	sabīka (f)	سبيكة
gold (n)	ðahab (m)	ذهب
gold, golden (adj)	ðahabiy	ذهبيّ
silver (n)	fiḍḍa (f)	فضّة
silver (as adj)	fiḍḍiy	فضّيّ
iron (n)	ḥadīd (m)	حديد
iron-, made of iron (adj)	ḥadīdiy	حديديّ
steel (n)	fūlāð (m)	فولاذ
steel (as adj)	fulāðiy	فولاذيّ
copper (n)	nuḥās (m)	نحاس
copper (as adj)	nuḥāsiy	نحاسيّ
aluminum (n)	alumīniyum (m)	الومينيوم
aluminum (as adj)	alumīniyum	الومينيوم
bronze (n)	brūnz (m)	برونز
bronze (as adj)	brūnziy	برونزيّ
brass	nuḥās aṣfar (m)	نحاس أصفر
nickel	nikil (m)	نيكل
platinum	blatīn (m)	بلاتين
mercury	zi'baq (m)	زئبق
tin	qaṣdīr (m)	قصدير
lead	ruṣāṣ (m)	رصاص
zinc	zink (m)	زنك

HUMAN BEING

Human being. The body

26. Humans. Basic concepts

human being	insān (m)	إنسان
man (adult male)	raʒul (m)	رجل
woman	imra'a (f)	إمرأة
child	ṭifl (m)	طفل
girl	bint (f)	بنت
boy	walad (m)	ولد
teenager	murāhiq (m)	مراهق
old man	ʿaʒūz (m)	عجوز
old woman	ʿaʒūza (f)	عجوزة

27. Human anatomy

organism (body)	ʒism (m)	جسم
heart	qalb (m)	قلب
blood	dam (m)	دم
artery	ʃaryān (m)	شريان
vein	ʿirq (m)	عرق
brain	muxx (m)	مخّ
nerve	ʿaṣab (m)	عصب
nerves	aʿṣāb (pl)	أعصاب
vertebra	faqra (f)	فقرة
spine (backbone)	ʿamūd faqriy (m)	عمود فقريّ
stomach (organ)	maʿida (f)	معدة
intestines, bowels	amʿāʾ (pl)	أمعاء
intestine (e.g., large ~)	miʿan (m)	معى
liver	kibd (f)	كبد
kidney	kilya (f)	كلية
bone	ʿaẓm (m)	عظم
skeleton	haykal ʿaẓmiy (m)	هيكل عظميّ
rib	ḍilʿ (m)	ضلع
skull	ʒumʒuma (f)	جمجمة
muscle	ʿaḍala (f)	عضلة
biceps	ʿaḍala ðāt ra'sayn (f)	عضلة ذات رأسين

triceps	ʿaḍla θulāθiyyat ar ruʾūs (f)	عضلة ثلائيّة الرءوس
tendon	watar (m)	وتر
joint	mafṣil (m)	مفصل
lungs	riʾatān (du)	رئتان
genitals	aʿḍāʾ ʒinsiyya (pl)	أعضاء جنسيّة
skin	buʃra (m)	بشرة

28. Head

head	raʾs (m)	رأس
face	waʒh (m)	وجه
nose	anf (m)	أنف
mouth	fam (m)	فم
eye	ʿayn (f)	عين
eyes	ʿuyūn (pl)	عيون
pupil	ḥadaqa (f)	حدقة
eyebrow	ḥāʒib (m)	حاجب
eyelash	rimʃ (m)	رمش
eyelid	ʒafn (m)	جفن
tongue	lisān (m)	لسان
tooth	sinn (f)	سنّ
lips	ʃifāh (pl)	شفاه
cheekbones	ʿizām waʒhiyya (pl)	عظام وجهيّة
gum	liθθa (f)	لئة
palate	ḥanak (m)	حنك
nostrils	minxarān (du)	منخران
chin	ðaqan (m)	ذقن
jaw	fakk (m)	فكّ
cheek	xadd (m)	خدّ
forehead	ʒabha (f)	جبهة
temple	ṣudɣ (m)	صدغ
ear	uðun (f)	أذن
back of the head	qafa (m)	قفا
neck	raqaba (f)	رقبة
throat	ḥalq (m)	حلق
hair	ʃaʿr (m)	شعر
hairstyle	tasrīḥa (f)	تسريحة
haircut	tasrīḥa (f)	تسريحة
wig	barūka (f)	باروكة
mustache	ʃawārib (pl)	شوارب
beard	liḥya (f)	لحية
to have (a beard, etc.)	ʿindahu	عنده
braid	ḍifīra (f)	ضفيرة
sideburns	sawālif (pl)	سوالف

red-haired (adj)	aḥmar aʃ ʃaʕr	أحمر الشعر
gray (hair)	abyaḍ	أبيض
bald (adj)	aṣlaʕ	أصلع
bald patch	ṣalaʕ (m)	صلع
ponytail	ðayl ḥiṣān (m)	ذيل حصان
bangs	quṣṣa (f)	قصّة

29. Human body

hand	yad (m)	يد
arm	ðirāʕ (f)	ذراع
finger	iṣbaʕ (m)	إصبع
toe	iṣbaʕ al qadam (m)	إصبع القدم
thumb	ibhām (m)	إبهام
little finger	χunṣur (m)	خنصر
nail	ẓufr (m)	ظفر
fist	qabḍa (f)	قبضة
palm	kaff (f)	كفّ
wrist	miʕṣam (m)	معصم
forearm	sāʕid (m)	ساعد
elbow	mirfaq (m)	مرفق
shoulder	katf (f)	كتف
leg	riʒl (f)	رجل
foot	qadam (f)	قدم
knee	rukba (f)	ركبة
calf (part of leg)	sammāna (f)	سمّانة
hip	faχð (f)	فخذ
heel	ʕaqb (m)	عقب
body	ʒism (m)	جسم
stomach	baṭn (m)	بطن
chest	ṣadr (m)	صدر
breast	θady (m)	ثدي
flank	ʒamb (m)	جنب
back	ẓahr (m)	ظهر
lower back	asfal az ẓahr (m)	أسفل الظهر
waist	χaṣr (m)	خصر
navel (belly button)	surra (f)	سرّة
buttocks	ardāf (pl)	أرداف
bottom	dubr (m)	دبر
beauty mark	ʃāma (f)	شامة
birthmark	waḥma	وحمة
(café au lait spot)		
tattoo	waʃm (m)	وشم
scar	nadba (f)	ندبة

Clothing & Accessories

30. Outerwear. Coats

clothes	malābis (pl)	ملابس
outerwear	malābis fawqāniyya (pl)	ملابس فوقانيّة
winter clothing	malābis ʃitawiyya (pl)	ملابس شتويّة
coat (overcoat)	mi'ṭaf (m)	معطف
fur coat	mi'ṭaf farw (m)	معطف فرو
fur jacket	ʒakīt farw (m)	جاكيت فرو
down coat	haʃiyyat rīʃ (m)	حشية ريش
jacket (e.g., leather ~)	ʒākīt (m)	جاكيت
raincoat (trenchcoat, etc.)	mi'ṭaf lil maṭar (m)	معطف للمطر
waterproof (adj)	ṣāmid lil mā'	صامد للماء

31. Men's & women's clothing

shirt (button shirt)	qamīṣ (m)	قميص
pants	banṭalūn (m)	بنطلون
jeans	ʒīnz (m)	جينز
suit jacket	sutra (f)	سترة
suit	badla (f)	بدلة
dress (frock)	fustān (m)	فستان
skirt	tannūra (f)	تنّورة
blouse	blūza (f)	بلوزة
knitted jacket (cardigan, etc.)	kardigān (m)	كارديجان
jacket (of woman's suit)	ʒākīt (m)	جاكيت
T-shirt	ti ʃirt (m)	تي شيرت
shorts (short trousers)	ʃūrt (m)	شورت
tracksuit	badlat at tadrīb (f)	بدلة التدريب
bathrobe	θawb hammām (m)	ثوب حمّام
pajamas	biʒāma (f)	بيجاما
sweater	bulūvir (m)	بلوفر
pullover	bulūvir (m)	بلوفر
vest	ṣudayriy (m)	صديريّ
tailcoat	badlat sahra (f)	بدلة سهرة
tuxedo	smūkin (m)	سموكن

uniform	zayy muwaḥḥad (m)	زي موحَّد
workwear	θiyāb al 'amal (m)	ثياب العمل
overalls	uvirūl (m)	اوفرول
coat (e.g., doctor's smock)	θawb (m)	ثوب

32. Clothing. Underwear

underwear	malābis dāχiliyya (pl)	ملابس داخليَّة
boxers, briefs	sirwāl dāχiliy riʒāliy (m)	سروال داخلي رجاليَ
panties	sirwāl dāχiliy nisā'iy (m)	سروال داخلي نسائيَ
undershirt (A-shirt)	qamīṣ bila aqmām (m)	قميص بلا أكمام
socks	ʒawārib (pl)	جوارب
nightgown	qamīṣ nawm (m)	قميص نوم
bra	ḥammālat ṣadr (f)	حمَّالة صدر
knee highs (knee-high socks)	ʒawārib ṭawīla (pl)	جوارب طويلة
pantyhose	ʒawārib kulūn (pl)	جوارب كولون
stockings (thigh highs)	ʒawārib nisā'iyya (pl)	جوارب نسائية
bathing suit	libās sibāḥa (m)	لباس سباحة

33. Headwear

hat	qubba'a (f)	قبَّعة
fedora	burnayṭa (f)	برنيطة
baseball cap	kāb baysbūl (m)	كاب بيسبول
flatcap	qubba'a musaṭṭaḥa (f)	قبَّعة مسطحة
beret	birīḥ (m)	بيريه
hood	χiṭā' (m)	غطاء
panama hat	qubba'at banāma (f)	قبَّعة بناما
knit cap (knitted hat)	qubbā'a maḥbūka (m)	قبَّعة محبوكة
headscarf	ʔiʃārb (m)	إيشارب
women's hat	burnayṭa (f)	برنيطة
hard hat	χūða (f)	خوذة
garrison cap	kāb (m)	كاب
helmet	χūða (f)	خوذة
derby	qubba'at dirbi (f)	قبَّعة ديربي
top hat	qubba'a 'āliya (f)	قبَّعة عالية

34. Footwear

footwear	aḥðiya (pl)	أحذية
shoes (men's shoes)	ʒazma (f)	جزمة

shoes (women's shoes)	ʒazma (f)	جزمة
boots (e.g., cowboy ~)	būt (m)	بوت
slippers	ʃibʃib (m)	شبشب
tennis shoes (e.g., Nike ~)	ḥiðā' riyāḍiy (m)	حذاء رياضيّ
sneakers	kutʃi (m)	كوتشي
(e.g., Converse ~)		
sandals	ṣandal (pl)	صندل
cobbler (shoe repairer)	iskāfiy (m)	إسكافيّ
heel	kaʿb (m)	كعب
pair (of shoes)	zawʒ (m)	زوج
shoestring	ʃarīṭ (m)	شريط
to lace (vt)	rabaṭ	ربط
shoehorn	labbāsat ḥiðā' (f)	لبّاسة حذاء
shoe polish	warnīʃ al ḥiðā' (m)	ورنيش الحذاء

35. Textile. Fabrics

cotton (n)	quṭn (m)	قطن
cotton (as adj)	min al quṭn	من القطن
flax (n)	kattān (m)	كتّان
flax (as adj)	min il kattān	من الكتّان
silk (n)	ḥarīr (m)	حرير
silk (as adj)	min al ḥarīr	من الحرير
wool (n)	ṣūf (m)	صوف
wool (as adj)	min aṣ ṣūf	من الصوف
velvet	muxmal (m)	مخمل
suede	ʒild ʃāmwāh (m)	جلد شامواه
corduroy	quṭn qaṭīfa (f)	قطن قطيفة
nylon (n)	naylūn (m)	نايلون
nylon (as adj)	min an naylūn	من النيلون
polyester (n)	bulyistir (m)	بوليستر
polyester (as adj)	min al bulyastar	من البوليستر
leather (n)	ʒild (m)	جلد
leather (as adj)	min al ʒild	من الجلد
fur (n)	farw (m)	فرو
fur (e.g., ~ coat)	min al farw	من الفرو

36. Personal accessories

gloves	quffāz (m)	قفّاز
mittens	quffāz muxlaq (m)	قفّاز مغلق

scarf (muffler)	'īʃārb (m)	إيشارب
glasses (eyeglasses)	nazzāra (f)	نظّارة
frame (eyeglass ~)	iṭār (m)	إطار
umbrella	ʃamsiyya (f)	شمسيّة
walking stick	ʻaṣa (f)	عصا
hairbrush	furʃat ʃaʻr (f)	فرشة شعر
fan	mirwaḥa yadawiyya (f)	مروحة يدويّة
tie (necktie)	karavatta (f)	كَرافتة
bow tie	babyūn (m)	بيبون
suspenders	ḥammāla (f)	حمّالة
handkerchief	mandīl (m)	منديل
comb	miʃṭ (m)	مشط
barrette	dabbūs (m)	دبّوس
hairpin	bansa (m)	بنسة
buckle	bukla (f)	بكلة
belt	ḥizām (m)	حزام
shoulder strap	ḥammalat al katf (f)	حمّالة الكتف
bag (handbag)	ʃanṭa (f)	شنطة
purse	ʃanṭat yad (f)	شنطة يد
backpack	ḥaqībat ẓahr (f)	حقيبة ظهر

37. Clothing. Miscellaneous

fashion	mūḍa (f)	موضة
in vogue (adj)	fil mūḍa	في الموضة
fashion designer	muṣammim azyāʼ (m)	مصمّم أزياء
collar	yāqa (f)	ياقة
pocket	ʒayb (m)	جيب
pocket (as adj)	ʒayb	جيب
sleeve	kumm (m)	كمّ
hanging loop	ʻallāqa (f)	علّاقة
fly (on trousers)	lisān (m)	لسان
zipper (fastener)	zimām munzaliq (m)	زمام منزلق
fastener	miʃbak (m)	مشبك
button	zirr (m)	زرّ
buttonhole	ʻurwa (f)	عروة
to come off (ab. button)	waqaʻ	وقع
to sew (vi, vt)	χāṭ	خاط
to embroider (vi, vt)	ṭarraz	طرّز
embroidery	taṭrīz (m)	تطريز
sewing needle	ibra (f)	إبرة
thread	χayṭ (m)	خيط
seam	darz (m)	درز

to get dirty (vi)	tawassax	توسَّخ
stain (mark, spot)	buqʻa (f)	بقعة
to crease, crumple (vi)	takarmaʃ	تكرمش
to tear, to rip (vt)	qaṭṭaʻ	قطّع
clothes moth	ʻuθθa (f)	عثّة

38. Personal care. Cosmetics

toothpaste	maʻʒūn asnān (m)	معجون أسنان
toothbrush	furʃat asnān (f)	فرشة أسنان
to brush one's teeth	nazzaf al asnān	نظّف الأسنان
razor	mūs ḥilāqa (m)	موس حلاقة
shaving cream	krīm ḥilāqa (m)	كريم حلاقة
to shave (vi)	ḥalaq	حلق
soap	ṣābūn (m)	صابون
shampoo	ʃāmbū (m)	شامبو
scissors	maqaṣṣ (m)	مقصّ
nail file	mibrad (m)	مبرد
nail clippers	milqaṭ (m)	ملقط
tweezers	milqaṭ (m)	ملقط
cosmetics	mawādd at taʒmīl (pl)	موادّ التجميل
face mask	mask (m)	ماسك
manicure	manikūr (m)	مانيكور
to have a manicure	ʻamal manikūr	عمل مانيكور
pedicure	badikīr (m)	باديكير
make-up bag	ḥaqībat adawāt at taʒmīl (f)	حقيبة أدوات التجميل
face powder	budrat waʒh (f)	بودرة وجه
powder compact	ʻulbat būdra (f)	علبة بودرة
blusher	aḥmar xudūd (m)	أحمر خدود
perfume (bottled)	ʻiṭr (m)	عطر
toilet water (lotion)	kulūnya (f)	كولونيا
lotion	lusiyun (m)	لوسيون
cologne	kulūniya (f)	كولونيا
eyeshadow	ay ʃaduw (m)	اي شادو
eyeliner	kuḥl al ʻuyūn (m)	كحل العيون
mascara	maskara (f)	ماسكارا
lipstick	aḥmar ʃifāh (m)	أحمر شفاه
nail polish, enamel	mulammiʻ al azāfir (m)	ملمّع الاظافر
hair spray	muθabbit aʃ ʃaʻr (m)	مثبّت الشعر
deodorant	muzīl rawāʾiḥ (m)	مزيل روائح
cream	krīm (m)	كريم
face cream	krīm lil waʒh (m)	كريم للوجه

hand cream	krīm lil yadayn (m)	كريم لليدين
anti-wrinkle cream	krīm muḍādd lit taӡāʿīd (m)	كريم مضادّ للتجاعيد
day cream	krīm an nahār (m)	كريم النهار
night cream	krīm al layl (m)	كريم الليل
day (as adj)	nahāriy	نهاريّ
night (as adj)	layliy	ليليّ
tampon	tambūn (m)	تانبون
toilet paper (toilet roll)	waraq ḥammām (m)	ورق حمّام
hair dryer	muӡaffif ʃaʿr (m)	مجفّف شعر

39. Jewelry

jewelry	muӡawharāt (pl)	مجوهرات
precious (e.g., ~ stone)	karīm	كريم
hallmark stamp	damɣa (f)	دمغة
ring	χātim (m)	خاتم
wedding ring	diblat al χuṭūba (m)	دبلة الخطوبة
bracelet	siwār (m)	سوار
earrings	ḥalaq (m)	حلق
necklace (~ of pearls)	ʿaqd (m)	عقد
crown	tāӡ (m)	تاج
bead necklace	ʿaqd χaraz (m)	عقد خرز
diamond	almās (m)	الماس
emerald	zumurrud (m)	زمرّد
ruby	yāqūt aḥmar (m)	ياقوت أحمر
sapphire	yāqūt azraq (m)	ياقوت أزرق
pearl	luʾluʾ (m)	لؤلؤ
amber	kahramān (m)	كهرمان

40. Watches. Clocks

watch (wristwatch)	sāʿa (f)	ساعة
dial	waӡh as sāʿa (m)	وجه الساعة
hand (of clock, watch)	ʿaqrab as sāʿa (m)	عقرب الساعة
metal watch band	siwār sāʿa maʿdaniyya (m)	سوار ساعة معدنية
watch strap	siwār sāʿa (m)	سوار ساعة
battery	baṭṭāriyya (f)	بطّاريّة
to be dead (battery)	tafarraɣ	تفرّغ
to change a battery	ɣayyar al baṭṭāriyya	غيّر البطّاريّة
to run fast	sabaq	سبق
to run slow	taʾaχχar	تأخّر
wall clock	sāʿat ḥāʾiṭ (f)	ساعة حائط
hourglass	sāʿa ramliyya (f)	ساعة رمليّة

sundial	sā'a ʃamsiyya (f)	ساعة شمسيّة
alarm clock	munabbih (m)	منبّه
watchmaker	sa'ātiy (m)	ساعاتيّ
to repair (vt)	aṣlaḥ	أصلح

Food. Nutricion

41. Food

meat	laḥm (m)	لحم
chicken	daʒāʒ (m)	دجاج
Rock Cornish hen (poussin)	farrūʒ (m)	فرّوج
duck	baṭṭa (f)	بطّة
goose	iwazza (f)	إوزّة
game	ṣayd (m)	صيد
turkey	daʒāʒ rūmiy (m)	دجاج رومي
pork	laḥm al xinzīr (m)	لحم الخنزير
veal	laḥm il ʿiʒl (m)	لحم العجل
lamb	laḥm aḍ ḍa'n (m)	لحم الضأن
beef	laḥm al baqar (m)	لحم البقر
rabbit	arnab (m)	أرنب
sausage (bologna, pepperoni, etc.)	suʒuq (m)	سجق
vienna sausage (frankfurter)	suʒuq (m)	سجق
bacon	bikūn (m)	بيكن
ham	hām (m)	هام
gammon	faxð xinzīr (m)	فخذ خنزير
pâté	maʿʒūn laḥm (m)	معجون لحم
liver	kibda (f)	كبدة
hamburger (ground beef)	haʃwa (f)	حشوة
tongue	lisān (m)	لسان
egg	bayḍa (f)	بيضة
eggs	bayḍ (m)	بيض
egg white	bayāḍ al bayḍ (m)	بياض البيض
egg yolk	ṣafār al bayḍ (m)	صفار البيض
fish	samak (m)	سمك
seafood	fawākih al baḥr (pl)	فواكه البحر
caviar	kaviyār (m)	كافيار
crab	salṭaʿūn (m)	سلطعون
shrimp	ʒambari (m)	جمبري
oyster	maḥār (m)	محار
spiny lobster	karkand ʃāik (m)	كركند شائك
octopus	uxṭubūṭ (m)	أخطبوط

squid	kalmāri (m)	كالماري
sturgeon	samak al ḥaff (m)	سمك الحفش
salmon	salmūn (m)	سلمون
halibut	samak al halbūt (m)	سمك الهلبوت
cod	samak al qudd (m)	سمك القدّ
mackerel	usqumriy (m)	أسقمريّ
tuna	tūna (f)	تونة
eel	ḥankalīs (m)	حنكليس
trout	salmūn muraqqaṭ (m)	سلمون مرقّط
sardine	sardīn (m)	سردين
pike	samak al karāki (m)	سمك الكراكي
herring	rinʒa (f)	رنجة
bread	χubz (m)	خبز
cheese	ʒubna (f)	جبنة
sugar	sukkar (m)	سكّر
salt	milḥ (m)	ملح
rice	urz (m)	أرز
pasta (macaroni)	makarūna (f)	مكرونة
noodles	nūdlis (f)	نودلز
butter	zubda (f)	زبدة
vegetable oil	zayt (m)	زيت
sunflower oil	zayt ʿabīd aʃ ʃams (m)	زيت عبيد الشمس
margarine	marɣarīn (m)	مرغرين
olives	zaytūn (m)	زيتون
olive oil	zayt az zaytūn (m)	زيت الزيتون
milk	ḥalīb (m)	حليب
condensed milk	ḥalīb mukaθθaf (m)	حليب مكثف
yogurt	yūɣurt (m)	يوغورت
sour cream	krīma ḥāmiḍa (f)	كريمة حامضة
cream (of milk)	krīma (f)	كريمة
mayonnaise	mayunīz (m)	مايونيز
buttercream	krīmat zubda (f)	كريمة زبدة
cereal grains (wheat, etc.)	ḥubūb (pl)	حبوب
flour	daqīq (m)	دقيق
canned food	muʿallabāt (pl)	معلّبات
cornflakes	kurn fliks (m)	كورن فليكس
honey	ʿasal (m)	عسل
jam	murabba (m)	مربّى
chewing gum	ʿilk (m)	علك

42. Drinks

water	mā' (m)	ماء
drinking water	mā' ʃurb (m)	ماء شرب
mineral water	mā' maʻdaniy (m)	ماء معدنيّ

still (adj)	bi dūn ɣāz	بدون غاز
carbonated (adj)	mukarban	مكربن
sparkling (adj)	bil ɣāz	بالغاز
ice	θalʒ (m)	ثلج
with ice	biθ θalʒ	بالثلج

non-alcoholic (adj)	bi dūn kuḥūl	بدون كحول
soft drink	maʃrūb ɣāziy (m)	مشروب غازي
refreshing drink	maʃrūb muθallaʒ (m)	مشروب مثلج
lemonade	ʃarāb laymūn (m)	شراب ليمون

liquors	maʃrūbāt kuḥūliyya (pl)	مشروبات كحوليّة
wine	nabīð (f)	نبيذ
white wine	nibīð abyaḍ (m)	نبيذ أبيض
red wine	nabīð aḥmar (m)	نبيذ أحمر

liqueur	liqiūr (m)	ليكيور
champagne	ʃambāniya (f)	شمبانيا
vermouth	virmut (m)	فيرموث

whiskey	wiski (m)	وسكي
vodka	vudka (f)	فودكا
gin	ʒīn (m)	جين
cognac	kunyāk (m)	كونياك
rum	rum (m)	رم

coffee	qahwa (f)	قهوة
black coffee	qahwa sāda (f)	قهوة سادة
coffee with milk	qahwa bil ḥalīb (f)	قهوة بالحليب
cappuccino	kaputʃinu (m)	كابتشينو
instant coffee	niskafi (m)	نيسكافيه

milk	ḥalīb (m)	حليب
cocktail	kuktayl (m)	كوكتيل
milkshake	milk ʃiyk (m)	ميلك شيك

juice	ʻaṣīr (m)	عصير
tomato juice	ʻaṣīr ṭamāṭim (m)	عصير طماطم
orange juice	ʻaṣīr burtuqāl (m)	عصير برتقال
freshly squeezed juice	ʻaṣīr ṭāziʒ (m)	عصير طازج

beer	bīra (f)	بيرة
light beer	bīra xafifa (f)	بيرة خفيفة
dark beer	bīra ɣāmiqa (f)	بيرة غامقة
tea	ʃāy (m)	شاي

| black tea | ʃāy aswad (m) | شاي أسود |
| green tea | ʃāy axḍar (m) | شاي أخضر |

43. Vegetables

vegetables	xuḍār (pl)	خضار
greens	xuḍrawāt waraqiyya (pl)	خضروات ورقيّة
tomato	ṭamāṭim (f)	طماطم
cucumber	xiyār (m)	خيار
carrot	ʒazar (m)	جزر
potato	baṭāṭis (f)	بطاطس
onion	baṣal (m)	بصل
garlic	θūm (m)	ثوم
cabbage	kurumb (m)	كرنب
cauliflower	qarnabīṭ (m)	قرنبيط
Brussels sprouts	kurumb brūksil (m)	كرنب بروكسل
broccoli	brukuli (m)	بركولي
beetroot	banʒar (m)	بنجر
eggplant	bātinʒān (m)	باذنجان
zucchini	kūsa (f)	كوسة
pumpkin	qarʿ (m)	قرع
turnip	lift (m)	لفت
parsley	baqdūnis (m)	بقدونس
dill	ʃabat (m)	شبت
lettuce	xass (m)	خسّ
celery	karafs (m)	كرفس
asparagus	halyūn (m)	هليون
spinach	sabānix (m)	سبانخ
pea	bisilla (f)	بسلّة
beans	fūl (m)	فول
corn (maize)	ðura (f)	ذرّة
kidney bean	faṣūliya (f)	فاصوليا
bell pepper	filfil (m)	فلفل
radish	fiʒl (m)	فجل
artichoke	xurʃūf (m)	خرشوف

44. Fruits. Nuts

fruit	fākiha (f)	فاكهة
apple	tuffāḥa (f)	تفّاحة
pear	kummaθra (f)	كمّثرى
lemon	laymūn (m)	ليمون

orange	burtuqāl (m)	برتقال
strawberry (garden ~)	farawla (f)	فراولة
mandarin	yūsufiy (m)	يوسفي
plum	barqūq (m)	برقوق
peach	durrāq (m)	دراق
apricot	miʃmiʃ (f)	مشمش
raspberry	tūt al ʿullayq al aḥmar (m)	توت العليق الأحمر
pineapple	ananās (m)	أناناس
banana	mawz (m)	موز
watermelon	baṭṭīx aḥmar (m)	بطيخ أحمر
grape	ʿinab (m)	عنب
cherry	karaz (m)	كرز
melon	baṭṭīx aṣfar (f)	بطيخ أصفر
grapefruit	zinbāʿ (m)	زنباع
avocado	avukādu (f)	افوكاتو
papaya	babāya (m)	بابايا
mango	mangu (m)	مانجو
pomegranate	rummān (m)	رمان
redcurrant	kiʃmiʃ aḥmar (m)	كشمش أحمر
blackcurrant	ʿinab aθ θaʿlab al aswad (m)	عنب الثعلب الأسود
gooseberry	ʿinab aθ θaʿlab (m)	عنب الثعلب
bilberry	ʿinab al aḥrāʒ (m)	عنب الأحراج
blackberry	θamar al ʿullayk (m)	ثمر العليّق
raisin	zabīb (m)	زبيب
fig	tīn (m)	تين
date	tamr (m)	تمر
peanut	fūl sudāniy (m)	فول سودانيّ
almond	lawz (m)	لوز
walnut	ʿayn al ʒamal (f)	عين الجمل
hazelnut	bunduq (m)	بندق
coconut	ʒawz al hind (m)	جوز هند
pistachios	fustuq (m)	فستق

45. Bread. Candy

bakers' confectionery (pastry)	ḥalawiyyāt (pl)	حلويّات
bread	xubz (m)	خبز
cookies	baskawīt (m)	بسكويت
chocolate (n)	ʃukulāta (f)	شكولاتة
chocolate (as adj)	biʃ ʃukulāta	بالشكولاتة
candy (wrapped)	bumbūn (m)	بونبون

cake (e.g., cupcake)	ka'k (m)	كعك
cake (e.g., birthday ~)	tūrta (f)	تورتة
pie (e.g., apple ~)	fatīra (f)	فطيرة
filling (for cake, pie)	ḥaʃwa (f)	حشوة
jam (whole fruit jam)	murabba (m)	مربّى
marmalade	marmalād (f)	مرملاد
waffles	wāfil (m)	وافل
ice-cream	muθallaʒāt (pl)	مثلّجات
pudding	būding (m)	بودنج

46. Cooked dishes

course, dish	waʒba (f)	وجبة
cuisine	matbaχ (m)	مطبخ
recipe	waṣfa (f)	وصفة
portion	waʒba (f)	وجبة
salad	sulṭa (f)	سلطة
soup	ʃūrba (f)	شوربة
clear soup (broth)	maraq (m)	مرق
sandwich (bread)	sandawitʃ (m)	ساندويتش
fried eggs	bayḍ maqliy (m)	بيض مقليّ
hamburger (beefburger)	hamburger (m)	هامبورجر
beefsteak	biftīk (m)	بفتيك
side dish	ṭabaq ʒānibiy (m)	طبق جانبيّ
spaghetti	spaɣitti (m)	سباغيتي
mashed potatoes	harīs baṭāṭis (m)	هريس بطاطس
pizza	bītza (f)	بيتزا
porridge (oatmeal, etc.)	'aṣīda (f)	عصيدة
omelet	bayḍ maχfūq (m)	بيض مخفوق
boiled (e.g., ~ beef)	maslūq	مسلوق
smoked (adj)	mudaχχin	مدخّن
fried (adj)	maqliy	مقليّ
dried (adj)	muʒaffaf	مجفّف
frozen (adj)	muʒammad	مجمّد
pickled (adj)	muχallil	مخلّل
sweet (sugary)	musakkar	مسكّر
salty (adj)	māliḥ	مالح
cold (adj)	bārid	بارد
hot (adj)	sāχin	ساخن
bitter (adj)	murr	مرّ
tasty (adj)	laðīð	لذيذ
to cook in boiling water	ṭabaχ	طبخ

to cook (dinner)	ḥaḍḍar	حضّر
to fry (vt)	qala	قلى
to heat up (food)	saxxan	سخّن
to salt (vt)	mallaḥ	ملّح
to pepper (vt)	falfal	فلفل
to grate (vt)	baʃar	بشر
peel (n)	qiʃra (f)	قشرة
to peel (vt)	qaʃʃar	قشّر

47. Spices

salt	milḥ (m)	ملح
salty (adj)	māliḥ	مالح
to salt (vt)	mallaḥ	ملّح
black pepper	filfil aswad (m)	فلفل أسود
red pepper (milled ~)	filfil aḥmar (m)	فلفل أحمر
mustard	ṣalṣat al xardal (f)	صلصة الخردل
horseradish	fiʒl ḥārr (m)	فجل حارّ
condiment	tābil (m)	تابل
spice	bahār (m)	بهار
sauce	ṣalṣa (f)	صلصة
vinegar	xall (m)	خلّ
anise	yānsūn (m)	يانسون
basil	rīḥān (m)	ريحان
cloves	qurumful (m)	قرنفل
ginger	zanʒabīl (m)	زنجبيل
coriander	kuzbara (f)	كزبرة
cinnamon	qirfa (f)	قرفة
sesame	simsim (m)	سمسم
bay leaf	awrāq al xār (pl)	أوراق الغار
paprika	babrika (f)	بابريكا
caraway	karāwiya (f)	كراوية
saffron	za'farān (m)	زعفران

48. Meals

food	akl (m)	أكل
to eat (vi, vt)	akal	أكل
breakfast	futūr (m)	فطور
to have breakfast	aftar	أفطر
lunch	yadā' (m)	غداء
to have lunch	tayadda	تغدّى

| dinner | 'aʃā' (m) | عشاء |
| to have dinner | ta'aʃʃa | تعشّى |

| appetite | ʃahiyya (f) | شهيّة |
| Enjoy your meal! | hanī'an marī'an! | هنيئًا مريئًا! |

to open (~ a bottle)	fataḥ	فتح
to spill (liquid)	dalaq	دلق
to spill out (vi)	indalaq	إندلق
to boil (vi)	ɣala	غلى
to boil (vt)	ɣala	غلى
boiled (~ water)	maɣliy	مغليّ
to chill, cool down (vt)	barrad	برّد
to chill (vi)	tabarrad	تبرّد

| taste, flavor | ṭa'm (m) | طعم |
| aftertaste | al maðāq al 'āliq fil fam (m) | المذاق العالق فى الفم |

to slim down (lose weight)	faqad al wazn	فقد الوزن
diet	ḥimya ɣaðā'iyya (f)	حمية غذائية
vitamin	vitamīn (m)	فيتامين
calorie	su'ra ḥarāriyya (f)	سعرة حراريّة
vegetarian (n)	nabātiy (m)	نباتيّ
vegetarian (adj)	nabātiy	نباتيّ

fats (nutrient)	duhūn (pl)	دهون
proteins	brutināt (pl)	بروتينات
carbohydrates	naʃawiyyāt (pl)	نشويّات
slice (of lemon, ham)	ʃarīḥa (f)	شريحة
piece (of cake, pie)	qiṭ'a (f)	قطعة
crumb (of bread, cake, etc.)	futāta (f)	فتاتة

49. Table setting

spoon	mil'aqa (f)	ملعقة
knife	sikkīn (m)	سكّين
fork	ʃawka (f)	شوكة
cup (e.g., coffee ~)	finʒān (m)	فنجان
plate (dinner ~)	ṭabaq (m)	طبق
saucer	ṭabaq finʒān (m)	طبق فنجان
napkin (on table)	mandīl (m)	منديل
toothpick	xallat asnān (f)	خلّة أسنان

50. Restaurant

| restaurant | maṭ'am (m) | مطعم |
| coffee house | kafé (m), maqha (m) | كافيه, مقهى |

pub, bar	bār (m)	بار
tearoom	ṣālun ʃāy (m)	صالون شاي
waiter	nādil (m)	نادل
waitress	nādila (f)	نادلة
bartender	bārman (m)	بارمان
menu	qā'imat aṭ ṭa'ām (f)	قائمة طعام
wine list	qā'imat al xumūr (f)	قائمة خمور
to book a table	ḥaʒaz mā'ida	حجز مائدة
course, dish	waʒba (f)	وجبة
to order (meal)	ṭalab	طلب
to make an order	ṭalab	طلب
aperitif	ʃarāb (m)	شراب
appetizer	muqabbilāt (pl)	مقبّلات
dessert	ḥalawiyyāt (pl)	حلويّات
check	ḥisāb (m)	حساب
to pay the check	dafa' al ḥisāb	دفع الحساب
to give change	a'ṭa al bāqi	أعطى الباقي
tip	baqʃiʃ (m)	بقشيش

Family, relatives and friends

51. Personal information. Forms

name (first name)	ism (m)	إسم
surname (last name)	ism al 'ā'ila (m)	إسم العائلة
date of birth	tarīx al mīlād (m)	تاريخ الميلاد
place of birth	makān al mīlād (m)	مكان الميلاد
nationality	ʒinsiyya (f)	جنسية
place of residence	maqarr al iqāma (m)	مقر الإقامة
country	balad (m)	بلد
profession (occupation)	mihna (f)	مهنة
gender, sex	ʒins (m)	جنس
height	ṭūl (m)	طول
weight	wazn (m)	وزن

52. Family members. Relatives

mother	umm (f)	أمَ
father	ab (m)	أب
son	ibn (m)	إبن
daughter	ibna (f)	إبنة
younger daughter	al ibna aṣ ṣayīra (f)	الإبنة الصغيرة
younger son	al ibn aṣ ṣayīr (m)	الابن الصغير
eldest daughter	al ibna al kabīra (f)	الإبنة الكبيرة
eldest son	al ibn al kabīr (m)	الإبن الكبير
brother	ax (m)	أخ
elder brother	al ax al kabīr (m)	الأخ الكبير
younger brother	al ax aṣ ṣayīr (m)	الأخ الصغير
sister	uxt (f)	أخت
elder sister	al uxt al kabīra (f)	الأخت الكبيرة
younger sister	al uxt aṣ ṣayīra (f)	الأخت الصغيرة
cousin (masc.)	ibn 'amm (m), ibn xāl (m)	إبن عمّ، إبن خال
cousin (fem.)	ibnat 'amm (f), ibnat xāl (f)	إبنة عمّ، إبنة خال
mom, mommy	mama (f)	ماما
dad, daddy	baba (m)	بابا
parents	wālidān (du)	والدان
child	ṭifl (m)	طفل
children	aṭfāl (pl)	أطفال

grandmother	ʒidda (f)	جدّة
grandfather	ʒadd (m)	جدّ
grandson	ḥafīd (m)	حفيد
granddaughter	ḥafīda (f)	حفيدة
grandchildren	aḥfād (pl)	أحفاد
uncle	ʿamm (m), χāl (m)	عمّ, خال
aunt	ʿamma (f), χāla (f)	عمّة, خالة
nephew	ibn al aχ (m), ibn al uχt (m)	إبن الأخ, إبن الأخت
niece	ibnat al aχ (f), ibnat al uχt (f)	إبنة الأخ, إبنة الأخت
mother-in-law (wife's mother)	ḥamātt (f)	حماة
father-in-law (husband's father)	ḥamm (m)	حم
son-in-law (daughter's husband)	zawʒ al ibna (m)	زوج الأبنة
stepmother	zawʒat al ab (f)	زوجة الأب
stepfather	zawʒ al umm (m)	زوج الأمّ
infant	ṭifl raḍīʿ (m)	طفل رضيع
baby (infant)	mawlūd (m)	مولود
little boy, kid	walad ṣaɣīr (m)	ولد صغير
wife	zawʒa (f)	زوجة
husband	zawʒ (m)	زوج
spouse (husband)	zawʒ (m)	زوج
spouse (wife)	zawʒa (f)	زوجة
married (masc.)	mutazawwiʒ	متزوّج
married (fem.)	mutazawwiʒa	متزوّجة
single (unmarried)	aʿzab	أعزب
bachelor	aʿzab (m)	أعزب
divorced (masc.)	muṭallaq (m)	مطلّق
widow	armala (f)	أرملة
widower	armal (m)	أرمل
relative	qarīb (m)	قريب
close relative	nasīb qarīb (m)	نسيب قريب
distant relative	nasīb baʿīd (m)	نسيب بعيد
relatives	aqārib (pl)	أقارب
orphan (boy or girl)	yatīm (m)	يتيم
guardian (of a minor)	waliyy amr (m)	وليّ أمر
to adopt (a boy)	tabanna	تبنّى
to adopt (a girl)	tabanna	تبنّى

53. Friends. Coworkers

friend (masc.)	ṣadīq (m)	صديق
friend (fem.)	ṣadīqa (f)	صديقة

friendship	ṣadāqa (f)	صداقة
to be friends	ṣādaq	صادق
buddy (masc.)	ṣāḥib (m)	صاحب
buddy (fem.)	ṣaḥiba (f)	صاحبة
partner	rafīq (m)	رفيق
chief (boss)	raʾīs (m)	رئيس
superior (n)	raʾīs (m)	رئيس
owner, proprietor	ṣāḥib (m)	صاحب
subordinate (n)	tābiʿ (m)	تابع
colleague	zamīl (m)	زميل
acquaintance (person)	maʿruf (m)	معروف
fellow traveler	rafīq safar (m)	رفيق سفر
classmate	zamīl fiṣ ṣaff (m)	زميل في الصفّ
neighbor (masc.)	ʒār (m)	جار
neighbor (fem.)	ʒāra (f)	جارة
neighbors	ʒirān (pl)	جيران

54. Man. Woman

woman	imra'a (f)	إمرأة
girl (young woman)	fatāt (f)	فتاة
bride	ʿarūsa (f)	عروسة
beautiful (adj)	ʒamīla	جميلة
tall (adj)	ṭawīla	طويلة
slender (adj)	raʃīqa	رشيقة
short (adj)	qaṣīra	قصيرة
blonde (n)	ʃaqrāʾ (f)	شقراء
brunette (n)	sawdāʾ aʃ ʃaʿr (f)	سوداء الشعر
ladies' (adj)	sayyidāt	سيّدات
virgin (girl)	ʿaðrāʾ (f)	عذراء
pregnant (adj)	ḥāmil	حامل
man (adult male)	raʒul (m)	رجل
blond (n)	aʃqar (m)	أشقر
brunet (n)	aswad aʃ ʃaʿr (m)	أسود الشعر
tall (adj)	ṭawīl	طويل
short (adj)	qaṣīr	قصير
rude (rough)	waqiḥ	وقح
stocky (adj)	malyān	مليان
robust (adj)	matīn	متين
strong (adj)	qawiy	قويّ
strength	quwwa (f)	قوّة

stout, fat (adj)	θaxīn	ثخين
swarthy (adj)	asmar	أسمر
slender (well-built)	raʃīq	رشيق
elegant (adj)	anīq	أنيق

55. Age

age	'umr (m)	عمر
youth (young age)	ʃabāb (m)	شباب
young (adj)	ʃābb	شاب
younger (adj)	aşɣar	أصغر
older (adj)	akbar	أكبر
young man	ʃābb (m)	شاب
teenager	murāhiq (m)	مراهق
guy, fellow	ʃābb (m)	شاب
old man	'aʒūz (m)	عجوز
old woman	'aʒūza (f)	عجوزة
adult (adj)	bāliɣ (m)	بالغ
middle-aged (adj)	fi muntaşaf al 'umr	في منتصف العمر
elderly (adj)	'aʒūz	عجوز
old (adj)	'aʒūz	عجوز
retirement	ma'āʃ (m)	معاش
to retire (from job)	uhīl 'alal ma'āʃ	أحيل على المعاش
retiree	mutaqā'id (m)	متقاعد

56. Children

child	ţifl (m)	طفل
children	aţfāl (pl)	أطفال
twins	taw'amān (du)	توأمان
cradle	mahd (m)	مهد
rattle	xaʃxīʃa (f)	خشخيشة
diaper	hifāz aţfāl (m)	حفاظ أطفال
pacifier	bazzāza (f)	بزّازة
baby carriage	'arabat aţfāl (f)	عربة أطفال
kindergarten	rawdat aţfāl (f)	روضة أطفال
babysitter	murabbiyat aţfāl (f)	مربّية الأطفال
childhood	ţufūla (f)	طفولة
doll	dumya (f)	دمية
toy	lu'ba (f)	لعبة

construction set (toy)	muka''abāt (pl)	مكعّبات
well-bred (adj)	mu'addab	مؤدّب
ill-bred (adj)	qalīl al adab	قليل الأدب
spoiled (adj)	mutdalli'	متدلّع
to be naughty	la'ib	لعب
mischievous (adj)	la'ūb	لعوب
mischievousness	iz'āӡ (m)	إزعاج
mischievous child	ṭifl la'ūb (m)	طفل لعوب
obedient (adj)	muṭī'	مطيع
disobedient (adj)	'āq	عاق
docile (adj)	'āqil	عاقل
clever (smart)	ðakiy	ذكيّ
child prodigy	ṭifl mu'ӡiza (m)	طفل معجزة

57. Married couples. Family life

to kiss (vt)	bās	باس
to kiss (vi)	bās	باس
family (n)	'ā'ila (f)	عائلة
family (as adj)	'ā'iliy	عائليّ
couple	zawӡān (du)	زوجان
marriage (state)	zawāӡ (m)	زواج
hearth (home)	bayt (m)	بيت
dynasty	sulāla (f)	سلالة
date	maw'id (m)	موعد
kiss	būsa (f)	بوسة
love (for sb)	ḥubb (m)	حبّ
to love (sb)	aḥabb	أحبّ
beloved	ḥabīb	حبيب
tenderness	ḥanān (m)	حنان
tender (affectionate)	ḥanūn	حنون
faithfulness	iχlāṣ (m)	إخلاص
faithful (adj)	muχliṣ	مخلص
care (attention)	'ināya (f)	عناية
caring (~ father)	muhtamm	مهتمّ
newlyweds	'arūsān (du)	عروسان
honeymoon	ʃahr al 'asal (m)	شهر العسل
to get married (ab. woman)	tazawwaӡ	تزوّج
to get married (ab. man)	tazawwaӡ	تزوّج
wedding	zifāf (m)	زفاف
golden wedding	al yubīl að ðahabiy liz zawāӡ (m)	اليوبيل الذهبي للزواج

anniversary	ðikra sanawiyya (f)	ذكرى سنويّة
lover (masc.)	ḥabīb (m)	حبيب
mistress (lover)	ḥabība (f)	حبيبة
adultery	χiyāna zawʒiyya (f)	خيانة زوجية
to cheat on … (commit adultery)	χān	خان
jealous (adj)	ɣayūr	غيور
to be jealous	ɣār	غار
divorce	ṭalāq (m)	طلاق
to divorce (vi)	ṭallaq	طلّق
to quarrel (vi)	taʃāʒar	تشاجر
to be reconciled (after an argument)	taṣālaḥ	تصالح
together (adv)	maʻan	معًا
sex	ʒins (m)	جنس
happiness	saʻāda (f)	سعادة
happy (adj)	saʻīd	سعيد
misfortune (accident)	muṣība (m)	مصيبة
unhappy (adj)	taʻis	تعس

Character. Feelings. Emotions

58. Feelings. Emotions

feeling (emotion)	ʃuʿūr (m)	شعور
feelings	maʃāʿir (pl)	مشاعر
to feel (vt)	ʃaʿar	شعر
hunger	ʒawʿ (m)	جوع
to be hungry	arād an yaʾkul	أراد أن يأكل
thirst	ʿataʃ (m)	عطش
to be thirsty	arād an yaʃrab	أراد أن يشرب
sleepiness	nuʿās (m)	نعاس
to feel sleepy	arād an yanām	أراد أن ينام
tiredness	taʿab (m)	تعب
tired (adj)	taʿbān	تعبان
to get tired	taʿib	تعب
mood (humor)	ḥāla nafsiyya, mazāʒ (m)	حالة نفسيّة، مزاج
boredom	malal (m)	ملل
to be bored	ʃaʿar bil malal	شعر بالملل
seclusion	ʿuzla (f)	عزلة
to seclude oneself	inzawa	إنزوى
to worry (make anxious)	aqlaq	أقلق
to be worried	qalaq	قلق
worrying (n)	qalaq (m)	قلق
anxiety	qalaq (m)	قلق
preoccupied (adj)	maʃɣūl al bāl	مشغول البال
to be nervous	qalaq	قلق
to panic (vi)	uṣīb biθ ðaʿr	أصيب بالذعر
hope	amal (m)	أمل
to hope (vi, vt)	tamanna	تمنّى
certainty	yaqīn (m)	يقين
certain, sure (adj)	mutaʾakkid	متأكّد
uncertainty	ʿadam at taʾakkud (m)	عدم التأكّد
uncertain (adj)	ɣayr mutaʾakkid	غير متأكّد
drunk (adj)	sakrān	سكران
sober (adj)	ṣāḥi	صاح
weak (adj)	daʿīf	ضعيف
happy (adj)	saʿīd	سعيد
to scare (vt)	arhab	أرهب

fury (madness)	ɣaḍab ʃadīd (m)	غضب شديد
rage (fury)	ɣaḍab (m)	غضب
depression	ikti'āb (m)	إكتئاب
discomfort (unease)	ʿadam irtiyāḥ (m)	عدم إرتياح
comfort	rāḥa (f)	راحة
to regret (be sorry)	nadim	ندم
regret	nadam (m)	ندم
bad luck	sū' al ḥaẓẓ (m)	سوء الحظ
sadness	ḥuzn (f)	حزن
shame (remorse)	xaʒal (m)	خجل
gladness	faraḥ (m)	فرح
enthusiasm, zeal	ḥamās (m)	حماس
enthusiast	mutaḥammis (m)	متحمس
to show enthusiasm	taḥammas	تحمس

59. Character. Personality

character	ṭabʿ (m)	طبع
character flaw	ʿayb (m)	عيب
mind, reason	ʿaql (m)	عقل
conscience	ḍamīr (m)	ضمير
habit (custom)	ʿāda (f)	عادة
ability (talent)	qudra (f)	قدرة
can (e.g., ~ swim)	ʿaraf	عرف
patient (adj)	ṣābir	صابر
impatient (adj)	qalīl aṣ ṣabr	قليل الصبر
curious (inquisitive)	fuḍūliy	فضوليّ
curiosity	fuḍūl (m)	فضول
modesty	tawāḍuʿ (m)	تواضع
modest (adj)	mutawāḍiʿ	متواضع
immodest (adj)	ɣayr mutawāḍiʿ	غير متواضع
laziness	kasal (m)	كسل
lazy (adj)	kaslān	كسلان
lazy person (masc.)	kaslān (m)	كسلان
cunning (n)	makr (m)	مكر
cunning (as adj)	mākir	ماكر
distrust	ʿadam aθ θiqa (m)	عدم الثقة
distrustful (adj)	ʃakūk	شكوك
generosity	karam (m)	كرم
generous (adj)	karīm	كريم
talented (adj)	mawhūb	موهوب
talent	mawhiba (f)	موهبة

courageous (adj)	ʃuʒāʻ	شجاع
courage	ʃaʒāʻa (f)	شجاعة
honest (adj)	amīn	أمين
honesty	amāna (f)	أمانة
careful (cautious)	ḥāðir	حاذر
brave (courageous)	ʃuʒāʻ	شجاع
serious (adj)	ʒādd	جادّ
strict (severe, stern)	ṣārim	صارم
decisive (adj)	ḥazīm	حزيم
indecisive (adj)	mutaraddid	متردّد
shy, timid (adj)	χaʒūl	خجول
shyness, timidity	χaʒal (m)	خجل
confidence (trust)	θiqa (f)	ثقة
to believe (trust)	waθiq	وثق
trusting (credulous)	sarīʻ at taṣdīq	سريع التصديق
sincerely (adv)	bi ṣarāḥa	بصراحة
sincere (adj)	muχliṣ	مخلص
sincerity	iχlāṣ (m)	إخلاص
open (person)	ṣarīḥ	صريح
calm (adj)	hādi'	هادئ
frank (sincere)	ṣarīḥ	صريح
naïve (adj)	sāðiʒ	ساذج
absent-minded (adj)	ʃārid al fikr	شارد الفكر
funny (odd)	muḍḥik	مضحك
greed	buχl (m)	بخل
greedy (adj)	baχīl	بخيل
stingy (adj)	baχīl	بخيل
evil (adj)	ʃarīr	شرير
stubborn (adj)	ʻanīd	عنيد
unpleasant (adj)	karīh	كريه
selfish person (masc.)	anāniy (m)	أنانيّ
selfish (adj)	anāniy	أنانيّ
coward	ʒabān (m)	جبان
cowardly (adj)	ʒabān	جبان

60. Sleep. Dreams

to sleep (vi)	nām	نام
sleep, sleeping	nawm (m)	نوم
dream	ḥulm (m)	حلم
to dream (in sleep)	ḥalam	حلم
sleepy (adj)	naʻsān	نعسان
bed	sarīr (m)	سرير

mattress	martaba (f)	مرتبة
blanket (comforter)	baṭṭāniyya (f)	بطّانية
pillow	wisāda (f)	وسادة
sheet	milāya (f)	ملاية

insomnia	araq (m)	أرق
sleepless (adj)	ariq	أرق
sleeping pill	munawwim (m)	منوّم
to take a sleeping pill	tanāwal munawwim	تناول منوّمًا

to feel sleepy	arād an yanām	أراد أن ينام
to yawn (vi)	taθā'ab	تثاءب
to go to bed	ðahab ilā n nawm	ذهب إلى النوم
to make up the bed	a'add as sarīr	أعدّ السرير
to fall asleep	nām	نام

nightmare	kābūs (m)	كابوس
snore, snoring	ʃaxīr (m)	شخير
to snore (vi)	ʃaxxar	شخر

alarm clock	munabbih (m)	منبّه
to wake (vt)	ayqaz	أيقظ
to wake up	istayqaz	إستيقظ
to get up (vi)	qām	قام
to wash up (wash face)	ɣasal waʒhah	غسل وجهه

61. Humour. Laughter. Gladness

humor (wit, fun)	fukāha (f)	فكاهة
sense of humor	ḥiss (m)	حس
to enjoy oneself	istamta'	إستمتع
cheerful (merry)	farḥān	فرحان
merriment (gaiety)	faraḥ (m)	فرح

smile	ibtisāma (f)	إبتسامة
to smile (vi)	ibtasam	إبتسم
to start laughing	ḍaḥik	ضحك

| to laugh (vi) | ḍaḥik | ضحك |
| laugh, laughter | ḍaḥka (f) | ضحكة |

anecdote	ḥikāya muḍḥika (f)	حكاية مضحكة
funny (anecdote, etc.)	muḍḥik	مضحك
funny (odd)	muḍḥik	مضحك

to joke (vi)	mazaḥ	مزح
joke (verbal)	nukta (f)	نكتة
joy (emotion)	sa'āda (f)	سعادة
to rejoice (vi)	mariḥ	مرح
joyful (adj)	sa'īd	سعيد

62. Discussion, conversation. Part 1

communication	tawāṣul (m)	تواصل
to communicate	tawāṣal	تواصل
conversation	muḥādaθa (f)	محادثة
dialog	ḥiwār (m)	حوار
discussion (discourse)	munāqaʃa (f)	مناقشة
dispute (debate)	munāẓara (f)	مناظرة
to dispute	χālaf	خالف
interlocutor	muḥāwir (m)	محاور
topic (theme)	mawḍūʿ (m)	موضوع
point of view	wiʒhat naẓar (f)	وجهة نظر
opinion (point of view)	raʾy (m)	رأي
speech (talk)	χiṭāb (m)	خطاب
discussion (of report, etc.)	munāqaʃa (f)	مناقشة
to discuss (vt)	nāqaʃ	ناقش
talk (conversation)	ḥadīs (m)	حديث
to talk (to chat)	taḥādaθ	تحادث
meeting	liqāʾ (m)	لقاء
to meet (vi, vt)	qābal	قابل
proverb	maθal (m)	مثل
saying	qawl maʾθūr (m)	قول مأثور
riddle (poser)	luɣz (m)	لغز
to pose a riddle	alqa luɣz	ألقى لغزًا
password	kalimat al murūr (f)	كلمة مرور
secret	sirr (m)	سرّ
oath (vow)	qasam (m)	قسم
to swear (an oath)	aqsam	أقسم
promise	waʿd (m)	وعد
to promise (vt)	waʿad	وعد
advice (counsel)	naṣīḥa (f)	نصيحة
to advise (vt)	naṣaḥ	نصح
to follow one's advice	intaṣaḥ	إنتصح
to listen to … (obey)	aṭāʿ	أطاع
news	χabar (m)	خبر
sensation (news)	ḍaʒʒa (f)	ضجّة
information (data)	maʿlūmāt (pl)	معلومات
conclusion (decision)	istintāʒ (f)	إستنتاج
voice	ṣawt (m)	صوت
compliment	madḥ (m)	مدح
kind (nice)	laṭīf	لطيف
word	kalima (f)	كلمة
phrase	ʿibāra (f)	عبارة

answer	ʒawāb (m)	جواب
truth	ḥaqīqa (f)	حقيقة
lie	kiðb (m)	كذب

thought	fikra (f)	فكرة
idea (inspiration)	fikra (f)	فكرة
fantasy	xayāl (m)	خيال

63. Discussion, conversation. Part 2

respected (adj)	muḥtaram	محترم
to respect (vt)	iḥtaram	إحترم
respect	iḥtirām (m)	إحترام
Dear ... (letter)	ʿazīzi ...	عزيزي...

to introduce (sb to sb)	ʿarraf	عرّف
to make acquaintance	taʿarraf	تعرّف
intention	niyya (f)	نيّة
to intend (have in mind)	nawa	نوى
wish	tamanni (m)	تمنّ
to wish (~ good luck)	tamanna	تمنّى

surprise (astonishment)	ʿaʒab (m)	عجب
to surprise (amaze)	adhaʃ	أدهش
to be surprised	indahaʃ	إندهش

to give (vt)	aʿṭa	أعطى
to take (get hold of)	axað	أخذ
to give back	radd	ردّ
to return (give back)	arʒaʿ	أرجع

to apologize (vi)	iʿtaðar	إعتذر
apology	iʿtiðār (m)	إعتذار
to forgive (vt)	ʿafa	عفا

to talk (speak)	taḥaddaθ	تحدّث
to listen (vi)	istamaʿ	إستمع
to hear out	samiʿ	سمع
to understand (vt)	fahim	فهم

to show (to display)	ʿaraḍ	عرض
to look at ...	naẓar	نظر
to call (yell for sb)	nāda	نادى
to distract (disturb)	ʃaɣal	شغل
to disturb (vt)	azʿaʒ	أزعج
to pass (to hand sth)	sallam	سلّم

demand (request)	ṭalab (m)	طلب
to request (ask)	ṭalab	طلب
demand (firm request)	maṭlab (m)	مطلب

to demand (request firmly)	ṭālib	طالب
to tease (call names)	ɣāẓ	غاظ
to mock (make fun of)	saxar	سخر
mockery, derision	suxriyya (f)	سخرية
nickname	laqab (m)	لقب

insinuation	talmīḥ (m)	تلميح
to insinuate (imply)	lamaḥ	لمح
to mean (vt)	qaṣad	قصد

description	waṣf (m)	وصف
to describe (vt)	waṣaf	وصف
praise (compliments)	madḥ (m)	مدح
to praise (vt)	madaḥ	مدح

disappointment	xaybat amal (f)	خيبة أمل
to disappoint (vt)	xayyab	خيّب
to be disappointed	xābat ’āmāluh	خابت آماله

supposition	iftirāḍ (m)	إفتراض
to suppose (assume)	iftaraḍ	إفترض
warning (caution)	taḥ̄ōīr (m)	تحذير
to warn (vt)	ḥaððar	حذّر

64. Discussion, conversation. Part 3

| to talk into (convince) | aqnaʿ | أقنع |
| to calm down (vt) | ṭam’an | طمأن |

silence (~ is golden)	sukūt (m)	سكوت
to be silent (not speaking)	sakat	سكت
to whisper (vi, vt)	hamas	همس
whisper	hamsa (f)	همسة

| frankly, sincerely (adv) | bi ṣarāḥa | بصراحة |
| in my opinion ... | fi ra’yi ... | في رأيي... |

detail (of the story)	tafṣīl (m)	تفصيل
detailed (adj)	mufaṣṣal	مفصّل
in detail (adv)	bit tafāṣīl	بالتفاصيل

| hint, clue | iʃāra (f), talmīḥ (m) | إشارة، تلميح |
| to give a hint | aʿṭa talmīḥ | أعطى تلميحاً |

look (glance)	naẓra (f)	نظرة
to have a look	alqa naẓra	ألقى نظرة
fixed (look)	θābit	ثابت
to blink (vi)	ramaʃ	رمش
to wink (vi)	ɣamaz	غمز
to nod (in assent)	hazz ra’sah	هزّ رأسه

sigh	tanahhuda (f)	تنهّدة
to sigh (vi)	tanahhad	تنهّد
to shudder (vi)	irta'aʃ	إرتعش
gesture	iʃārat yad (f)	إشارة يد
to touch (one's arm, etc.)	lamas	لمس
to seize (e.g., ~ by the arm)	amsak	أمسك
to tap (on the shoulder)	ṣafaq	صفق

Look out!	χuð bālak!	خذ بالك!
Really?	wallahi?	والله؟
Are you sure?	hal anta muta'akkid?	هل أنت متأكّد؟
Good luck!	bit tawfīq!	بالتوفيق!
I see!	wāḍiḥ!	واضح!
What a pity!	ya lil asaf!	يا للأسف!

65. Agreement. Refusal

consent	muwāfaqa (f)	موافقة
to consent (vi)	wāfa'	وافق
approval	istiḥsān (m)	إستحسان
to approve (vt)	istiḥsan	إستحسن
refusal	rafḍ (m)	رفض
to refuse (vi, vt)	rafaḍ	رفض

Great!	'azīm!	عظيم!
All right!	ittafaqna!	إتّفقنا!
Okay! (I agree)	ittafaqna!	إتّفقنا!

forbidden (adj)	mamnū'	ممنوع
it's forbidden	mamnū'	ممنوع
it's impossible	mustaḥīl	مستحيل
incorrect (adj)	γalaṭ	غلط

to reject (~ a demand)	rafaḍ	رفض
to support (cause, idea)	ayyad	أيّد
to accept (~ an apology)	qabil	قبل

to confirm (vt)	aθbat	أثبت
confirmation	iθbāt (m)	إثبات
permission	samāḥ (m)	سماح
to permit (vt)	samaḥ	سمح
decision	qarār (m)	قرار
to say nothing (hold one's tongue)	ṣamat	صمت

condition (term)	ʃarṭ (m)	شرط
excuse (pretext)	'uðr (m)	عذر
praise (compliments)	madḥ (m)	مدح
to praise (vt)	madaḥ	مدح

66. Success. Good luck. Failure

success	naʒāḥ (m)	نجاح
successfully (adv)	bi naʒāḥ	بنجاح
successful (adj)	nāʒiḥ	ناجح
luck (good luck)	ḥazz (m)	حظ
Good luck!	bit tawfīq!	بالتوفيق!
lucky (e.g., ~ day)	murawaffiq	متوفق
lucky (fortunate)	maḥzūz	محظوظ
failure	faʃl (m)	فشل
misfortune	sū' al ḥazz (m)	سوء الحظ
bad luck	sū' al ḥazz (m)	سوء الحظ
unsuccessful (adj)	fāʃil	فاشل
catastrophe	kāriθa (f)	كارثة
pride	faχr (m)	فخر
proud (adj)	faχūr	فخور
to be proud	iftaχar	إفتخر
winner	fā'iz (m)	فائز
to win (vi)	fāz	فاز
to lose (not win)	χasir	خسر
try	muḥāwala (f)	محاولة
to try (vi)	ḥāwal	حاول
chance (opportunity)	furṣa (f)	فرصة

67. Quarrels. Negative emotions

shout (scream)	ṣarχa (f)	صرخة
to shout (vi)	ṣaraχ	صرخ
to start to cry out	ṣaraχ	صرخ
quarrel	muʃāʒara (f)	مشاجرة
to quarrel (vi)	taʃāʒar	تشاجر
fight (squabble)	muʃāʒara (f)	مشاجرة
to make a scene	taʃāʒar	تشاجر
conflict	χilāf (m)	خلاف
misunderstanding	sū'at tafāhum (m)	سوء التفاهم
insult	ihāna (f)	إهانة
to insult (vt)	ahān	أهان
insulted (adj)	muhān	مهان
resentment	ḍaym (m)	ضيم
to offend (vt)	asā'	أساء
to take offense	istā'	إستاء
indignation	istiyā' (m)	إستياء
to be indignant	istā'	إستاء

complaint	ʃakwa (f)	شكوى
to complain (vi, vt)	ʃaka	شكا
apology	iʻtiðār (m)	إعتذار
to apologize (vi)	iʻtaðar	إعتذر
to beg pardon	iʻtaðar	إعتذر
criticism	naqd (m)	نقد
to criticize (vt)	naqad	نقد
accusation	ittihām (m)	إتّهام
to accuse (vt)	ittaham	إتّهم
revenge	intiqām (m)	إنتقام
to avenge (get revenge)	intaqam	إنتقم
to pay back	radd	ردَ
disdain	iħtiqār (m)	إحتقار
to despise (vt)	iħtaqar	إحتقر
hatred, hate	karāha (f)	كراهة
to hate (vt)	karah	كره
nervous (adj)	ʻaṣabiy	عصبيَ
to be nervous	qalaq	قلق
angry (mad)	zaʻlān	زعلان
to make angry	azʻal	أزعل
humiliation	iðlāl (m)	إذلال
to humiliate (vt)	ðallal	ذلّل
to humiliate oneself	taðallal	تذلّل
shock	ṣadma (f)	صدمة
to shock (vt)	ṣadam	صدم
trouble (e.g., serious ~)	muʃkila (f)	مشكلة
unpleasant (adj)	karīh	كريه
fear (dread)	χawf (m)	خوف
terrible (storm, heat)	ʃadīd	شديد
scary (e.g., ~ story)	muχīf	مخيف
horror	ruʻb (m)	رعب
awful (crime, news)	murʻib	مرعب
to begin to tremble	irtaʻaʃ	إرتعش
to cry (weep)	baka	بكى
to start crying	baka	بكى
tear	damaʻa (f)	دمعة
fault	ɣalṭa (f)	غلطة
guilt (feeling)	ðamb (m)	ذنب
dishonor (disgrace)	ʻār (m)	عار
protest	iħtiʒāʒ (m)	إحتجاج
stress	tawattur (m)	توتّر

to disturb (vt)	az'aʒ	أزعج
to be furious	ɣaḍib	غضب
mad, angry (adj)	ɣaḍbān	غضبان
to end (~ a relationship)	anha	أنهى
to swear (at sb)	ʃātam	شاتم
to scare (become afraid)	χāf	خاف
to hit (strike with hand)	ḍarab	ضرب
to fight (street fight, etc.)	ta'ārak	تعارك
to settle (a conflict)	sawwa	سوّى
discontented (adj)	ɣayr rāḍi	غير راض
furious (adj)	'anīf	عنيف
It's not good!	laysa haða amr ʒayyid!	ليس هذا أمرًا جيّدًا!!
It's bad!	haða amr sayyi'!	هذا أمر سيّء!

Medicine

68. Diseases

sickness	maraḍ (m)	مرض
to be sick	maraḍ	مرض
health	ṣiḥḥa (f)	صحّة
runny nose (coryza)	zukām (m)	زكام
tonsillitis	iltihāb al lawzatayn (m)	التهاب اللوزتين
cold (illness)	bard (m)	برد
to catch a cold	aṣābahu al bard	أصابه البرد
bronchitis	iltihāb al qaṣabāt (m)	إلتهاب القصبات
pneumonia	iltihāb ar ri'atayn (m)	إلتهاب الرئتين
flu, influenza	inflūnza (f)	إنفلونزا
nearsighted (adj)	qaṣīr an naẓar	قصير النظر
farsighted (adj)	ba'īd an naẓar	بعيد النظر
strabismus (crossed eyes)	ḥawal (m)	حول
cross-eyed (adj)	aḥwal	أحول
cataract	katarakt (f)	كاتاراكت
glaucoma	glawkūma (f)	جلوكوما
stroke	sakta (f)	سكتة
heart attack	iḥtifā' (m)	إحتشاء
myocardial infarction	nawba qalbiya (f)	نوبة قلبية
paralysis	ʃalal (m)	شلل
to paralyze (vt)	ʃall	شلّ
allergy	ḥassāsiyya (f)	حسّاسيّة
asthma	rabw (m)	ربو
diabetes	ad dā' as sukkariy (m)	الداء السكّريّ
toothache	alam al asnān (m)	ألم الأسنان
caries	naxar al asnān (m)	نخر الأسنان
diarrhea	ishāl (m)	إسهال
constipation	imsāk (m)	إمساك
stomach upset	'usr al haḍm (m)	عسر الهضم
food poisoning	tasammum (m)	تسمّم
to get food poisoning	tasammam	تسمّم
arthritis	iltihāb al mafāṣil (m)	إلتهاب المفاصل
rickets	kusāḥ al aṭfāl (m)	كساح الأطفال
rheumatism	riumatizm (m)	روماتزم

atherosclerosis	taṣṣallub aʃ ʃarayīn (m)	تصلّب الشرايين
gastritis	iltihāb al maʿida (m)	إلتهاب المعدة
appendicitis	iltihāb az zāʾida ad dūdiyya (m)	إلتهاب الزائدة الدوديّة
cholecystitis	iltihāb al marāra (m)	إلتهاب المرارة
ulcer	qurḥa (f)	قرحة
measles	maraḍ al ḥaṣba (m)	مرض الحصبة
rubella (German measles)	ḥaṣba almāniyya (f)	حصبة ألمانية
jaundice	yaraqān (m)	يرقان
hepatitis	iltihāb al kabd al vayrūsiy (m)	إلتهاب الكبد الفيروسيّ
schizophrenia	ʃizufrīniya (f)	شيزوفرينيا
rabies (hydrophobia)	dāʾ al kalb (m)	داء الكلب
neurosis	ʿiṣāb (m)	عصاب
concussion	irtiʒāʒ al muxx (m)	إرتجاج المخ
cancer	saraṭān (m)	سرطان
sclerosis	taṣṣallub (m)	تصلّب
multiple sclerosis	taṣṣallub mutaʿaddid (m)	تصلّب متعدد
alcoholism	idmān al xamr (m)	إدمان الخمر
alcoholic (n)	mudmin al xamr (m)	مدمن الخمر
syphilis	sifilis az zuhariy (m)	سفلس الزهري
AIDS	al aydz (m)	الايدز
tumor	waram (m)	ورم
malignant (adj)	xabīθ	خبيث
benign (adj)	ḥamīd (m)	حميد
fever	ḥumma (f)	حمّى
malaria	malāriya (f)	ملاريا
gangrene	ɣanɣrīna (f)	غنغرينا
seasickness	duwār al baḥr (m)	دوار البحر
epilepsy	maraḍ aṣ ṣarʿ (m)	مرض الصرع
epidemic	wabāʾ (m)	وباء
typhus	tīfus (m)	تيفوس
tuberculosis	maraḍ as sull (m)	مرض السلّ
cholera	kulīra (f)	كوليرا
plague (bubonic ~)	ṭāʿūn (m)	طاعون

69. Symptoms. Treatments. Part 1

symptom	ʿaraḍ (m)	عرض
temperature	ḥarāra (f)	حرارة
high temperature (fever)	ḥumma (f)	حمّى
pulse	nabḍ (m)	نبض
dizziness (vertigo)	dawxa (f)	دوخة

hot (adj)	ḥārr	حارّ
shivering	nafaḍān (m)	نفضان
pale (e.g., ~ face)	aṣfar	أصفر
cough	suʿāl (m)	سعال
to cough (vi)	saʿal	سعل
to sneeze (vi)	ʿaṭas	عطس
faint	iɣmāʾ (m)	إغماء
to faint (vi)	ɣumiya ʿalayh	غمي عليه
bruise (hématome)	kadma (f)	كدمة
bump (lump)	tawarrum (m)	تورّم
to bang (bump)	iṣṭadam	إصطدم
contusion (bruise)	raḍḍ (m)	رضّ
to get a bruise	taraḍḍaḍ	ترضّض
to limp (vi)	ʿaraʒ	عرج
dislocation	xalʿ (m)	خلع
to dislocate (vt)	xalaʿ	خلع
fracture	kasr (m)	كسر
to have a fracture	inkasar	إنكسر
cut (e.g., paper ~)	ʒurḥ (m)	جرح
to cut oneself	ʒaraḥ nafsah	جرح نفسه
bleeding	nazf (m)	نزف
burn (injury)	ḥarq (m)	حرق
to get burned	taʃayyaṭ	تشيّط
to prick (vt)	waxaz	وخز
to prick oneself	waxaz nafsah	وخز نفسه
to injure (vt)	aṣāb	أصاب
injury	iṣāba (f)	إصابة
wound	ʒurḥ (m)	جرح
trauma	ṣadma (f)	صدمة
to be delirious	haða	هذى
to stutter (vi)	talaʿsam	تلعثم
sunstroke	ḍarbat ʃams (f)	ضربة شمس

70. Symptoms. Treatments. Part 2

pain, ache	alam (m)	ألم
splinter (in foot, etc.)	ʃaẓiyya (f)	شظيّة
sweat (perspiration)	ʿirq (m)	عرق
to sweat (perspire)	ʿariq	عرق
vomiting	taqayyuʿ (m)	تقيّؤ
convulsions	taʃannuʒāt (pl)	تشنّجات
pregnant (adj)	ḥāmil	حامل

to be born	wulid	وُلِد
delivery, labor	wilāda (f)	ولادة
to deliver (~ a baby)	walad	ولد
abortion	iʒhāḍ (m)	إجهاض

breathing, respiration	tanaffus (m)	تنفّس
in-breath (inhalation)	istinʃāq (m)	إستنشاق
out-breath (exhalation)	zafīr (m)	زفير
to exhale (breathe out)	zafar	زفر
to inhale (vi)	istanʃaq	إستنشق

disabled person	mu'āq (m)	معاق
cripple	muq'ad (m)	مقعد
drug addict	mudmin muxaddirāt (m)	مدمن مخدّرات

deaf (adj)	aṭraʃ	أطرش
mute (adj)	axras	أخرس
deaf mute (adj)	aṭraʃ axras	أطرش أخرس

mad, insane (adj)	maʒnūn (m)	مجنون
madman (demented person)	maʒnūn (m)	مجنون
madwoman	maʒnūna (f)	مجنونة
to go insane	ʒunn	جُنّ

gene	ʒīn (m)	جين
immunity	manā'a (f)	مناعة
hereditary (adj)	wirāθiy	وراثيّ
congenital (adj)	xilqiy munð al wilāda	خلقيّ منذ الولادة

virus	virūs (m)	فيروس
microbe	mikrūb (m)	ميكروب
bacterium	ʒurθūma (f)	جرثومة
infection	'adwa (f)	عدوى

71. Symptoms. Treatments. Part 3

| hospital | mustaʃfa (m) | مستشفى |
| patient | marīḍ (m) | مريض |

diagnosis	taʃxīṣ (m)	تشخيص
cure	'ilāʒ (m)	علاج
medical treatment	'ilāʒ (m)	علاج
to get treatment	ta'ālaʒ	تعالج
to treat (~ a patient)	'ālaʒ	عالج
to nurse (look after)	marraḍ	مرّض
care (nursing ~)	'ināya (f)	عناية

| operation, surgery | 'amaliyya ʒaraḥiyya (f) | عمليّة جرحيّة |
| to bandage (head, limb) | ḍammad | ضمّد |

bandaging	taḍmīd (m)	تضميد
vaccination	talqīḥ (m)	تلقيح
to vaccinate (vt)	laqqaḥ	لقّح
injection, shot	ḥuqna (f)	حقنة
to give an injection	ḥaqan ibra	حقن إبرة

attack	nawba (f)	نوبة
amputation	batr (m)	بتر
to amputate (vt)	batar	بتر
coma	ɣaybūba (f)	غيبوبة
to be in a coma	kān fi ḥālat ɣaybūba	كان في حالة غيبوبة
intensive care	al 'ināya al murakkaza (f)	العناية المركّزة

to recover (~ from flu)	ʃufiy	شفي
condition (patient's ~)	ḥāla (f)	حالة
consciousness	wa'y (m)	وعي
memory (faculty)	ðākira (f)	ذاكرة

to pull out (tooth)	xala'	خلع
filling	haʃw (m)	حشو
to fill (a tooth)	haʃa	حشا

| hypnosis | at tanwīm al maɣnaṭīsiy (m) | التنويم المغناطيسيّ |
| to hypnotize (vt) | nawwam | نوّم |

72. Doctors

doctor	ṭabīb (m)	طبيب
nurse	mumarriḍa (f)	ممرّضة
personal doctor	duktūr ʃaxṣiy (m)	دكتور شخصيّ

dentist	ṭabīb al asnān (m)	طبيب الأسنان
eye doctor	ṭabīb al 'uyūn (m)	طبيب العيون
internist	ṭabīb bāṭiniy (m)	طبيب باطنيّ
surgeon	ʒarrāḥ (m)	جرّاح

psychiatrist	ṭabīb nafsiy (m)	طبيب نفسيّ
pediatrician	ṭabīb al aṭfāl (m)	طبيب الأطفال
psychologist	sikulūʒiy (m)	سيكولوجيّ
gynecologist	ṭabīb an nisā' (m)	طبيب النساء
cardiologist	ṭabīb al qalb (m)	طبيب القلب

73. Medicine. Drugs. Accessories

medicine, drug	dawā' (m)	دواء
remedy	'ilāʒ (m)	علاج
to prescribe (vt)	waṣaf	وصف
prescription	waṣfa (f)	وصفة

tablet, pill	quṣ (m)	قرص
ointment	marham (m)	مرهم
ampule	ambūla (f)	أمبولة
mixture	dawā' ʃarāb (m)	دواء شراب
syrup	ʃarāb (m)	شراب
pill	ḥabba (f)	حبّة
powder	ðarūr (m)	ذرور
gauze bandage	ḍammāda (f)	ضمادة
cotton wool	quṭn (m)	قطن
iodine	yūd (m)	يود
Band-Aid	blāstir (m)	بلاستر
eyedropper	māṣṣat al bastara (f)	ماصّة البسترة
thermometer	tirmūmitr (m)	ترمومتر
syringe	miḥqana (f)	محقنة
wheelchair	kursiy mutaḥarrik (m)	كرسي متحرّك
crutches	ʻukkāzān (du)	عكّازان
painkiller	musakkin (m)	مسكّن
laxative	mulayyin (m)	ملين
spirits (ethanol)	iθanūl (m)	إيثانول
medicinal herbs	aʻʃāb ṭibbiyya (pl)	أعشاب طبية
herbal (~ tea)	ʻuʃbiy	عشبي

74. Smoking. Tobacco products

tobacco	tabγ (m)	تبغ
cigarette	sīʒāra (f)	سيجارة
cigar	sīʒār (m)	سيجار
pipe	γalyūn (m)	غليون
pack (of cigarettes)	ʻulba (f)	علبة
matches	kibrīt (m)	كبريت
matchbox	ʻulbat kibrīt (f)	علبة كبريت
lighter	wallāʻa (f)	ولّاعة
ashtray	ṭaqṭūqa (f)	طقطقة
cigarette case	ʻulbat saʒāʼir (f)	علبة سجائر
cigarette holder	ḥamilat sīʒāra (f)	حاملة سيجارة
filter (cigarette tip)	filtir (m)	فلتر
to smoke (vi, vt)	daxxan	دخّن
to light a cigarette	aʃʻal siʒāra	أشعل سيجارة
smoking	tadxīn (m)	تدخين
smoker	mudaxxin (m)	مدخّن
stub, butt (of cigarette)	ʻuqb siʒāra (m)	عقب سيجارة
smoke, fumes	duxān (m)	دخان
ash	ramād (m)	رماد

HUMAN HABITAT

City

75. City. Life in the city

city, town	madīna (f)	مدينة
capital city	ʿāṣima (f)	عاصمة
village	qarya (f)	قرية
city map	xarīṭat al madīna (f)	خريطة المدينة
downtown	markaz al madīna (m)	مركز المدينة
suburb	ḍāhiya (f)	ضاحية
suburban (adj)	aḍ ḍawāhi	الضواحي
outskirts	aṭrāf al madīna (pl)	أطراف المدينة
environs (suburbs)	ḍawāhi al madīna (pl)	ضواحي المدينة
city block	ḥayy (m)	حي
residential block (area)	ḥayy sakaniy (m)	حي سكني
traffic	ḥarakat al murūr (f)	حركة المرور
traffic lights	iʃārāt al murūr (pl)	إشارات المرور
public transportation	wasāʾil an naql (pl)	وسائل النقل
intersection	taqāṭuʿ (m)	تقاطع
crosswalk	maʿbar al muʃāt (m)	معبر المشاة
pedestrian underpass	nafaq muʃāt (m)	نفق مشاة
to cross (~ the street)	ʿabar	عبر
pedestrian	māʃi (m)	ماش
sidewalk	raṣīf (m)	رصيف
bridge	ʒisr (m)	جسر
embankment (river walk)	kurnīʃ (m)	كورنيش
fountain	nāfūra (f)	نافورة
allée (garden walkway)	mamʃa (m)	ممشى
park	ḥadīqa (f)	حديقة
boulevard	bulvār (m)	بولفار
square	maydān (m)	ميدان
avenue (wide street)	ʃāriʿ (m)	شارع
street	ʃāriʿ (m)	شارع
side street	zuqāq (m)	زقاق
dead end	ṭarīq masdūd (m)	طريق مسدود
house	bayt (m)	بيت
building	mabna (m)	مبنى

skyscraper	nāṭiḥat saḥāb (f)	ناطحة سحاب
facade	wāǯiha (f)	واجهة
roof	saqf (m)	سقف
window	ʃubbāk (m)	شبّاك
arch	qaws (m)	قوس
column	ʿamūd (m)	عمود
corner	zāwiya (f)	زاوية

store window	vatrīna (f)	فترينة
signboard (store sign, etc.)	lāfita (f)	لافتة
poster	mulṣaq (m)	ملصق
advertising poster	mulṣaq iʿlāniy (m)	ملصق إعلاني
billboard	lawḥat iʿlānāt (f)	لوحة إعلانات

garbage, trash	zubāla (f)	زبالة
trashcan (public ~)	ṣundūq zubāla (m)	صندوق زبالة
to litter (vi)	rama zubāla	رمى زبالة
garbage dump	mazbala (f)	مزبلة

phone booth	kuʃk tilifūn (m)	كشك تليفون
lamppost	ʿamūd al miṣbāḥ (m)	عمود المصباح
bench (park ~)	dikka (f), kursiy (m)	دكّة, كرسيّ

police officer	ʃurṭiy (m)	شرطيّ
police	ʃurṭa (f)	شرطة
beggar	ʃaḥḥāð (m)	شحّاذ
homeless (n)	mutaʃarrid (m)	متشرّد

76. Urban institutions

store	maḥall (m)	محلّ
drugstore, pharmacy	ṣaydaliyya (f)	صيدليّة
eyeglass store	al adawāt al baṣariyya (pl)	الأدوات البصريّة
shopping mall	markaz tiǯāriy (m)	مركز تجاريّ
supermarket	subirmarkit (m)	سوبرماركت

bakery	maxbaz (m)	مخبز
baker	xabbāz (m)	خبّاز
pastry shop	dukkān ḥalawāniy (m)	دكّان حلوانيّ
grocery store	baqqāla (f)	بقّالة
butcher shop	malḥama (f)	ملحمة

| produce store | dukkān xuḍār (m) | دكّان خضار |
| market | sūq (f) | سوق |

coffee house	kafé (m), maqha (m)	كافيه, مقهى
restaurant	maṭʿam (m)	مطعم
pub, bar	ḥāna (f)	حانة
pizzeria	maṭʿam pizza (m)	مطعم بيتزا
hair salon	ṣālūn ḥilāqa (m)	صالون حلاقة

post office	maktab al barīd (m)	مكتب البريد
dry cleaners	tanzīf ʒāff (m)	تنظيف جافّ
photo studio	istūdiyu taṣwīr (m)	إستوديو تصوير
shoe store	maḥall aḥðiya (m)	محلّ أحذية
bookstore	maḥall kutub (m)	محلّ كتب
sporting goods store	maḥall riyāḍiy (m)	محلّ رياضيّ
clothes repair shop	maḥall xiyāṭat malābis (m)	محلّ خياطة ملابس
formal wear rental	maḥall taʾʒīr malābis rasmiyya (m)	محلّ تأجير ملابس رسمية
video rental store	maḥal taʾʒīr vidiyu (m)	محلّ تأجير فيديو
circus	sirk (m)	سيرك
zoo	ḥadīqat al ḥayawān (f)	حديقة حيوان
movie theater	sinima (f)	سينما
museum	matḥaf (m)	متحف
library	maktaba (f)	مكتبة
theater	masraḥ (m)	مسرح
opera (opera house)	ubra (f)	أوبرا
nightclub	malha layliy (m)	ملهى ليليّ
casino	kazinu (m)	كازينو
mosque	masʒid (m)	مسجد
synagogue	kanīs maʿbad yahūdiy (m)	كنيس معبد يهوديّ
cathedral	katidrāʾiyya (f)	كاتدرائيّة
temple	maʿbad (m)	معبد
church	kanīsa (f)	كنيسة
college	kulliyya (m)	كلّيّة
university	ʒāmiʿa (f)	جامعة
school	madrasa (f)	مدرسة
prefecture	muqāṭaʿa (f)	مقاطعة
city hall	baladiyya (f)	بلديّة
hotel	funduq (m)	فندق
bank	bank (m)	بنك
embassy	safāra (f)	سفارة
travel agency	ʃarikat siyāḥa (f)	شركة سياحة
information office	maktab al istiʿlāmāt (m)	مكتب الإستعلامات
currency exchange	ṣarrāfa (f)	صرّافة
subway	mitru (m)	مترو
hospital	mustaʃfa (m)	مستشفى
gas station	maḥaṭṭat banzīn (f)	محطّة بنزين
parking lot	mawqif as sayyārāt (m)	موقف السيّارات

77. Urban transportation

bus	bāṣ (m)	باص
streetcar	trām (m)	ترام
trolley bus	truli bāṣ (m)	ترولي باص
route (of bus, etc.)	χaṭṭ (m)	خطّ
number (e.g., bus ~)	raqm (m)	رقم
to go by ...	rakib ...	ركب...
to get on (~ the bus)	rakib	ركب
to get off ...	nazil min	نزل من
stop (e.g., bus ~)	mawqif (m)	موقف
next stop	al maḥaṭṭa al qādima (f)	المحطّة القادمة
terminus	āχir maḥaṭṭa (f)	آخر محطّة
schedule	ʒadwal (m)	جدول
to wait (vt)	intaẓar	إنتظر
ticket	taðkira (f)	تذكرة
fare	uʒra (f)	أجرة
cashier (ticket seller)	ṣarrāf (m)	صرّاف
ticket inspection	taftīʃ taðkira (m)	تفتيش تذكرة
ticket inspector	mufattiʃ taðākir (m)	مفتّش تذاكر
to be late (for ...)	ta'aχχar	تأخّر
to miss (~ the train, etc.)	ta'aχχar	تأخّر
to be in a hurry	ista'ʒal	إستعجل
taxi, cab	taksi (m)	تاكسي
taxi driver	sā'iq taksi (m)	سائق تاكسي
by taxi	bit taksi	بالتاكسي
taxi stand	mawqif taksi (m)	موقف تاكسي
to call a taxi	kallam tāksi	كلّم تاكسي
to take a taxi	aχað taksi	أخذ تاكسي
traffic	ḥarakat al murūr (f)	حركة المرور
traffic jam	zaḥmat al murūr (f)	زحمة المرور
rush hour	sā'at að ðurwa (f)	ساعة الذروة
to park (vi)	awqaf	أوقف
to park (vt)	awqaf	أوقف
parking lot	mawqif as sayyārāt (m)	موقف السيارات
subway	mitru (m)	مترو
station	maḥaṭṭa (f)	محطّة
to take the subway	rakib al mitru	ركب المترو
train	qiṭār (m)	قطار
train station	maḥaṭṭat qiṭār (f)	محطّة قطار

78. Sightseeing

monument	timθāl (m)	تمثال
fortress	qal'a (f), ḥiṣn (m)	قلعة، حصن
palace	qaṣr (m)	قصر
castle	qal'a (f)	قلعة
tower	burʒ (m)	برج
mausoleum	ḍarīḥ (m)	ضريح
architecture	handasa mi'māriyya (f)	هندسة معماريّة
medieval (adj)	min al qurūn al wusṭa	من القرون الوسطى
ancient (adj)	qadīm	قديم
national (adj)	waṭaniy	وطنيّ
famous (monument, etc.)	maʃhūr	مشهور
tourist	sā'iḥ (m)	سائح
guide (person)	murʃid (m)	مرشد
excursion, sightseeing tour	ʒawla (f)	جولة
to show (vt)	'araḍ	عرض
to tell (vt)	ḥaddaθ	حدّث
to find (vt)	waʒad	وجد
to get lost (lose one's way)	ḍā'	ضاع
map (e.g., subway ~)	χarīṭa (f)	خريطة
map (e.g., city ~)	χarīṭa (f)	خريطة
souvenir, gift	tiðkār (m)	تذكار
gift shop	maḥall hadāya (m)	محلّ هدايا
to take pictures	ṣawwar	صوّر
to have one's picture taken	taṣawwar	تصوّر

79. Shopping

to buy (purchase)	iʃtara	إشترى
purchase	ʃay' (m)	شيء
to go shopping	iʃtara	إشترى
shopping	ʃubinɣ (m)	شوبينغ
to be open (ab. store)	maftūḥ	مفتوح
to be closed	muɣlaq	مغلق
footwear, shoes	aḥðiya (pl)	أحذية
clothes, clothing	malābis (pl)	ملابس
cosmetics	mawādd at taʒmīl (pl)	موادّ التجميل
food products	ma'kūlāt (pl)	مأكولات
gift, present	hadiyya (f)	هديّة
salesman	bā'i' (m)	بائع
saleswoman	bā'i'a (f)	بائعة

check out, cash desk	ṣundū' ad dafʿ (m)	صندوق الدفع
mirror	mir'āt (f)	مرآة
counter (store ~)	minḍada (f)	منضدة
fitting room	ɣurfat al qiyās (f)	غرفة القياس

to try on	ʒarrab	جرّب
to fit (ab. dress, etc.)	nāsab	ناسب
to like (I like ...)	aʿʒab	أعجب

price	siʿr (m)	سعر
price tag	tikit as siʿr (m)	تيكت السعر
to cost (vt)	kallaf	كلّف
How much?	bikam?	بكم؟
discount	xaṣm (m)	خصم

inexpensive (adj)	ɣayr ɣāli	غير غال
cheap (adj)	raxīṣ	رخيص
expensive (adj)	ɣāli	غال
It's expensive	haða ɣāli	هذا غال

rental (n)	isti'ʒār (m)	إستئجار
to rent (~ a tuxedo)	ista'ʒar	إستأجر
credit (trade credit)	i'timān (m)	إئتمان
on credit (adv)	bid dayn	بالدين

80. Money

money	nuqūd (pl)	نقود
currency exchange	taḥwīl ʿumla (m)	تحويل عملة
exchange rate	siʿr aṣ ṣarf (m)	سعر الصرف
ATM	ṣarrāf 'āliy (m)	صرّاف آليّ
coin	qiṭʿa naqdiyya (f)	قطعة نقديّة

| dollar | dulār (m) | دولار |
| euro | yuru (m) | يورو |

lira	lira iṭāliyya (f)	ليرة إيطالية
Deutschmark	mark almāniy (m)	مارك ألماني
franc	frank (m)	فرنك
pound sterling	ʒunayh istirlīniy (m)	جنيه استرلينيّ
yen	yīn (m)	ين

debt	dayn (m)	دين
debtor	mudīn (m)	مدين
to lend (money)	sallaf	سلّف
to borrow (vi, vt)	istalaf	إستلف

bank	bank (m)	بنك
account	ḥisāb (m)	حساب
to deposit (vt)	awdaʿ	أودع

to deposit into the account	awda' fil ḥisāb	أودع في الحساب
to withdraw (vt)	saḥab min al ḥisāb	سحب من الحساب
credit card	biṭāqat i'timān (f)	بطاقة إئتمان
cash	nuqūd (pl)	نقود
check	ʃīk (m)	شيك
to write a check	katab ʃīk	كتب شيكًا
checkbook	daftar ʃīkāt (m)	دفتر شيكات
wallet	maḥfaẓat ʒīb (f)	محفظة جيب
change purse	maḥfaẓat fakka (f)	محفظة فكّة
safe	χizāna (f)	خزانة
heir	wāris (m)	وارث
inheritance	wirāθa (f)	وراثة
fortune (wealth)	θarwa (f)	ثروة
lease	ʾīʒār (m)	إيجار
rent (money)	uʒrat as sakan (f)	أجرة السكن
to rent (sth from sb)	ista'ʒar	إستأجر
price	si'r (m)	سعر
cost	θaman (m)	ثمن
sum	mablaɣ (m)	مبلغ
to spend (vt)	ṣaraf	صرف
expenses	maṣārīf (pl)	مصاريف
to economize (vi, vt)	waffar	وفّر
economical	muwaffir	موفّر
to pay (vi, vt)	dafa'	دفع
payment	daf' (m)	دفع
change (give the ~)	al bāqi (m)	الباقي
tax	ḍarība (f)	ضريبة
fine	ɣarāma (f)	غرامة
to fine (vt)	faraḍ ɣarāma	فرض غرامة

81. Post. Postal service

post office	maktab al barīd (m)	مكتب البريد
mail (letters, etc.)	al barīd (m)	البريد
mailman	sā'i al barīd (m)	ساعي البريد
opening hours	awqāt al 'amal (pl)	أوقات العمل
letter	risāla (f)	رسالة
registered letter	risāla musaʒʒala (f)	رسالة مسجّلة
postcard	biṭāqa barīdiyya (f)	بطاقة بريديّة
telegram	barqiyya (f)	برقيّة
package (parcel)	ṭard (m)	طرد

money transfer	ḥawāla māliyya (f)	حوالة ماليّة
to receive (vt)	istalam	إستلم
to send (vt)	arsal	أرسل
sending	irsāl (m)	إرسال
address	'unwān (m)	عنوان
ZIP code	raqm al barīd (m)	رقم البريد
sender	mursil (m)	مرسل
receiver	mursal ilayh (m)	مرسل إليه
name (first name)	ism (m)	إسم
surname (last name)	ism al 'ā'ila (m)	إسم العائلة
postage rate	ta'rīfa (f)	تعريفة
standard (adj)	'ādiy	عاديّ
economical (adj)	muwaffir	موفّر
weight	wazn (m)	وزن
to weigh (~ letters)	wazan	وزن
envelope	ẓarf (m)	ظرف
postage stamp	ṭābi' (m)	طابع
to stamp an envelope	alṣaq ṭābi'	ألصق طابعا

Dwelling. House. Home

82. House. Dwelling

house	bayt (m)	بيت
at home (adv)	fil bayt	في البيت
yard	finā' (m)	فناء
fence (iron ~)	sūr (m)	سور
brick (n)	tūb (m)	طوب
brick (as adj)	min at tūb	من الطوب
stone (n)	haʒar (m)	حجر
stone (as adj)	haʒariy	حجريّ
concrete (n)	xarasāna (f)	خرسانة
concrete (as adj)	xarasāniy	خرسانيّ
new (new-built)	ʒadīd	جديد
old (adj)	qadīm	قديم
decrepit (house)	'āyil lis suqūt	آيل للسقوط
modern (adj)	mu'āsir	معاصر
multistory (adj)	muta'addid at tawābiq	متعدّد الطوابق
tall (~ building)	'āli	عال
floor, story	tābiq (m)	طابق
single-story (adj)	ðu tābiq wāhid	ذو طابق واحد
1st floor	tābiq sufliy (m)	طابق سفليّ
top floor	tābiq 'ulwiy (m)	طابق علويّ
roof	saqf (m)	سقف
chimney	madxana (f)	مدخنة
roof tiles	qirmīd (m)	قرميد
tiled (adj)	min al qirmīd	من القرميد
attic (storage place)	'ullayya (f)	عليّة
window	ʃubbāk (m)	شبّاك
glass	zuʒāʒ (m)	زجاج
window ledge	raff ʃubbāk (f)	رف شبّاك
shutters	darf ʃubbāk (m)	درف شبّاك
wall	hā'it (m)	حائط
balcony	ʃurfa (f)	شرفة
downspout	masūrat at tasrīf (f)	ماسورة التصريف
upstairs (to be ~)	fawq	فوق
to go upstairs	sa'ad	صعد
to come down (the stairs)	nazil	نزل
to move (to new premises)	intaqal	إنتقل

91

83. House. Entrance. Lift

entrance	madχal (m)	مدخل
stairs (stairway)	sullam (m)	سلّم
steps	daraʒāt (pl)	درجات
banister	drabizīn (m)	درابزين
lobby (hotel ~)	ṣāla (f)	صالة
mailbox	ṣundūq al barīd (m)	صندوق البريد
garbage can	ṣundūq az zubāla (m)	صندوق الزبالة
trash chute	manfað að ðubāla (m)	منفذ الزبالة
elevator	miṣ'ad (m)	مصعد
freight elevator	miṣ'ad aʃʃaḥn (m)	مصعد الشحن
elevator cage	kabīna (f)	كابينة
to take the elevator	rakib al miṣ'ad	ركب المصعد
apartment	ʃaqqa (f)	شقّة
residents (~ of a building)	sukkān al 'imāra (pl)	سكّان العمارة
neighbor (masc.)	ʒār (m)	جار
neighbor (fem.)	ʒāra (f)	جارة
neighbors	ʒirān (pl)	جيران

84. House. Doors. Locks

door	bāb (m)	باب
gate (vehicle ~)	bawwāba (f)	بوّابة
handle, doorknob	qabḍat al bāb (f)	قبضة الباب
to unlock (unbolt)	fataḥ	فتح
to open (vt)	fataḥ	فتح
to close (vt)	aɣlaq	أغلق
key	miftāḥ (m)	مفتاح
bunch (of keys)	rabṭa (f)	ربطة
to creak (door, etc.)	ṣarr	صرّ
creak	ṣarīr (m)	صرير
hinge (door ~)	mufaṣṣala (f)	مفصّلة
doormat	siʒāda (f)	سجادة
door lock	qifl al bāb (m)	قفل الباب
keyhole	θaqb al bāb (m)	ثقب الباب
crossbar (sliding bar)	tirbās (m)	ترباس
door latch	mizlāʒ (m)	مزلاج
padlock	qifl (m)	قفل
to ring (~ the door bell)	rann	رنّ
ringing (sound)	ranīn (m)	رنين
doorbell	ʒaras (m)	جرس
doorbell button	zirr (m)	زرّ

| knock (at the door) | ṭarq, daqq (m) | طرق، دقّ |
| to knock (vi) | daqq | دقّ |

code	kūd (m)	كـود
combination lock	kūd (m)	كـود
intercom	ʒaras al bāb (m)	جرس الباب
number (on the door)	raqm (m)	رقم
doorplate	lawḥa (f)	لوحة
peephole	al ʿayn as siḥriyya (m)	العين السحريّة

85. Country house

village	qarya (f)	قرية
vegetable garden	bustān χuḍār (m)	بستان خضار
fence	sūr (m)	سور
picket fence	sūr (m)	سور
wicket gate	bawwāba farʿiyya (f)	بوّابة فرعيّة

granary	ʃawna (f)	شونة
root cellar	sirdāb (m)	سرداب
shed (garden ~)	saqīfa (f)	سقيفة
well (water)	biʾr (m)	بئر

stove (wood-fired ~)	furn (m)	فرن
to stoke the stove	awqad	أوقد
firewood	ḥaṭab (m)	حطب
log (firewood)	qiṭʿat ḥaṭab (f)	قطعة حطب

veranda	virānda (f)	فيراندة
deck (terrace)	ʃurfa (f)	شرفة
stoop (front steps)	sullam (m)	سلّم
swing (hanging seat)	urʒūḥa (f)	أرجوحة

86. Castle. Palace

castle	qalʿa (f)	قلعة
palace	qaṣr (m)	قصر
fortress	qalʿa (f), ḥiṣn (m)	قلعة، حصن

wall (round castle)	sūr (m)	سور
tower	burʒ (m)	برج
keep, donjon	burʒ raʾīsiy (m)	برج رئيسيّ

portcullis	bāb mutaḥarrik (m)	باب متحرّك
underground passage	sirdāb (m)	سرداب
moat	χandaq māʾiy (m)	خندق مائيّ
chain	silsila (f)	سلسلة
arrow loop	mazɣal (m)	مزغل

magnificent (adj)	rā'i'	رائع
majestic (adj)	muhīb	مهيب
impregnable (adj)	manī'	منيع
medieval (adj)	min al qurūn al wusṭa	من القرون الوسطى

87. Apartment

apartment	ʃaqqa (f)	شقّة
room	ɣurfa (f)	غرفة
bedroom	ɣurfat an nawm (f)	غرفة الوم
dining room	ɣurfat il akl (f)	غرفة الأكل
living room	ṣālat al istiqbāl (f)	صالة الإستقبال
study (home office)	maktab (m)	مكتب
entry room	madχal (m)	مدخل
bathroom (room with a bath or shower)	ḥammām (m)	حمّام
half bath	ḥammām (m)	حمّام
ceiling	saqf (m)	سقف
floor	arḍ (f)	أرض
corner	zāwiya (f)	زاوية

88. Apartment. Cleaning

to clean (vi, vt)	nazzaf	نظّف
to put away (to stow)	ʃāl	شال
dust	ɣubār (m)	غبار
dusty (adj)	muɣabbar	مغبَر
to dust (vt)	masaḥ al ɣubār	مسح الغبار
vacuum cleaner	miknasa kahraba'iyya (f)	مكنسة كهربائيّة
to vacuum (vt)	nazzaf bi miknasa kahrabā'iyya	نظّف بمكنسة كهربائيّة
to sweep (vi, vt)	kanas	كنس
sweepings	qumāma (f)	قمامة
order	niẓām (m)	نظام
disorder, mess	'adam an niẓām (m)	عدم النظام
mop	mimsaḥa ṭawīla (f)	ممسحة طويلة
dust cloth	mimsaḥa (f)	ممسحة
short broom	miqaʃʃa (f)	مقشّة
dustpan	ʒārūf (m)	جاروف

89. Furniture. Interior

furniture	aθāθ (m)	أثاث
table	maktab (m)	مكتب

| chair | kursiy (m) | كرسيّ |
| bed | sarīr (m) | سرير |

| couch, sofa | kanaba (f) | كنبة |
| armchair | kursiy (m) | كرسيّ |

| bookcase | xizānat kutub (f) | خزانة كتب |
| shelf | raff (m) | رفّ |

wardrobe	dūlāb (m)	دولاب
coat rack (wall-mounted ~)	ʃammāʿa (f)	شمّاعة
coat stand	ʃammāʿa (f)	شمّاعة

| bureau, dresser | dulāb adrāʒ (m) | دولاب أدراج |
| coffee table | ṭāwilat al qahwa (f) | طاولة القهوة |

mirror	mir'āt (f)	مرآة
carpet	siʒāda (f)	سجادة
rug, small carpet	siʒāda (f)	سجادة

fireplace	midfa'a ḥā'iṭiyya (f)	مدفأة حائطيّة
candle	ʃamʿa (f)	شمعة
candlestick	ʃamʿadān (m)	شمعدان

drapes	satā'ir (pl)	ستائر
wallpaper	waraq ḥī'ṭān (m)	ورق حيطان
blinds (jalousie)	haṣīrat ʃubbāk (f)	حصيرة شبّاك

| table lamp | miṣbāḥ aṭ ṭāwila (m) | مصباح الطاولة |
| wall lamp (sconce) | miṣbāḥ al ḥā'iṭ (f) | مصباح الحائط |

| floor lamp | miṣbāḥ arḍiy (m) | مصباح أرضيّ |
| chandelier | naʒafa (f) | نجفة |

| leg (of chair, table) | riʒl (f) | رجل |
| armrest | masnad (m) | مسند |

| back (backrest) | masnad (m) | مسند |
| drawer | durʒ (m) | درج |

90. Bedding

| bedclothes | bayāḍāt as sarīr (pl) | بياضات السرير |
| pillow | wisāda (f) | وسادة |

| pillowcase | kīs al wisāda (m) | كيس الوسادة |
| duvet, comforter | baṭṭāniyya (f) | بطّانيّة |

| sheet | milāya (f) | ملاية |
| bedspread | ɣiṭā' as sarīr (m) | غطاء السرير |

91. Kitchen

kitchen	maṭbaχ (m)	مطبخ
gas	ɣāz (m)	غاز
gas stove (range)	butuɣāz (m)	بوتوغاز
electric stove	furn kaharabāʼiy (m)	فرن كهربائيّ
oven	furn (m)	فرن
microwave oven	furn al mikruwayv (m)	فرن الميكروويف
refrigerator	θallāʒa (f)	ثلاجة
freezer	frīzir (m)	فريزير
dishwasher	ɣassāla (f)	غسّالة
meat grinder	farrāmat laḥm (f)	فرّامة لحم
juicer	ʻaṣṣāra (f)	عصّارة
toaster	maḥmaṣat χubz (f)	محمصة خبز
mixer	χallāṭ (m)	خلّاط
coffee machine	mākinat ṣanʻ al qahwa (f)	ماكينة صنع القهوة
coffee pot	kanaka (f)	كنكة
coffee grinder	maṭhanat qahwa (f)	مطحنة قهوة
kettle	barrād (m)	برّاد
teapot	barrād aʃʃāy (m)	برّاد الشاي
lid	ɣiṭāʼ (m)	غطاء
tea strainer	miṣfāt (f)	مصفاة
spoon	milʻaqa (f)	ملعقة
teaspoon	milʻaqat ʃāy (f)	ملعقة شاي
soup spoon	milʻaqa kabīra (f)	ملعقة كبيرة
fork	ʃawka (f)	شوكة
knife	sikkīn (m)	سكّين
tableware (dishes)	ṣuḥūn (pl)	صحون
plate (dinner ~)	ṭabaq (m)	طبق
saucer	ṭabaq finʒān (m)	طبق فنجان
shot glass	kaʼs (f)	كأس
glass (tumbler)	kubbāya (f)	كبّاية
cup	finʒān (m)	فنجان
sugar bowl	sukkariyya (f)	سكّريّة
salt shaker	mamlaḥa (f)	مملحة
pepper shaker	mabhara (f)	مبهرة
butter dish	ṣuḥn zubda (m)	صحن زبدة
stock pot (soup pot)	kassirūlla (f)	كاسرولة
frying pan (skillet)	ṭāsa (f)	طاسة
ladle	miɣrafa (f)	مغرفة
colander	miṣfāt (f)	مصفاة
tray (serving ~)	ṣīniyya (f)	صينيّة

bottle	zuʒāʒa (f)	زجاجة
jar (glass)	barṭamān (m)	برطمان
can	tanaka (f)	تنكة
bottle opener	fattāḥa (f)	فتّاحة
can opener	fattāḥa (f)	فتّاحة
corkscrew	barrīma (f)	بريمة
filter	filtir (m)	فلتر
to filter (vt)	ṣaffa	صفّى
trash, garbage (food waste, etc.)	zubāla (f)	زبالة
trash can (kitchen ~)	ṣundūq az zubāla (m)	صندوق الزبالة

92. Bathroom

bathroom	ḥammām (m)	حمّام
water	mā' (m)	ماء
faucet	ḥanafiyya (f)	حنفيّة
hot water	mā' sāxin (m)	ماء ساخن
cold water	mā' bārid (m)	ماء بارد
toothpaste	ma'ʒūn asnān (m)	معجون أسنان
to brush one's teeth	naẓẓaf al asnān	نظّف الأسنان
toothbrush	furʃat asnān (f)	فرشة أسنان
to shave (vi)	ḥalaq	حلق
shaving foam	raɣwa lil ḥilāqa (f)	رغفة للحلاقة
razor	mūs ḥilāqa (m)	موس حلاقة
to wash (one's hands, etc.)	ɣasal	غسل
to take a bath	istaḥamm	إستحمّ
shower	dūʃ (m)	دوش
to take a shower	axað ad duʃ	أخذ الدش
bathtub	ḥawḍ istiḥmām (m)	حوض استحمام
toilet (toilet bowl)	mirḥāḍ (m)	مرحاض
sink (washbasin)	ḥawḍ (m)	حوض
soap	ṣābūn (m)	صابون
soap dish	ṣabbāna (f)	صبّانة
sponge	līfa (f)	ليفة
shampoo	ʃāmbū (m)	شامبو
towel	fūṭa (f)	فوطة
bathrobe	θawb ḥammām (m)	ثوب حمّام
laundry (process)	ɣasīl (m)	غسيل
washing machine	ɣassāla (f)	غسّالة
to do the laundry	ɣasal al malābis	غسل الملابس
laundry detergent	masḥūq ɣasīl (m)	مسحوق غسيل

93. Household appliances

TV set	tilivizyūn (m)	تليفزيون
tape recorder	ʒihāz tasʒīl (m)	جهاز تسجيل
VCR (video recorder)	ʒihāz tasʒīl vidiyu (m)	جهاز تسجيل فيديو
radio	ʒihāz radiyu (m)	جهاز راديو
player (CD, MP3, etc.)	blayir (m)	بلير

video projector	'āriḍ vidiyu (m)	عارض فيديو
home movie theater	sinima manziliyya (f)	سينما منزليّة
DVD player	di vi di (m)	دي في دي
amplifier	mukabbir aṣ ṣawt (m)	مكبّر الصوت
video game console	'atāri (m)	أتاري

video camera	kamira vidiyu (f)	كاميرا فيديو
camera (photo)	kamira (f)	كاميرا
digital camera	kamira diʒital (f)	كاميرا ديجيتال

vacuum cleaner	miknasa kahrabā'iyya (f)	مكنسة كهربائيّة
iron (e.g., steam ~)	makwāt (f)	مكواة
ironing board	lawḥat kayy (f)	لوحة كيّ

telephone	hātif (m)	هاتف
cell phone	hātif maḥmūl (m)	هاتف محمول
typewriter	'āla katiba (f)	آلة كاتبة
sewing machine	'ālat al xiyāṭa (f)	آلة الخياطة

microphone	mikrufūn (m)	ميكروفون
headphones	sammā'āt ra'siya (pl)	سمّاعات رأسيّة
remote control (TV)	rimuwt kuntrūl (m)	ريموت كنترول

CD, compact disc	si di (m)	سي دي
cassette, tape	ʃarīṭ (m)	شريط
vinyl record	usṭuwāna (f)	أسطوانة

94. Repairs. Renovation

renovations	taʒdīdāt (m)	تجديدات
to renovate (vt)	ʒaddad	جدّد
to repair, to fix (vt)	aṣlaḥ	أصلح
to put in order	naẓẓam	نظّم
to redo (do again)	a'ād	أعاد

paint	dihān (m)	دهان
to paint (~ a wall)	dahan	دهن
house painter	dahhān (m)	دهّان
paintbrush	furʃat lit talwīn (f)	فرشة للتلوين
whitewash	maḥlūl mubayyiḍ (m)	محلول مبيّض
to whitewash (vt)	bayyaḍ	بيّض

wallpaper	waraq ḥī'ṭān (m)	ورق حيطان
to wallpaper (vt)	laṣaq waraq al ḥīṭān	لصق ورق الحيطان
varnish	warnīʃ (m)	ورنيش
to varnish (vt)	ṭala bil warnīʃ	طلى بالورنيش

95. Plumbing

water	māʼ (m)	ماء
hot water	māʼ sāxin (m)	ماء ساخن
cold water	māʼ bārid (m)	ماء بارد
faucet	ḥanafiyya (f)	حنفيّة

drop (of water)	qaṭara (f)	قطرة
to drip (vi)	qaṭar	قطر
to leak (ab. pipe)	sarab	سرب
leak (pipe ~)	tasarrub (m)	تسرّب
puddle	birka (f)	بركة

pipe	māsūra (f)	ماسورة
valve (e.g., ball ~)	ṣimām (m)	صمام
to be clogged up	kān masdūdan	كان مسدودًا

tools	adawāt (pl)	أدوات
adjustable wrench	miftāḥ inʒlīziy (m)	مفتاح إنجليزيّ
to unscrew (lid, filter, etc.)	fataḥ	فتح
to screw (tighten)	aḥkam aʃ ʃadd	أحكم الشدّ

to unclog (vt)	sallak	سلَك
plumber	sabbāk (m)	سبّاك
basement	sirdāb (m)	سرداب
sewerage (system)	ʃabakit il maʒāry (f)	شبكة مياه المجاري

96. Fire. Conflagration

fire (accident)	ḥarīq (m)	حريق
flame	ʃuʻla (f)	شعلة
spark	ʃarāra (f)	شرارة
smoke (from fire)	duxān (m)	دخان
torch (flaming stick)	ʃuʻla (f)	شعلة
campfire	nār muxayyam (m)	نار مخيّم

gas, gasoline	banzīn (m)	بنزين
kerosene (type of fuel)	kirusīn (m)	كيروسين
flammable (adj)	qābil lil iḥtirāq	قابل للإحتراق
explosive (adj)	mutafaʒʒir	متفجّر
NO SMOKING	mamnūʻ at tadxīn	ممنوع التدخين
safety	amn (m)	أمن
danger	xaṭar (m)	خطر

dangerous (adj)	xaṭīr	خطير
to catch fire	iʃtaʿal	إشتعل
explosion	infiʒār (m)	إنفجار
to set fire	aʃʿal an nār	أشعل النار
arsonist	muʃʿil ḥarīq (m)	مشعل حريق
arson	iḥrāq (m)	إحراق
to blaze (vi)	talahhab	تلهّب
to burn (be on fire)	iḥtaraq	إحترق
to burn down	iḥtaraq	إحترق
to call the fire department	istadʿa qism al ḥarīq	إستدعى قسم الحريق
firefighter, fireman	raʒul iṭfāʾ (m)	رجل إطفاء
fire truck	sayyārat iṭfāʾ (f)	سيّارة إطفاء
fire department	qism iṭfāʾ (m)	قسم إطفاء
fire truck ladder	sullam iṭfāʾ (m)	سلّم إطفاء
fire hose	xarṭūm al māʾ (m)	خرطوم الماء
fire extinguisher	miṭfaʾat ḥarīq (f)	مطفأة حريق
helmet	xūða (f)	خوذة
siren	ṣaffārat inðār (f)	صفّارة إنذار
to cry (for help)	ṣarax	صرخ
to call for help	istayāθ	إستغاث
rescuer	munqið (m)	منقذ
to rescue (vt)	anqað	أنقذ
to arrive (vi)	waṣal	وصل
to extinguish (vt)	aṭfaʾ	أطفأ
water	māʾ (m)	ماء
sand	raml (m)	رمل
ruins (destruction)	ḥiṭām (pl)	حطام
to collapse (building, etc.)	inhār	إنهار
to fall down (vi)	inhār	إنهار
to cave in (ceiling, floor)	inhār	إنهار
piece of debris	ḥiṭma (f)	حطمة
ash	ramād (m)	رماد
to suffocate (die)	ixtanaq	إختنق
to be killed (perish)	halak	هلك

HUMAN ACTIVITIES

Job. Business. Part 1

97. Banking

bank	bank (m)	بنك
branch (of bank, etc.)	far' (m)	فرع
bank clerk, consultant	muwaẓẓaf bank (m)	موظّف بنك
manager (director)	mudīr (m)	مدير
bank account	ḥisāb (m)	حساب
account number	raqm al ḥisāb (m)	رقم الحساب
checking account	ḥisāb ǧāri (m)	حساب جار
savings account	ḥisāb tawfīr (m)	حساب توفير
to open an account	fataḥ ḥisāb	فتح حسابا
to close the account	aɣlaq ḥisāb	أغلق حسابا
to deposit into the account	awda' fil ḥisāb	أودع في الحساب
to withdraw (vt)	saḥab min al ḥisāb	سحب من الحساب
deposit	wadī'a (f)	وديعة
to make a deposit	awda'	أودع
wire transfer	ḥawāla (f)	حوالة
to wire, to transfer	ḥawwal	حوّل
sum	mablaɣ (m)	مبلغ
How much?	kam?	كم؟
signature	tawqī' (m)	توقيع
to sign (vt)	waqqa'	وقّع
credit card	biṭāqat i'timān (f)	بطاقة ائتمان
code (PIN code)	kūd (m)	كود
credit card number	raqm biṭāqat i'timān (m)	رقم بطاقة إئتمان
ATM	ṣarrāf 'āliy (m)	صرّاف آليّ
check	ʃīk (m)	شيك
to write a check	katab ʃīk	كتب شيكًا
checkbook	daftar ʃīkāt (m)	دفتر شيكات
loan (bank ~)	qarḍ (m)	قرض
to apply for a loan	qaddam ṭalab lil ḥuṣūl 'ala qarḍ	قدّم طلبا للحصول على قرض

to get a loan	ḥaṣal ʿala qarḍ	حصل على قرض
to give a loan	qaddam qarḍ	قدمَ قرضا
guarantee	ḍamān (m)	ضمان

98. Telephone. Phone conversation

telephone	hātif (m)	هاتف
cell phone	hātif maḥmūl (m)	هاتف محمول
answering machine	muʒīb al hātif (m)	مجيب الهاتف
to call (by phone)	ittaṣal	إتّصل
phone call	mukālama tilifuniyya (f)	مكالمة تليفونية
to dial a number	ittaṣal bi raqm	إتّصل برقم
Hello!	alu!	ألو!
to ask (vt)	sa'al	سأل
to answer (vi, vt)	radd	ردَ
to hear (vt)	samiʿ	سمع
well (adv)	ʒayyidan	جيّداً
not well (adv)	sayyi'an	سيّئًا
noises (interference)	taʃwīʃ (m)	تشويش
receiver	sammāʿa (f)	سمّاعة
to pick up (~ the phone)	rafaʿ as sammāʿa	رفع السمّاعة
to hang up (~ the phone)	qafal as sammāʿa	قفل السمّاعة
busy (engaged)	maʃɣūl	مشغول
to ring (ab. phone)	rann	رنَ
telephone book	dalīl at tilifūn (m)	دليل التليفون
local (adj)	maḥalliyya	ة محلّية
local call	mukālama hātifiyya maḥalliyya (f)	مكالمة هاتفيّة محلّية
long distance (~ call)	baʿīd al mada	بعيد المدى
long-distance call	mukālama baʿīdat al mada (f)	مكالمة بعيدة المدى
international (adj)	duwaliy	دوليّ
international call	mukālama duwaliyya (f)	مكالمة دوليّة

99. Cell phone

cell phone	hātif maḥmūl (m)	هاتف محمول
display	ʒihāz ʿarḍ (m)	جهاز عرض
button	zirr (m)	زرّ
SIM card	sim kart (m)	سيم كارت
battery	baṭṭāriyya (f)	بطّاريّة
to be dead (battery)	xalaṣat	خلصت

charger	ʃāḥin (m)	شاحن
menu	qāʼima (f)	قائمة
settings	awḍāʻ (pl)	أوضاع
tune (melody)	naɣma (f)	نغمة
to select (vt)	ixtār	إختار
calculator	ʼāla ḥāsiba (f)	آلة حاسبة
voice mail	barīd ṣawtiy (m)	بريد صوتيّ
alarm clock	munabbih (m)	منبّه
contacts	ʒihāt al ittiṣāl (pl)	جهات الإتّصال
SMS (text message)	risāla qaṣīra ɛsɛmɛs (f)	sms رسالة قصيرة
subscriber	muʃtarik (m)	مشترك

100. Stationery

ballpoint pen	qalam ʒāf (m)	قلم جاف
fountain pen	qalam rīʃa (m)	قلم ريشة
pencil	qalam ruṣāṣ (m)	قلم رصاص
highlighter	markir (m)	ماركر
felt-tip pen	qalam xaṭṭāṭ (m)	قلم خطاط
notepad	muðakkira (f)	مذكّرة
agenda (diary)	ʒadwal al aʻmāl (m)	جدول الأعمال
ruler	masṭara (f)	مسطرة
calculator	ʼāla ḥāsiba (f)	آلة حاسبة
eraser	astīka (f)	استيكة
thumbtack	dabbūs (m)	دبّوس
paper clip	dabbūs waraq (m)	دبّوس ورق
glue	ṣamɣ (m)	صمغ
stapler	dabbāsa (f)	دبّاسة
hole punch	xarrāma (m)	خرّامة
pencil sharpener	mibrāt (f)	مبراة

Job. Business. Part 2

101. Mass Media

newspaper	ӡarīda (f)	جريدة
magazine	maӡalla (f)	مجلّة
press (printed media)	ṣiḥāfa (f)	صحافة
radio	iðā'a (f)	إذاعة
radio station	maḥaṭṭat iðā'a (f)	محطّة إذاعة
television	tilivizyūn (m)	تليفزيون
presenter, host	mu'addim (m)	مقدّم
newscaster	muðī' (m)	مذيع
commentator	mu'alliq (m)	معلّق
journalist	ṣuḥufiy (m)	صحفيّ
correspondent (reporter)	murāsil (m)	مراسل
press photographer	muṣawwir ṣuḥufiy (m)	مصوّر صحفيّ
reporter	ṣuḥufiy (m)	صحفيّ
editor	muḥarrir (m)	محرّر
editor-in-chief	ra'īs taḥrīr (m)	رئيس تحرير
to subscribe (to ...)	iſtarak	إشترك
subscription	iſtirāk (m)	إشتراك
subscriber	muſtarik (m)	مشترك
to read (vi, vt)	qara'	قرأ
reader	qāri' (m)	قارئ
circulation (of newspaper)	tadāwul (m)	تداول
monthly (adj)	ſahriy	شهريّ
weekly (adj)	usbū'iy	أسبوعيّ
issue (edition)	'adad (m)	عدد
new (~ issue)	ӡadīd	جديد
headline	'unwān (m)	عنوان
short article	maqāla qaṣīra (f)	مقالة قصيرة
column (regular article)	'amūd (m)	عمود
article	maqāla (f)	مقالة
page	ṣafḥa (f)	صفحة
reportage, report	taqrīr (m)	تقرير
event (happening)	ḥadaθ (m)	حدث
sensation (news)	ḍaӡӡa (f)	ضجّة
scandal	faḍīḥa (f)	فضيحة
scandalous (adj)	fāḍiḥ	فاضح

great (~ scandal)	ʃahīr	شهير
show (e.g., cooking ~)	barnāmaʒ (m)	برنامج
interview	muqābala (f)	مقابلة
live broadcast	iðā'a mubāʃira (f)	إذاعة مباشرة
channel	qanāt (f)	قناة

102. Agriculture

agriculture	zirā'a (f)	زراعة
peasant (masc.)	fallāḥ (m)	فلاح
peasant (fem.)	fallāḥa (f)	فلاحة
farmer	muzāri' (m)	مزارع
tractor (farm ~)	ʒarrār (m)	جرّار
combine, harvester	ḥaṣṣāda (f)	حصّادة
plow	miḥrāθ (m)	محراث
to plow (vi, vt)	ḥaraθ	حرث
plowland	ḥaql maḥrūθ (m)	حقل محروث
furrow (in field)	talam (m)	تلم
to sow (vi, vt)	baðar	بذر
seeder	baððāra (f)	بذّارة
sowing (process)	zar' (m)	زرع
scythe	miḥaʃ (m)	محشّ
to mow, to scythe	ḥaʃʃ	حشّ
spade (tool)	karīk (m)	مجرفة
to till (vt)	ḥafar	حفر
hoe	mi'zaqa (f)	معزقة
to hoe, to weed	ista'ṣal nabātāt	إستأصل نباتات
weed (plant)	ḥaʃīʃa (m)	حشيشة
watering can	miraʃʃa al miyāh (f)	مرشّة المياه
to water (plants)	saqa	سقى
watering (act)	saqy (m)	سقي
pitchfork	maðrāt (f)	مذراة
rake	midamma (f)	مدمّة
fertilizer	samād (m)	سماد
to fertilize (vt)	sammad	سمّد
manure (fertilizer)	zibd (m)	زبل
field	ḥaql (m)	حقل
meadow	marʒ (m)	مرج
vegetable garden	bustān χuḍār (m)	بستان خضار
orchard (e.g., apple ~)	bustān (m)	بستان

to graze (vt)	ra'a	رعى
herder (herdsman)	rā'i (m)	راع
pasture	mar'a (m)	مرعى
cattle breeding	tarbiyat al mawāʃi (f)	تربية المواشي
sheep farming	tarbiyat aɣnām (f)	تربية أغنام
plantation	mazra'a (f)	مزرعة
row (garden bed ~s)	ħawḍ (m)	حوض
hothouse	daffi'a (f)	دفيئة
drought (lack of rain)	ʒafāf (m)	جفاف
dry (~ summer)	ʒāff	جافّ
grain	ħubūb (pl)	حبوب
cereal crops	maħāṣīl al ħubūb (pl)	محاصيل الحبوب
to harvest, to gather	ħaṣad	حصد
miller (person)	ṭaħħān (m)	طحّان
mill (e.g., gristmill)	ṭāħūna (f)	طاحونة
to grind (grain)	ṭaħan al ħubūb	طحن الحبوب
flour	daqīq (m)	دقيق
straw	qaʃʃ (m)	قشّ

103. Building. Building process

construction site	arḍ binā' (f)	أرض بناء
to build (vt)	bana	بنى
construction worker	'āmil binā' (m)	عامل بناء
project	maʃrū' (m)	مشروع
architect	muhandis mi'māriy (m)	مهندس معماريّ
worker	'āmil (m)	عامل
foundation (of a building)	asās (m)	أساس
roof	saqf (m)	سقف
foundation pile	watad al asās (f)	وتد الأساس
wall	ħā'iṭ (m)	حائط
reinforcing bars	ħadīd taslīħ (m)	حديد تسليح
scaffolding	saqāla (f)	سقالة
concrete	χarasāna (f)	خرسانة
granite	granīt (m)	جرانيت
stone	ħaʒar (m)	حجر
brick	ṭūb (m)	طوب
sand	raml (m)	رمل
cement	ismant (m)	إسمنت
plaster (for walls)	qiṣāra (m)	قصارة

to plaster (vt)	ṭala bil ʒiṣṣ	طلى بالجصّ
paint	dihān (m)	دهان
to paint (~ a wall)	dahhan	دهّن
barrel	barmīl (m)	برميل
crane	rāfiʻa (f)	رافعة
to lift, to hoist (vt)	rafaʻ	رفع
to lower (vt)	anzal	أنزل
bulldozer	ʒarrāfa (f)	جرّافة
excavator	ḥaffāra (f)	حفّارة
scoop, bucket	dalw (m)	دلو
to dig (excavate)	ḥafar	حفر
hard hat	xūða (f)	خوذة

Professions and occupations

104. Job search. Dismissal

job	'amal (m)	عمل
staff (work force)	kawādir (pl)	كوادر
personnel	ṭāqim al 'āmilīn (m)	طاقم العاملين
career	masār mihniy (m)	مسار مهنيّ
prospects (chances)	'āfāq (pl)	آفاق
skills (mastery)	mahārāt (pl)	مهارات
selection (screening)	iḫtiyār (m)	إختيار
employment agency	wikālat tawẓīf (f)	وكالة توظيف
résumé	sīra ðātiyya (f)	سيرة ذاتيّة
job interview	mu'ābalat 'amal (f)	مقابلة عمل
vacancy, opening	waẓīfa ḫāliya (f)	وظيفة خالية
salary, pay	murattab (m)	مرتّب
fixed salary	rātib θābit (m)	راتب ثابت
pay, compensation	uʒra (f)	أجرة
position (job)	manṣib (m)	منصب
duty (of employee)	wāʒib (m)	واجب
range of duties	maʒmū'a min al wāʒibāt (f)	مجموعة من الواجبات
busy (I'm ~)	maʃɣūl	مشغول
to fire (dismiss)	aqāl	أقال
dismissal	iqāla (m)	إقالة
unemployment	biṭāla (f)	بطالة
unemployed (n)	'āṭil (m)	عاطل
retirement	ma'āʃ (m)	معاش
to retire (from job)	uḥīl 'alal ma'āʃ	أحيل على المعاش

105. Business people

director	mudīr (m)	مدير
manager (director)	mudīr (m)	مدير
boss	mudīr (m), raʾīs (m)	مدير, رئيس
superior	raʾīs (m)	رئيس
superiors	ru'asā' (pl)	رؤساء
president	raʾīs (m)	رئيس

chairman	raʾīs (m)	رئيس
deputy (substitute)	nāʾib (m)	نائب
assistant	musāʿid (m)	مساعد
secretary	sikirtīr (m)	سكرتير
personal assistant	sikritīr xāṣṣ (m)	سكرتير خاصّ
businessman	raʒul aʿmāl (m)	رجل أعمال
entrepreneur	rāʾid aʿmāl (m)	رائد أعمال
founder	muʾassis (m)	مؤسِّس
to found (vt)	assas	أسّس
incorporator	muʾassis (m)	مؤسِّس
partner	ʃarīk (m)	شريك
stockholder	musāhim (m)	مساهم
millionaire	milyunīr (m)	مليونير
billionaire	milyardīr (m)	ملياردير
owner, proprietor	ṣāḥib (m)	صاحب
landowner	ṣāḥib al arḍ (m)	صاحب الأرض
client	ʿamīl (m)	عميل
regular client	ʿamīl dāʾim (m)	عميل دائم
buyer (customer)	muʃtari (m)	مشتر
visitor	zāʾir (m)	زائر
professional (n)	muḥtarif (m)	محترف
expert	xabīr (m)	خبير
specialist	mutaxaṣṣiṣ (m)	متخصّص
banker	ṣāḥib maṣraf (m)	صاحب مصرف
broker	simsār (m)	سمسار
cashier, teller	ṣarrāf (m)	صرّاف
accountant	muḥāsib (m)	محاسب
security guard	ḥāris amn (m)	حارس أمن
investor	mustaθmir (m)	مستثمر
debtor	mudīn (m)	مدين
creditor	dāʾin (m)	دائن
borrower	muqtariḍ (m)	مقترض
importer	mustawrid (m)	مستورد
exporter	muṣaddir (m)	مصدِّر
manufacturer	aʃ ʃarika al muṣniʿa (f)	الشركة المصنعة
distributor	muwazziʿ (m)	موزِّع
middleman	wasīṭ (m)	وسيط
consultant	mustaʃār (m)	مستشار
sales representative	mandūb mabiʿāt (m)	مندوب مبيعات
agent	wakīl (m)	وكيل
insurance agent	wakīl at taʾmīn (m)	وكيل التأمين

106. Service professions

cook	ṭabbāχ (m)	طبّاخ
chef (kitchen chef)	ʃāf (m)	شاف
baker	χabbāz (m)	خبّاز
bartender	bārman (m)	بارمان
waiter	nādil (m)	نادل
waitress	nādila (f)	نادلة
lawyer, attorney	muḥāmi (m)	محام
lawyer (legal expert)	muḥāmi (m)	محام
notary	muwaθθaq (m)	موئق
electrician	kahrabā'iy (m)	كهربائيّ
plumber	sabbāk (m)	سبّاك
carpenter	naʒʒār (m)	نجّار
masseur	mudallik (m)	مدلّك
masseuse	mudallika (f)	مدلّكة
doctor	ṭabīb (m)	طبيب
taxi driver	sā'iq taksi (m)	سائق تاكسي
driver	sā'iq (m)	سائق
delivery man	sā'i (m)	ساع
chambermaid	'āmilat tanẓīf χuraf (f)	عاملة تنظيف غرف
security guard	ḥāris amn (m)	حارس أمن
flight attendant (fem.)	muḍīfat ṭayarān (f)	مضيفة طيران
schoolteacher	mudarris madrasa (m)	مدرّس مدرسة
librarian	amīn maktaba (m)	أمين مكتبة
translator	mutarʒim (m)	مترجم
interpreter	mutarʒim fawriy (m)	مترجم فوريّ
guide	murʃid (m)	مرشد
hairdresser	ḥallāq (m)	حلّاق
mailman	sā'i al barīd (m)	ساعي البريد
salesman (store staff)	bā'i' (m)	بائع
gardener	bustāniy (m)	بستانيّ
domestic servant	χādim (m)	خادم
maid (female servant)	χādima (f)	خادمة
cleaner (cleaning lady)	'āmilat tanẓīf (f)	عاملة تنظيف

107. Military professions and ranks

private	ʒundiy (m)	جنديّ
sergeant	raqīb (m)	رقيب

lieutenant	mulāzim (m)	ملازم
captain	naqīb (m)	نقيب
major	rā'id (m)	رائد
colonel	ʿaqīd (m)	عقيد
general	ʒinirāl (m)	جنرال
marshal	mārʃāl (m)	مارشال
admiral	amirāl (m)	أميرال
military (n)	ʿaskariy (m)	عسكريّ
soldier	ʒundiy (m)	جنديّ
officer	ḍābiṭ (m)	ضابط
commander	qā'id (m)	قائد
border guard	ḥāris ḥudūd (m)	حارس حدود
radio operator	ʿāmil lāsilkiy (m)	عامل لاسلكيّ
scout (searcher)	mustakʃif (m)	مستكشف
pioneer (sapper)	muhandis ʿaskariy (m)	مهندس عسكريّ
marksman	rāmi (m)	رام
navigator	mallāḥ (m)	مّلاح

108. Officials. Priests

king	malik (m)	ملك
queen	malika (f)	ملكة
prince	amīr (m)	أمير
princess	amīra (f)	أميرة
czar	qayṣar (m)	قيصر
czarina	qayṣara (f)	قيصرة
president	raʾīs (m)	رئيس
Secretary (minister)	wazīr (m)	وزير
prime minister	raʾīs wuzarā' (m)	رئيس وزراء
senator	ʿuḍw maʒlis aʃ ʃuyūχ (m)	عضو مجلس الشيوخ
diplomat	diblumāsiy (m)	دبلوماسيّ
consul	qunṣul (m)	قنصل
ambassador	safīr (m)	سفير
counsilor (diplomatic officer)	mustaʃār (m)	مستشار
official, functionary (civil servant)	muwazzaf (m)	موظّف
prefect	raʾīs idārat al ḥayy (m)	رئيس إدارة الحيّ
mayor	raʾīs al baladiyya (m)	رئيس البلديّة
judge	qāḍi (m)	قاض
prosecutor (e.g., district attorney)	mudda'i (m)	مدّع

missionary	mubaʃʃir (m)	مبشّر
monk	rāhib (m)	راهب
abbot	raʔīs ad dayr (m)	رئيس الدير
rabbi	ḥāxām (m)	حاخام

vizier	wazīr (m)	وزير
shah	ʃāh (m)	شاه
sheikh	ʃɛyx (m)	شيخ

109. Agricultural professions

beekeeper	naḥḥāl (m)	نحّال
herder, shepherd	rāʿi (m)	راع
agronomist	muhandis zirāʿiy (m)	مهندس زراعيّ
cattle breeder	murabbi al mawāʃi (m)	مربّي المواشي
veterinarian	ṭabīb bayṭariy (m)	طبيب بيطريّ

farmer	muzāriʿ (m)	مزارع
winemaker	ṣāniʿ an nabīð (m)	صانع النبيذ
zoologist	xabīr fi ʿilm al ḥayawān (m)	خبير في علم الحيوان
cowboy	rāʿi al baqar (m)	راعي البقر

110. Art professions

actor	mumaθθil (m)	ممثّل
actress	mumaθθila (f)	ممثّلة

singer (masc.)	muɣanni (m)	مغنّ
singer (fem.)	muɣanniya (f)	مغنّية

dancer (masc.)	rāqiṣ (m)	راقص
dancer (fem.)	rāqiṣa (f)	راقصة

performer (masc.)	fannān (m)	فنّان
performer (fem.)	fannāna (f)	فنّانة

musician	ʿāzif (m)	عازف
pianist	ʿāzif biyānu (m)	عازف بيانو
guitar player	ʿāzif gitār (m)	عازف جيتار

conductor (orchestra ~)	qāʾid urkistra (m)	قائد أركسترا
composer	mulaḥḥin (m)	ملحّن
impresario	mudīr firqa (m)	مدير فرقة

film director	muxriʒ (m)	مخرج
producer	muntiʒ (m)	منتج
scriptwriter	kātib sināriyu (m)	كاتب سيناريو
critic	nāqid (m)	ناقد

writer	kātib (m)	كاتب
poet	ʃāʿir (m)	شاعر
sculptor	nahhāt (m)	نحّات
artist (painter)	rassām (m)	رسّام

juggler	bahlawān (m)	بهلوان
clown	muharriʒ (m)	مهرّج
acrobat	bahlawān (m)	بهلوان
magician	sāhir (m)	ساحر

111. Various professions

doctor	ṭabīb (m)	طبيب
nurse	mumarriḍa (f)	ممرّضة
psychiatrist	ṭabīb nafsiy (m)	طبيب نفسيّ
dentist	ṭabīb al asnān (m)	طبيب الأسنان
surgeon	ʒarrāḥ (m)	جرّاح

astronaut	rāʾid faḍāʾ (m)	رائد فضاء
astronomer	ʿālim falak (m)	عالم فلك
pilot	ṭayyār (m)	طيّار

driver (of taxi, etc.)	sāʾiq (m)	سائق
engineer (train driver)	sāʾiq (m)	سائق
mechanic	mikanīkiy (m)	ميكانيكيّ

miner	ʿāmil manʒam (m)	عامل منجم
worker	ʿāmil (m)	عامل
locksmith	qaffāl (m)	قفّال
joiner (carpenter)	naʒʒār (m)	نجّار
turner (lathe machine operator)	χarrāṭ (m)	خرّاط

| construction worker | ʿāmil bināʾ (m) | عامل بناء |
| welder | lahhām (m) | لحّام |

professor (title)	brufissūr (m)	بروفيسور
architect	muhandis miʿmāriy (m)	مهندس معماريّ
historian	muʾarriχ (m)	مؤرّخ
scientist	ʿālim (m)	عالم
physicist	fizyāʾiy (m)	فيزيائيّ
chemist (scientist)	kimyāʾiy (m)	كيميائيّ

archeologist	ʿālimʾāθār (m)	عالم آثار
geologist	ʒiulūʒiy (m)	جيولوجيّ
researcher (scientist)	bāḥiθ (m)	باحث

babysitter	murabbiyat aṭfāl (f)	مربّية الأطفال
teacher, educator	muʿallim (m)	معلّم
editor	muharrir (m)	محرّر
editor-in-chief	raʾīs tahrīr (m)	رئيس تحرير

correspondent	murāsil (m)	مراسل
typist (fem.)	kāteba 'ala el 'āla el kāteba (f)	كاتبة على الآلة الكاتبة
designer	muṣammim (m)	مصمّم
computer expert	mutaxaṣṣiṣ bil kumbyūtir (m)	متخصص بالكمبيوتر
programmer	mubarmiʒ (m)	مبرمج
engineer (designer)	muhandis (m)	مهندس
sailor	baḥḥār (m)	بحّار
seaman	baḥḥār (m)	بحّار
rescuer	munqið (m)	منقذ
fireman	raʒul iṭfā' (m)	رجل إطفاء
police officer	ʃurṭiy (m)	شرطيّ
watchman	ḥāris (m)	حارس
detective	muḥaqqiq (m)	محقق
customs officer	muwazzaf al ʒamārik (m)	موظّف الجمارك
bodyguard	ḥāris ʃaxṣiy (m)	حارس شخصيّ
prison guard	ḥāris siʒn (m)	حارس سجن
inspector	mufattiʃ (m)	مفتّش
sportsman	riyāḍiy (m)	رياضيّ
trainer, coach	mudarrib (m)	مدرّب
butcher	ʒazzār (m)	جزّار
cobbler (shoe repairer)	iskāfiy (m)	إسكافيّ
merchant	tāʒir (m)	تاجر
loader (person)	ḥammāl (m)	حمّال
fashion designer	muṣammim azyā' (m)	مصمّم أزياء
model (fem.)	mudīl (f)	موديل

112. Occupations. Social status

schoolboy	tilmīð (m)	تلميذ
student (college ~)	ṭālib (m)	طالب
philosopher	faylasūf (m)	فيلسوف
economist	iqtiṣādiy (m)	إقتصاديّ
inventor	muxtariʕ (m)	مخترع
unemployed (n)	'āṭil (m)	عاطل
retiree	mutaqāʕid (m)	متقاعد
spy, secret agent	ʒāsūs (m)	جاسوس
prisoner	saʒīn (m)	سجين
striker	muḍrib (m)	مضرب
bureaucrat	buruqrāṭiy (m)	بيوروقراطيّ

traveler (globetrotter)	raḥḥāla (m)	رحّالة
gay, homosexual (n)	miθliy ʒinsiyyan (m)	مثليّ جنسيًا
hacker	hākir (m)	هاكِر
hippie	hippi (m)	هِبِي
bandit	qāṭiʿ ṭarīq (m)	قاطِع طريق
hit man, killer	qātil maʾʒūr (m)	قاتِل مأجور
drug addict	mudmin muxaddirāt (m)	مدمِن مخدّرات
drug dealer	tāʒir muxaddirāt (m)	تاجِر مخدّرات
prostitute (fem.)	ʿāhira (f)	عاهِرة
pimp	qawwād (m)	قوّاد
sorcerer	sāḥir (m)	ساحِر
sorceress (evil ~)	sāḥira (f)	ساحِرة
pirate	qurṣān (m)	قرصان
slave	ʿabd (m)	عبد
samurai	samurāy (m)	ساموراي
savage (primitive)	mutawaḥḥiʃ (m)	متوحّش

Sports

113. Kinds of sports. Sportspersons

sportsman	riyāḍiy (m)	رياضيّ
kind of sports	nawʿ min ar riyāḍa (m)	نوع من الرياضة
basketball	kurat as salla (f)	كرة السلّة
basketball player	lāʿib kūrat as salla (m)	لاعب كرة السلّة
baseball	kurat al qāʿida (f)	كرة القاعدة
baseball player	lāʿib kurat al qāʿida (m)	لاعب كرة القاعدة
soccer	kurat al qadam (f)	كرة القدم
soccer player	lāʿib kurat al qadam (m)	لاعب كرة القدم
goalkeeper	ḥāris al marma (m)	حارس المرمى
hockey	huki (m)	هوكي
hockey player	lāʿib huki (m)	لاعب هوكي
volleyball	al kura aṭ ṭāʿira (m)	الكرة الطائرة
volleyball player	lāʿib al kura aṭ ṭāʿira (m)	لاعب الكرة الطائرة
boxing	mulākama (f)	ملاكمة
boxer	mulākim (m)	ملاكم
wrestling	muṣāraʿa (f)	مصارعة
wrestler	muṣāriʿ (m)	مصارع
karate	karatī (m)	كاراتيه
karate fighter	lāʿib karatī (m)	لاعب كاراتيه
judo	ʒudu (m)	جودو
judo athlete	lāʿib ʒudu (m)	لاعب جودو
tennis	tinis (m)	تنس
tennis player	lāʿib tinnis (m)	لاعب تنس
swimming	sibāḥa (f)	سباحة
swimmer	sabbāḥ (m)	سبّاح
fencing	musāyafa (f)	مسايفة
fencer	mubāriz (m)	مبارز
chess	ʃaṭranʒ (m)	شطرنج
chess player	lāʿib ʃaṭranʒ (m)	لاعب شطرنج

alpinism	tasalluq al ʒibāl (m)	تسلّق الجبال
alpinist	mutasalliq al ʒibāl (m)	متسلّق الجبال
running	ʒary (m)	جري
runner	'addā' (m)	عدّاء
athletics	al'āb al qiwa (pl)	ألعاب القوى
athlete	lā'ib riyāḍiy (m)	لاعب رياضيّ
horseback riding	riyāḍat al furūsiyya (f)	رياضة الفروسيّة
horse rider	fāris (m)	فارس
figure skating	tazalluʒ fanniy 'alal ʒalīd (m)	تزلّج فنّيّ على الجليد
figure skater (masc.)	mutazalliʒ fanniy (m)	متزلّج فنّيّ
figure skater (fem.)	mutazalliʒa fanniyya (f)	متزلّجة فنّيّة
powerlifting	raf' al aθqāl (m)	رفع الأثقال
powerlifter	rāfi' al aθqāl (m)	رافع الأثقال
car racing	sibāq as sayyārāt (m)	سباق السيّارات
racing driver	sā'iq sibāq (m)	سائق سباق
cycling	sibāq ad darrāʒāt (m)	سباق الدرّاجات
cyclist	lā'ib ad darrāʒāt (m)	لاعب الدرّاجات
broad jump	al qafz aṭ ṭawīl (m)	القفز الطويل
pole vault	al qafz biz zāna (m)	القفز بالزانة
jumper	qāfiz (m)	قافز

114. Kinds of sports. Miscellaneous

football	kurat al qadam (f)	كرة القدم
badminton	kurat ar rīʃa (f)	كرة الريشة
biathlon	al biatlūn (m)	البياثلون
billiards	bilyārdu (m)	بليّاردو
bobsled	zallāʒa ʒama'iyya (f)	زلّاجة جماعيّة
bodybuilding	kamāl aʒsām (m)	كمال أجسام
water polo	kurat al mā' (f)	كرة الماء
handball	kurat al yad (f)	كرة اليد
golf	gūlf (m)	جولف
rowing, crew	taʒðīf (m)	تجذيف
scuba diving	al ɣawṣ taḥt al mā' (m)	الغوص تحت الماء
cross-country skiing	riyāḍat al iski (f)	رياضة الإسكي
table tennis (ping-pong)	kurat aṭ ṭāwila (f)	كرة الطاولة
sailing	riyāḍa ibḥār al marākib (f)	رياضة إبحار المراكب
rally racing	sibāq as sayyārāt (m)	سباق السيّارات

rugby	raɣbi (m)	رغبي
snowboarding	tazalluʒ 'laθ θuluʒ (m)	تزلّج على الثلوج
archery	rimāya (f)	رماية

115. Gym

barbell	ḥadīda (f)	حديدة
dumbbells	dambilz (m)	دمبلز
training machine	ʒihāz tadrīb (m)	جهاز تدريب
exercise bicycle	darrāʒat tadrīb (f)	درّاجة تدريب
treadmill	ʒihāz al maʃy (m)	جهاز المشي
horizontal bar	'uqla (f)	عقلة
parallel bars	al mutawāzi (m)	المتوازي
vault (vaulting horse)	hisān al maqābiḍ (m)	حصان المقابض
mat (exercise ~)	ḥaṣīra (f)	حصيرة
jump rope	ḥabl an naṭṭ (m)	حبل النطّ
aerobics	at tamrīnāt al hiwā'iyya (pl)	التمرينات الهوائية
yoga	yūga (f)	يوجا

116. Sports. Miscellaneous

Olympic Games	al'āb ulumbiyya (pl)	ألعاب أولمبيّة
winner	fā'iz (m)	فائز
to be winning	fāz	فاز
to win (vi)	fāz	فاز
leader	za'īm (m)	زعيم
to lead (vi)	taqaddam	تقدّم
first place	al martaba al ūla (f)	المرتبة الأولى
second place	al martaba aθ θāniya (f)	المرتبة الثانية
third place	al martaba aθ θāliθa (f)	المرتبة الثالثة
medal	midāliyya (f)	ميداليّة
trophy	ʒā'iza (f)	جائزة
prize cup (trophy)	ka's (m)	كأس
prize (in game)	ʒā'iza (f)	جائزة
main prize	akbar ʒā'iza (f)	أكبر جائزة
record	raqm qiyāsiy (m)	رقم قياسيّ
to set a record	fāz bi raqm qiyāsiy	فاز برقم قياسيّ
final	mubarāt nihā'iyya (f)	مباراة نهائيّة
final (adj)	nihā'iy	نهائيّ
champion	baṭal (m)	بطل

championship	buṭūla (f)	بطولة
stadium	mal'ab (m)	ملعب
stand (bleachers)	mudarraʒ (m)	مدرّج
fan, supporter	muʃaʒʒi' (m)	مشجّع
opponent, rival	'aduww (m)	عدو
start (start line)	χaṭṭ al bidāya (m)	خطّ البداية
finish line	χaṭṭ an nihāya (m)	خطّ النهاية
defeat	hazīma (f)	هزيمة
to lose (not win)	χasir	خسر
referee	ḥakam (m)	حكم
jury (judges)	hay'at al ḥukm (f)	هيئة الحكم
score	natīʒa (f)	نتيجة
tie	ta'ādul (m)	تعادل
to tie (vi)	ta'ādal	تعادل
point	nuqṭa (f)	نقطة
result (final score)	natīʒa nihā'iyya (f)	نتيجة نهائية
period	ʃawṭ (m)	شوط
half-time	istirāḥa ma bayn aʃ ʃawṭayn (f)	إستراحة ما بين الشوطين
doping	munaʃʃiṭāt (pl)	منشّطات
to penalize (vt)	'āqab	عاقب
to disqualify (vt)	ḥaram	حرم
apparatus	ma'add riyāḍiy (f)	معدّ رياضيّ
javelin	rumḥ (m)	رمح
shot (metal ball)	ʒulla (f)	جلّة
ball (snooker, etc.)	kura (f)	كرة
aim (target)	hadaf (m)	هدف
target	hadaf (m)	هدف
to shoot (vi)	aṭlaq an nār	أطلق النار
accurate (~ shot)	maḍbūṭ	مضبوط
trainer, coach	mudarrib (m)	مدرّب
to train (sb)	darrab	درّب
to train (vi)	tadarrab	تدرّب
training	tadrīb (m)	تدريب
gym	markaz li liyāqa badaniyya (m)	مركز للياقة بدنيّة
exercise (physical)	tamrīn (m)	تمرين
warm-up (athlete ~)	tasχīn (m)	تسخين

Education

117. School

school	madrasa (f)	مدرسة
principal (headmaster)	mudīr madrasa (m)	مدير مدرسة
pupil (boy)	tilmīð (m)	تلميذ
pupil (girl)	tilmīða (f)	تلميذة
schoolboy	tilmīð (m)	تلميذ
schoolgirl	tilmīða (f)	تلميذة
to teach (sb)	'allam	علّم
to learn (language, etc.)	ta'allam	تعلّم
to learn by heart	ḥafaẓ	حفظ
to learn (~ to count, etc.)	ta'allam	تعلّم
to be in school	daras	درس
to go to school	ðahab ilal madrasa	ذهب إلى المدرسة
alphabet	alifbā' (m)	الفباء
subject (at school)	mādda (f)	مادّة
classroom	faṣl (m)	فصل
lesson	dars (m)	درس
recess	istirāḥa (f)	إستراحة
school bell	ʒaras al madrasa (m)	جرس المدرسة
school desk	taxta lil madrasa (m)	تخته للمدرسة
chalkboard	sabbūra (f)	سبّورة
grade	daraʒa (f)	درجة
good grade	daraʒa ʒayyida (f)	درجة جيّدة
bad grade	daraʒa ɣayr ʒayyida (f)	درجة غير جيّدة
to give a grade	a'ṭa daraʒa	أعطى درجة
mistake, error	xaṭa' (m)	خطأ
to make mistakes	axṭa'	أخطأ
to correct (an error)	ṣaḥḥaḥ	صحّح
cheat sheet	waraqat ɣaʃʃ (f)	ورقة غشّ
homework	wāʒib manziliy (m)	واجب منزليّ
exercise (in education)	tamrīn (m)	تمرين
to be present	ḥaḍar	حضر
to be absent	ɣāb	غاب
to miss school	taɣayyab 'an al madrasa	تغيّب عن المدرسة

to punish (vt)	ʿāqab	عاقب
punishment	ʿuqūba (f), ʿiqāb (m)	عقوبة, عقاب
conduct (behavior)	sulūk (m)	سلوك

report card	at taqrīr al madrasiy (m)	التقرير المدرسيّ
pencil	qalam ruṣāṣ (m)	قلم رصاص
eraser	astīka (f)	استيكة
chalk	ṭabāʃīr (m)	طباشير
pencil case	maqlama (f)	مقلمة

schoolbag	ʃanṭat al madrasa (f)	شنطة المدرسة
pen	qalam (m)	قلم
school notebook	daftar (m)	دفتر
textbook	kitāb taʿlīm (m)	كتاب تعليم
compasses	barʒal (m)	برجل

| to make technical drawings | rasam rasm taqniy | رسم رسمًا تقنيًا |
| technical drawing | rasm taqniy (m) | رسم تقنيّ |

poem	qaṣīda (f)	قصيدة
by heart (adv)	ʿan ẓahr qalb	عن ظهر قلب
to learn by heart	ḥafaẓ	حفظ

school vacation	ʿuṭla madrasiyya (f)	عطلة مدرسيّة
to be on vacation	ʿindahu ʿuṭla	عنده عطلة
to spend one's vacation	qaḍa al ʿuṭla	قضى العطلة

test (written math ~)	imtiḥān (m)	إمتحان
essay (composition)	inʃāʾ (m)	إنشاء
dictation	imlāʾ (m)	إملاء
exam (examination)	imtiḥān (m)	إمتحان
to take an exam	marr al imtiḥān	مرّ الإمتحان
experiment (e.g., chemistry ~)	taʒriba (f)	تجربة

118. College. University

academy	akadīmiyya (f)	أكاديميّة
university	ʒāmiʿa (f)	جامعة
faculty (e.g., ~ of Medicine)	kulliyya (f)	كلّيّة

student (masc.)	ṭālib (m)	طالب
student (fem.)	ṭāliba (f)	طالبة
lecturer (teacher)	muḥāḍir (m)	محاضر

lecture hall, room	mudarraʒ (m)	مدرّج
graduate	mutaxarriʒ (m)	متخرّج
diploma	diblūma (f)	دبلومة

dissertation	risāla 'ilmiyya (f)	رسالة علميّة
study (report)	dirāsa (f)	دراسة
laboratory	muxtabar (m)	مختبر
lecture	muḥāḍara (f)	محاضرة
coursemate	zamīl fiṣ ṣaff (m)	زميل في الصفّ
scholarship	minḥa dirāsiyya (f)	منحة دراسيّة
academic degree	daraʒa 'ilmiyya (f)	درجة علميّة

119. Sciences. Disciplines

mathematics	riyāḍīyyāt (pl)	رياضيّات
algebra	al ʒabr (m)	الجبر
geometry	handasa (f)	هندسة
astronomy	'ilm al falak (m)	علم الفلك
biology	'ilm al aḥyā' (m)	علم الأحياء
geography	ʒuɣrāfiya (f)	جغرافيا
geology	ʒiulūʒiya (f)	جيولوجيا
history	tarīx (m)	تاريخ
medicine	ṭibb (m)	طبّ
pedagogy	'ilm at tarbiya (f)	علم التربية
law	qānūn (m)	قانون
physics	fizyā' (f)	فيزياء
chemistry	kimyā' (f)	كيمياء
philosophy	falsafa (f)	فلسفة
psychology	'ilm an nafs (m)	علم النفس

120. Writing system. Orthography

grammar	an naḥw waṣ ṣarf (m)	النحو والصرف
vocabulary	mufradāt al luɣa (pl)	مفردات اللغة
phonetics	ṣawtīyyāt (pl)	صوتيّات
noun	ism (m)	إسم
adjective	ṣifa (f)	صفة
verb	fi'l (m)	فعل
adverb	ẓarf (m)	ظرف
pronoun	ḍamīr (m)	ضمير
interjection	ḥarf nidā' (m)	حرف نداء
preposition	ḥarf al ʒarr (m)	حرف الجرّ
root	ʒiðr al kalima (m)	جذر الكلمة
ending	nihāya (f)	نهاية
prefix	sābiqa (f)	سابقة

syllable	maqṭaʻ lafẓiy (m)	مقطع لفظيّ
suffix	lāḥiqa (f)	لاحقة
stress mark	nabra (f)	نبرة
apostrophe	ʻalāmat ḥaðf (f)	علامة حذف
period, dot	nuqṭa (f)	نقطة
comma	fāṣila (f)	فاصلة
semicolon	nuqṭa wa fāṣila (f)	نقطة وفاصلة
colon	nuqṭatān raʼsiyyatān (du)	نقطتان رأسيتان
ellipsis	θalāθ nuqaṭ (pl)	ثلاث نقط
question mark	ʻalāmat istifhām (f)	علامة إستفهام
exclamation point	ʼalāmat taʻaʒʒub (f)	علامة تعجّب
quotation marks	ʼalāmāt al iqtibās (pl)	علامات الإقتباس
in quotation marks	bayn ʻalāmatay al iqtibās	بين علامتي الإقتباس
parenthesis	qawsān (du)	قوسان
in parenthesis	bayn al qawsayn	بين القوسين
hyphen	ʼalāmat waṣl (f)	علامة وصل
dash	ʃurṭa (f)	شرطة
space (between words)	farāɣ (m)	فراغ
letter	ḥarf (m)	حرف
capital letter	ḥarf kabīr (m)	حرف كبير
vowel (n)	ḥarf ṣawtiy (m)	حرف صوتيّ
consonant (n)	ḥarf sākin (m)	حرف ساكن
sentence	ʒumla (f)	جملة
subject	fāʻil (m)	فاعل
predicate	musnad (m)	مسند
line	saṭr (m)	سطر
on a new line	min bidāyat as saṭr	من بداية السطر
paragraph	fiqra (f)	فقرة
word	kalima (f)	كلمة
group of words	maʒmūʻa min al kalimāt (pl)	مجموعة من الكلمات
expression	ʼibāra (f)	عبارة
synonym	murādif (m)	مرادف
antonym	mutaḍādd luɣawiy (m)	متضادّ
rule	qāʻida (f)	قاعدة
exception	istiθnāʼ (m)	إستثناء
correct (adj)	ṣaḥīḥ	صحيح
conjugation	ṣarf (m)	صرف
declension	taṣrīf al asmāʼ (m)	تصريف الأسماء
nominal case	ḥāla ismiyya (f)	حالة إسميّة
question	suʼāl (m)	سؤال

| to underline (vt) | waḍaʿ ҳaṭṭ taḥt | وضع خطًا تحت |
| dotted line | ҳaṭṭ munaqqaṭ (m) | خط منقط |

121. Foreign languages

language	luɣa (f)	لغة
foreign (adj)	aӡnabiy	أجنبيّ
foreign language	luɣa aӡnabiyya (f)	لغة أجنبيّة
to study (vt)	daras	درس
to learn (language, etc.)	taʿallam	تعلّم

to read (vi, vt)	qara'	قرأ
to speak (vi, vt)	takallam	تكلّم
to understand (vt)	fahim	فهم
to write (vt)	katab	كتب

fast (adv)	bi surʿa	بسرعة
slowly (adv)	bi buṭ'	بيطء
fluently (adv)	bi ṭalāqa	بطلاقة

rules	qawāʿid (pl)	قواعد
grammar	an naḥw waṣ ṣarf (m)	النحو والصرف
vocabulary	mufradāt al luɣa (pl)	مفردات اللغة
phonetics	ṣawtīyyāt (pl)	صوتيّات

textbook	kitāb taʿlīm (m)	كتاب تعليم
dictionary	qāmūs (m)	قاموس
teach-yourself book	kitāb taʿlīm ðātiy (m)	كتاب تعليم ذاتيّ
phrasebook	kitāb lil ʿibārāt aʃ ʃā'iʿa (m)	كتاب للعبارت الشائعة

cassette, tape	ʃarīṭ (m)	شريط
videotape	ʃarīṭ vidiyu (m)	شريط فيديو
CD, compact disc	si di (m)	سي دي
DVD	di vi di (m)	دي في دي

alphabet	alifbā' (m)	الفباء
to spell (vt)	tahaӡӡa	تهجّى
pronunciation	nuṭq (m)	نطق

accent	lukna (f)	لكنة
with an accent	bi lukna	بلكنة
without an accent	bi dūn lukna	بدون لكنة

| word | kalima (f) | كلمة |
| meaning | maʿna (m) | معنى |

course (e.g., a French ~)	dawra (f)	دورة
to sign up	saӡӡal ismahu	سجّل إسمه
teacher	mudarris (m)	مدرّس
translation (process)	tarӡama (f)	ترجمة

translation (text, etc.)	tarʒama (f)	ترجمة
translator	mutarʒim (m)	مترجم
interpreter	mutarʒim fawriy (m)	مترجم فوريّ
polyglot	'alīm bi 'iddat luɣāt (m)	عليم بعدّة لغات
memory	ðākira (f)	ذاكرة

122. Fairy tale characters

Santa Claus	baba nuwīl (m)	بابا نويل
Cinderella	sindrīla	سيندريلا
mermaid	ḥūriyyat al baḥr (f)	حوريّة البحر
Neptune	nibtūn (m)	نبتون
magician, wizard	sāḥir (m)	ساحر
fairy	sāḥira (f)	ساحرة
magic (adj)	siḥriy	سحريّ
magic wand	'aṣa siḥriyya (f)	عصا سحريّة
fairy tale	ḥikāya xayāliyya (f)	حكاية خياليّة
miracle	mu'ʒiza (f)	معجزة
dwarf	qazam (m)	قزم
to turn into ...	taḥawwal ila ...	تحوّل إلى...
ghost	ʃabaḥ (m)	شبح
phantom	ʃabaḥ (m)	شبح
monster	waḥʃ (m)	وحش
dragon	tinnīn (m)	تنّين
giant	'imlāq (m)	عملاق

123. Zodiac Signs

Aries	burʒ al ḥamal (m)	برج الحمل
Taurus	burʒ aθ θawr (m)	برج الثور
Gemini	burʒ al ʒawzā' (m)	برج الجوزاء
Cancer	burʒ as saraṭān (m)	برج السرطان
Leo	burʒ al asad (m)	برج الأسد
Virgo	burʒ al 'aðrā' (m)	برج العذراء
Libra	burʒ al mīzān (m)	برج الميزان
Scorpio	burʒ al 'aqrab (m)	برج العقرب
Sagittarius	burʒ al qaws (m)	برج القوس
Capricorn	burʒ al ʒaday (m)	برج الجدي
Aquarius	burʒ ad dalw (m)	برج الدلو
Pisces	burʒ al ḥūt (m)	برج الحوت
character	ṭab' (m)	طبع
character traits	aṣ ṣifāt aʃ ʃaxṣiyya (pl)	الصفات الشخصيّة

behavior	sulūk (m)	سلوك
to tell fortunes	tanabba'	تنبأ
fortune-teller	'arrāfa (f)	عرّافة
horoscope	tawaqqu'āt al abrāʒ (pl)	توقّعات الأبراج

Arts

124. Theater

theater	masraḥ (m)	مسرح
opera	ubra (f)	أوبرا
operetta	ubirīt (f)	أوبريت
ballet	balīh (m)	باليه
theater poster	mulṣaq (m)	ملصق
troupe (theatrical company)	firqa (f)	فرقة
tour	ʒawlat fannānīn (f)	جولة فنّانين
to be on tour	taʒawwal	تجوّل
to rehearse (vi, vt)	aʒra bruvāt	أجرى بروفات
rehearsal	brūva (f)	بروفة
repertoire	barnāmaʒ al masraḥ (m)	برنامج المسرح
performance	adāʾ fanniy (m)	أداء فنّيّ
theatrical show	ʿarḍ masraḥiy (m)	عرض مسرحيّ
play	masraḥiyya (f)	مسرحيّة
ticket	taðkira (f)	تذكرة
box office (ticket booth)	ʃubbāk at taðākir (m)	شبّاك التذاكر
lobby, foyer	ṣāla (f)	صالة
coat check (cloakroom)	ɣurfat al maʿāṭif (f)	غرفة المعاطف
coat check tag	biṭāqat īdāʿ al maʿāṭif (f)	بطاقة إيداع المعاطف
binoculars	minzār (m)	منظار
usher	ḥāʒib (m)	حاجب
orchestra seats	karāsi al urkistra (pl)	كراسي الأوركسترا
balcony	balakūna (f)	بلكونة
dress circle	ʃurfa (f)	شرفة
box	lūʒ (m)	لوج
row	ṣaff (m)	صفّ
seat	maqʿad (m)	مقعد
audience	ʒumhūr (m)	جمهور
spectator	muʃāhid (m)	مشاهد
to clap (vi, vt)	ṣaffaq	صفّق
applause	taṣfīq (m)	تصفيق
ovation	taṣfīq ḥārr (m)	تصفيق حارّ
stage	xaʃabat al masraḥ (f)	خشبة المسرح
curtain	sitāra (f)	ستارة
scenery	dikūr (m)	ديكور

backstage	kawalīs (pl)	كواليس
scene (e.g., the last ~)	maʃhad (m)	مشهد
act	faṣl (m)	فصل
intermission	istirāḥa (f)	إستراحة

125. Cinema

actor	mumaθθil (m)	ممثّل
actress	mumaθθila (f)	ممثّلة
movies (industry)	sinima (f)	سينما
movie	film sinimā'iy (m)	فيلم سينمائيّ
episode	ʒuz' min al film (m)	جزء من الفيلم
detective movie	film bulīsiy (m)	فيلم بوليسيّ
action movie	film ḥaraka (m)	فيلم حركة
adventure movie	film muɣāmarāt (m)	فيلم مغامرات
science fiction movie	film ɣayāl 'ilmiy (m)	فيلم خيال علميّ
horror movie	film ru'b (m)	فيلم رعب
comedy movie	film kumīdiya (f)	فيلم كوميديا
melodrama	miludrāma (m)	ميلودراما
drama	drāma (f)	دراما
fictional movie	film fanniy (m)	فيلم فنّيّ
documentary	film waθā'iqiy (m)	فيلم وثائقيّ
cartoon	film kartūn (m)	فيلم كرتون
silent movies	sinima ṣāmita (f)	سينما صامتة
role (part)	dawr (m)	دور
leading role	dawr ra'īsi (m)	دور رئيسي
to play (vi, vt)	maθθal	مثّل
movie star	naʒm sinimā'iy (m)	نجم سينمائيّ
well-known (adj)	ma'rūf	معروف
famous (adj)	maʃhūr	مشهور
popular (adj)	maḥbūb	محبوب
script (screenplay)	sināriyu (m)	سيناريو
scriptwriter	kātib sināriyu (m)	كاتب سيناريو
movie director	muɣriʒ (m)	مخرج
producer	muntiʒ (m)	منتج
assistant	musā'id (m)	مساعد
cameraman	muṣawwir (m)	مصوّر
stuntman	mu'addi maʃāhid ɣaṭīra (m)	مؤدّي مشاهد خطيرة
double (stuntman)	mumaθθil badīl (m)	ممثّل بديل
to shoot a movie	ṣawwar film	صوّر فيلمًا
audition, screen test	taʒribat adā' (f)	تجربة أداء
shooting	taṣwīr (m)	تصوير

movie crew	ṭāqim al film (m)	طاقم الفيلم
movie set	mintaqat at taṣwīr (f)	منطقة التصوير
camera	kamira sinimā'iyya (f)	كاميرا سينمائية
movie theater	sinima (f)	سينما
screen (e.g., big ~)	ʃāʃa (f)	شاشة
to show a movie	'araḍ film	عرض فيلمًا
soundtrack	musīqa taṣwīriyya (f)	موسيقى تصويرية
special effects	mu'aθθirāt χāṣṣa (pl)	مؤثرات خاصة
subtitles	tarʒamat al ḥiwār (f)	ترجمة الحوار
credits	ʃārat an nihāya (f)	شارة النهاية
translation	tarʒama (f)	ترجمة

126. Painting

art	fann (m)	فنّ
fine arts	funūn ʒamīla (pl)	فنون جميلة
art gallery	maʿraḍ fanniy (m)	معرض فنّي
art exhibition	maʿraḍ fanniy (m)	معرض فنّي
painting (art)	taṣwīr (m)	تصوير
graphic art	rusūmiyyāt (pl)	رسوميّات
abstract art	fann taʒrīdiy (m)	فنّ تجريديّ
impressionism	al intibāʿiyya (f)	الإنطباعيّة
picture (painting)	lawḥa (f)	لوحة
drawing	rasm (m)	رسم
poster	mulṣaq i'lāniy (m)	ملصق إعلانيّ
illustration (picture)	rasm tawḍīḥiy (m)	رسم توضيحيّ
miniature	ṣūra muṣaɣɣara (f)	صورة مصغّرة
copy (of painting, etc.)	nusχa (f)	نسخة
reproduction	nusχa ṭibq al aṣl (f)	نسخة طبق الأصل
mosaic	fusayfisā' (f)	فسيفساء
stained glass window	zuʒāʒ muʿaʃʃaq (m)	زجاج معشّق
fresco	taṣwīr ʒiṣṣiy (m)	تصوير جصّي
engraving	naqʃ (m)	نقش
bust (sculpture)	timθāl niṣfiy (m)	تمثال نصفيّ
sculpture	naḥt (m)	نحت
statue	timθāl (m)	تمثال
plaster of Paris	ʒībs (m)	جيبس
plaster (as adj)	min al ʒībs	من الجيبس
portrait	burtrī (m)	بورتريه
self-portrait	burtrīh ðātiy (m)	بورتريه ذاتيّ
landscape painting	lawḥat manẓar ṭabīʿiy (f)	لوحة منظر طبيعيّ
still life	ṭabīʿa ṣāmita (f)	طبيعة صامتة

caricature	ṣūra karikaturiyya (f)	صورة كاريكاتورِيّة
sketch	rasm tamhīdiy (m)	رسم تمهيدي
paint	lawn (m)	لون
watercolor paint	alwān māʾiyya (m)	ألوان مائية
oil (paint)	zayt (m)	زيت
pencil	qalam ruṣāṣ (m)	قلم رصاص
India ink	ḥibr hindiy (m)	حبر هندي
charcoal	faḥm (m)	فحم
to draw (vi, vt)	rasam	رسم
to paint (vi, vt)	rasam	رسم
to pose (vi)	qaʿad	قعد
artist's model (masc.)	mudil ḥay (m)	موديل حيّ
artist's model (fem.)	mudil ḥay (m)	موديل حي
artist (painter)	rassām (m)	رسّام
work of art	ʿamal fanniy (m)	عمل فنّيّ
masterpiece	tuḥfa fanniyya (f)	تحفة فنّية
studio (artist's workroom)	warʃa (f)	ورشة
canvas (cloth)	kanava (f)	كانفا
easel	musnad ar rasm (m)	مسند الرسم
palette	lawḥat al alwān (f)	لوحة الألوان
frame (picture ~, etc.)	iṭār (m)	إطار
restoration	tarmīm (m)	ترميم
to restore (vt)	rammam	رمّم

127. Literature & Poetry

literature	adab (m)	أدب
author (writer)	muʾallif (m)	مؤلف
pseudonym	ism mustaʿār (m)	إسم مستعار
book	kitāb (m)	كتاب
volume	muʒallad (m)	مجلّد
table of contents	fihris (m)	فهرس
page	ṣafḥa (f)	صفحة
main character	aʃ ʃaxṣiyya ar raʾīsiyya (f)	الشخصيّة الرئيسيّة
autograph	tawqīʿ al muʾallif (m)	توقيع المؤلف
short story	qiṣṣa qaṣīra (f)	قصّة قصيرة
story (novella)	qiṣṣa (f)	قصّة
novel	riwāya (f)	رواية
work (writing)	muʾallif (m)	مؤلف
fable	ḥikāya (f)	حكاية
detective novel	riwāya bulīsiyya (f)	رواية بوليسيّة
poem (verse)	qaṣīda (f)	قصيدة
poetry	ʃiʿr (m)	شعر

| poem (epic, ballad) | qaṣīda (f) | قصيدة |
| poet | ʃā'ir (m) | شاعر |

fiction	adab ʒamīl (m)	أدب جميل
science fiction	χayāl 'ilmiy (m)	خيال علميّ
adventures	adab al muɣāmarāt (m)	أدب المغامرات
educational literature	adab tarbawiy (m)	أدب تربويّ
children's literature	adab al aṭfāl (m)	أدب الأطفال

128. Circus

circus	sirk (m)	سيرك
traveling circus	sirk mutanaqqil (m)	سيرك متنقّل
program	barnāmaʒ (m)	برنامج
performance	adā' fanniy (m)	أداء فنّيّ

| act (circus ~) | dawr (m) | دور |
| circus ring | ḥalbat as sirk (f) | حلبة السيرك |

| pantomime (act) | 'arḍ 'īmā'y (m) | عرض إيمائي |
| clown | muḥarriʒ (m) | مهرّج |

acrobat	bahlawān (m)	بهلوان
acrobatics	al'āb bahlawāniyya (f)	ألعاب بهلوانيّة
gymnast	lā'ib ʒumbāz (m)	لاعب جنباز
gymnastics	ʒumbāz (m)	جنباز
somersault	ʃaqlaba (f)	شقلبة

athlete (strongman)	lā'ib riyāḍiy (m)	لاعب رياضيّ
tamer (e.g., lion ~)	murawwiḍ (m)	مروّض
rider (circus horse ~)	fāris (m)	فارس
assistant	musā'id (m)	مساعد

stunt	al'āb bahlawāniyya (f)	ألعاب بهلوانيّة
magic trick	χid'a siḥriyya (f)	خدعة سحريّة
conjurer, magician	sāḥir (m)	ساحر

juggler	bahlawān (m)	بهلوان
to juggle (vi, vt)	la'ib bi kurāt 'adīda	لعب بكرات عديدة
animal trainer	mudarrib ḥayawānāt (m)	مدرّب حيوانات
animal training	tadrīb al ḥayawānāt (m)	تدريب الحيوانات
to train (animals)	darrab	درّب

129. Music. Pop music

music	musīqa (f)	موسيقى
musician	'āzif (m)	عازف
musical instrument	'āla musiqiyya (f)	آلة موسيقيّة

to play ...	ʿazaf ...	عزف...
guitar	gitār (m)	جيتار
violin	kamān (m)	كمان
cello	tʃīlu (m)	تشيلو
double bass	kamān aʒhar (m)	كمان أجهر
harp	qiθār (m)	قيثار
piano	biānu (m)	بيانو
grand piano	biānu kibīr (m)	بيانو كبير
organ	arɣan (m)	أرغن
wind instruments	ʾālāt nafχiyya (pl)	آلات نفخيّة
oboe	ubwa (m)	أويوا
saxophone	saksufūn (m)	ساكسوفون
clarinet	klarnīt (m)	كلارنيت
flute	flut (m)	فلوت
trumpet	būq (m)	بوق
accordion	ukurdiūn (m)	أكورديون
drum	ṭabla (f)	طبلة
duo	θunāʾiy (m)	ثنائيّ
trio	θulāθy (m)	ثلاثيّ
quartet	rubāʿiy (m)	رباعيّ
choir	χūrus (m)	خورس
orchestra	urkistra (f)	أوركسترا
pop music	musīqa al bub (f)	موسيقى البوب
rock music	musīqa ar rūk (f)	موسيقى الروك
rock group	firqat ar rūk (f)	فرقة الروك
jazz	ʒāz (m)	جاز
idol	maʿbūd (m)	معبود
admirer, fan	muʿʒab (m)	معجب
concert	ḥafla mūsiqiyya (f)	حفلة موسيقيّة
symphony	simfūniyya (f)	سمفونيّة
composition	qiṭʿa mūsiqiyya (f)	قطعة موسيقيّة
to compose (write)	allaf	ألّف
singing (n)	ɣināʾ (m)	غناء
song	uɣniyya (f)	أغنيّة
tune (melody)	laḥn (m)	لحن
rhythm	ʾīqāʿ (m)	إيقاع
blues	musīqa al blūz (f)	موسيقى البلوز
sheet music	nutāt (pl)	نوتات
baton	ʿaṣa al mayistru (m)	عصا المايسترو
bow	qaws (m)	قوس
string	watar (m)	وتر
case (e.g., guitar ~)	ʃanṭa (f)	شنطة

Rest. Entertainment. Travel

130. Trip. Travel

tourism, travel	siyāḥa (f)	سياحة
tourist	sā'iḥ (m)	سائح
trip, voyage	riḥla (f)	رحلة
adventure	muɣāmara (f)	مغامرة
trip, journey	riḥla (f)	رحلة
vacation	ʿuṭla (f)	عطلة
to be on vacation	ʿindahu ʿuṭla	عنده عطلة
rest	istirāḥa (f)	إستراحة
train	qiṭār (m)	قطار
by train	bil qiṭār	بالقطار
airplane	ṭā'ira (f)	طائرة
by airplane	biṭ ṭā'ira	بالطائرة
by car	bis sayyāra	بالسيّارة
by ship	bis safīna	بالسفينة
luggage	aʃ ʃunaṭ (pl)	الشنط
suitcase	ḥaqībat safar (f)	حقيبة سفر
luggage cart	ʿarabat ʃunaṭ (f)	عربة شنط
passport	ʒawāz as safar (m)	جواز السفر
visa	ta'ʃīra (f)	تأشيرة
ticket	taðkira (f)	تذكرة
air ticket	taðkirat ṭā'ira (f)	تذكرة طائرة
guidebook	dalīl (m)	دليل
map (tourist ~)	χarīṭa (f)	خريطة
area (rural ~)	mintaqa (f)	منطقة
place, site	makān (m)	مكان
exotica (n)	ɣarāba (f)	غرابة
exotic (adj)	ɣarīb	غريب
amazing (adj)	mudhiʃ	مدهش
group	maʒmūʿa (f)	مجموعة
excursion, sightseeing tour	ʒawla (f)	جولة
guide (person)	murʃid (m)	مرشد

131. Hotel

hotel	funduq (m)	فندق
motel	mutīl (m)	موتيل
three-star (~ hotel)	θalāθat nuʒūm	ثلاثة نجوم
five-star	xamsat nuʒūm	خمسة نجوم
to stay (in a hotel, etc.)	nazal	نزل
room	ɣurfa (f)	غرفة
single room	ɣurfa li ʃaxṣ wāhid (f)	غرفة لشخص واحد
double room	ɣurfa li ʃaxṣayn (f)	غرفة لشخصين
to book a room	haʒaz ɣurfa	حجز غرفة
half board	waʒbitān fil yawm (du)	وجبتان في اليوم
full board	θalāθ waʒabāt fil yawm	ثلاث وجبات في اليوم
with bath	bi hawḍ al istihmām	بحوض الإستحمام
with shower	bid duʃ	بالدوش
satellite television	tilivizyūn faḍā'iy (m)	تلفزيون فضائيّ
air-conditioner	takyīf (m)	تكييف
towel	fūṭa (f)	فوطة
key	miftāh (m)	مفتاح
administrator	mudīr (m)	مدير
chambermaid	'āmilat tanẓīf ɣuraf (f)	عاملة تنظيف غرف
porter, bellboy	hammāl (m)	حمّال
doorman	bawwāb (m)	بوّاب
restaurant	maṭ'am (m)	مطعم
pub, bar	bār (m)	بار
breakfast	futūr (m)	فطور
dinner	'aʃā' (m)	عشاء
buffet	bufīh (m)	بوفيه
lobby	radha (f)	ردهة
elevator	miṣ'ad (m)	مصعد
DO NOT DISTURB	ar raʒā' 'adam al iz'āʒ	الرجاء عدم الإزعاج
NO SMOKING	mamnū' at tadxīn	ممنوع التدخين

132. Books. Reading

book	kitāb (m)	كتاب
author	mu'allif (m)	مؤلف
writer	kātib (m)	كاتب
to write (~ a book)	allaf	ألف
reader	qāri' (m)	قارئ
to read (vi, vt)	qara'	قرأ

reading (activity)	qirā'a (f)	قراءة
silently (to oneself)	sirran	سرًّا
aloud (adv)	bi ṣawt 'āli	بصوت عال
to publish (vt)	naʃar	نشر
publishing (process)	naʃr (m)	نشر
publisher	nāʃir (m)	ناشر
publishing house	dār aṭ ṭibā'a wan naʃr (f)	دار الطباعة والنشر
to come out (be released)	ṣadar	صدر
release (of a book)	ṣudūr (m)	صدور
print run	'adad an nusaχ (m)	عدد النسخ
bookstore	maḥall kutub (m)	محلّ كتب
library	maktaba (f)	مكتبة
story (novella)	qiṣṣa (f)	قصّة
short story	qiṣṣa qaṣīra (f)	قصّة قصيرة
novel	riwāya (f)	رواية
detective novel	riwāya bulīsiyya (f)	رواية بوليسيّة
memoirs	muðakkirāt (pl)	مذكّرات
legend	usṭūra (f)	أسطورة
myth	χurāfa (f)	خرافة
poetry, poems	ʃi'r (m)	شعر
autobiography	sīrat ḥayāt (f)	سيرة حياة
selected works	muχtārāt (pl)	مختارات
science fiction	χayāl 'ilmiy (m)	خيال علميّ
title	'unwān (m)	عنوان
introduction	muqaddima (f)	مقدّمة
title page	ṣafḥat al 'unwān (f)	صفحة العنوان
chapter	faṣl (m)	فصل
extract	qiṭ'a (f)	قطعة
episode	maʃhad (m)	مشهد
plot (storyline)	mawdū' (m)	موضوع
contents	muḥtawayāt (pl)	محتويات
table of contents	fihris (m)	فهرس
main character	aʃ ʃaχṣiyya ar ra'īsiyya (f)	الشخصيّة الرئيسيّة
volume	muʒallad (m)	مجلّد
cover	ɣilāf (m)	غلاف
binding	taʒlīd (m)	تجليد
bookmark	ʃarīṭ (m)	شريط
page	ṣafḥa (f)	صفحة
to page through	qallab aṣ ṣafaḥāt	قلّب الصفحات
margins	hāmiʃ (m)	هامش
annotation (marginal note, etc.)	mulāḥaza (f)	ملاحظة

footnote	mulāḥaza (f)	ملاحظة
text	naṣṣ (m)	نص
type, font	nawʿ al ẖaṭṭ (m)	نوع الخط
misprint, typo	ẖaṭaʾ maṭbaʿiy (m)	خطأ مطبعي
translation	tarʒama (f)	ترجمة
to translate (vt)	tarʒam	ترجم
original (n)	aṣliy (m)	أصلي
famous (adj)	maʃhūr	مشهور
unknown (not famous)	ɣayr maʿrūf	غير معروف
interesting (adj)	mumtiʿ	ممتع
bestseller	akθar mabīʿan (m)	أكثر مبيعًا
dictionary	qāmūs (m)	قاموس
textbook	kitāb taʿlīm (m)	كتاب تعليم
encyclopedia	mawsūʿa (f)	موسوعة

133. Hunting. Fishing

hunting	ṣayd (m)	صيد
to hunt (vi, vt)	iṣṭād	إصطاد
hunter	ṣayyād (m)	صياد
to shoot (vi)	aṭlaq an nār	أطلق النار
rifle	bunduqiyya (f)	بندقية
bullet (shell)	ruṣāṣa (f)	رصاصة
shot (lead balls)	raʃʃ (m)	رش
steel trap	maṣyada (f)	مصيدة
snare (for birds, etc.)	faẖẖ (m)	فخ
to fall into the steel trap	waqaʿ fi faẖẖ	وقع في فخ
to lay a steel trap	naṣab faẖẖ	نصب فخًا
poacher	sāriq aṣ ṣayd (m)	سارق الصيد
game (in hunting)	ṣayd (m)	صيد
hound dog	kalb ṣayd (m)	كلب صيد
safari	safāri (m)	سفاري
mounted animal	ḥayawān muḥannaṭ (m)	حيوان محنّط
fisherman, angler	ṣayyād as samak (m)	صياد السمك
fishing (angling)	ṣayd as samak (m)	صيد السمك
to fish (vi)	iṣṭād as samak	إصطاد السمك
fishing rod	ṣannāra (f)	صنارة
fishing line	ẖayṭ (m)	خيط
hook	ʃaṣṣ aṣ ṣayd (m)	شص الصيد
float, bobber	ʿawwāma (f)	عوّامة
bait	tuʿm (m)	طعم
to cast a line	ṭaraḥ aṣ ṣinnāra	طرح الصنارة

to bite (ab. fish)	'aḍḍ	عضّ
catch (of fish)	as samak al muṣṭād (m)	السمك المصطاد
ice-hole	fatḥa fil ʒalīd (f)	فتحة في الجليد

fishing net	ʃabakat aṣ ṣayd (f)	شبكة الصيد
boat	markab (m)	مركب
to net (to fish with a net)	iṣṭād biʃ ʃabaka	إصطاد بالشبكة
to cast[throw] the net	rama ʃabaka	رمى شبكة
to haul the net in	axraʒ ʃabaka	أخرج شبكة
to fall into the net	waqaʻ fi ʃabaka	وقع في شبكة

whaler (person)	ṣayyād al ḥūt (m)	صيّاد الحوت
whaleboat	safīnat ṣayd al ḥītān (f)	سفينة صيد الحيتان
harpoon	ḥarba (f)	حربة

134. Games. Billiards

billiards	bilyārdu (m)	بلياردو
billiard room, hall	qāʻat bilyārdu (m)	قاعة بلياردو
ball (snooker, etc.)	kura (f)	كرة

to pocket a ball	aṣqaṭ kura	أصقط كرة
cue	'aṣa bilyardu (f)	عصا بلياردو
pocket	ʒayb bilyārdu (m)	جيب بلياردو

135. Games. Playing cards

diamonds	ad dināriy (m)	الديناريّ
spades	al bastūniy (m)	البستونيّ
hearts	al kūba (f)	الكوبة
clubs	as sibātiy (m)	السباتيّ

ace	'ās (m)	آس
king	malik (m)	ملك
queen	malika (f)	ملكة
jack, knave	walad (m)	ولد

| playing card | waraqa (f) | ورقة |
| cards | waraq (m) | ورق |

| trump | waraqa rābiḥa (f) | ورقة رابحة |
| deck of cards | dasta waraq al laʻb (f) | دستة ورق اللعب |

point	nuqta (f)	نقطة
to deal (vi, vt)	farraq	فرّق
to shuffle (cards)	xallaṭ	خلط
lead, turn (n)	dawr (m)	دور
cardsharp	muḥtāl fil qimār (m)	محتال في القمار

136. Rest. Games. Miscellaneous

to stroll (vi, vt)	tanazzah	تنزّه
stroll (leisurely walk)	tanazzuh (m)	تنزّه
car ride	ȝawla bis sayyāra (f)	جولة بالسيّارة
adventure	muɣāmara (f)	مغامرة
picnic	nuzha (f)	نزهة
game (chess, etc.)	luʿba (f)	لعبة
player	lāʿib (m)	لاعب
game (one ~ of chess)	dawr (m)	دور
collector (e.g., philatelist)	ȝāmiʿ (m)	جامع
to collect (stamps, etc.)	ȝamaʿ	جمع
collection	maȝmūʿa (f)	مجموعة
crossword puzzle	kalimāt mutaqāṭiʿa (pl)	كلمات متقاطعة
racetrack (horse racing venue)	ḥalbat sibāq al ҳuyūl (f)	حلبة سباق الخيول
disco (discotheque)	disku (m)	ديسكو
sauna	sāuna (f)	ساونا
lottery	yanaṣīb (m)	يانصيب
camping trip	riḥlat taҳyīm (f)	رحلة تخييم
camp	muҳayyam (m)	مخيّم
tent (for camping)	ҳayma (f)	خيمة
compass	būṣila (f)	بوصلة
camper	muҳayyim (m)	مخيّم
to watch (movie, etc.)	ʃāhid	شاهد
viewer	muʃāhid (m)	مشاهد
TV show (TV program)	barnāmaȝ tiliviziyūniy (m)	برنامج تليفزيونيّ

137. Photography

camera (photo)	kamira (f)	كاميرا
photo, picture	ṣūra (f)	صورة
photographer	muṣawwir (m)	مصوّر
photo studio	istūdiyu taṣwīr (m)	إستوديو تصوير
photo album	albūm aṣ ṣuwar (m)	ألبوم الصور
camera lens	ʿadasa (f)	عدسة
telephoto lens	ʿadasa tiliskūpiyya (f)	عدسة تلسكوبيّة
filter	filtir (m)	فلتر
lens	ʿadasa (f)	عدسة
optics (high-quality ~)	aȝhiza baṣariyya (pl)	أجهزة بصريّة
diaphragm (aperture)	buʾra (f)	بؤرة

| exposure time (shutter speed) | muddat at ta'rīḍ (f) | مدّة التعريض |
| viewfinder | al 'ayn al fāḥiṣa (f) | العين الفاحصة |

digital camera	kamira raqmiyya (f)	كاميرا رقميّة
tripod	ḥāmil θulāθiy (m)	حامل ثلاثيّ
flash	flāʃ (m)	فلاش

to photograph (vt)	ṣawwar	صوّر
to take pictures	ṣawwar	صوّر
to have one's picture taken	taṣawwar	تصوّر

focus	bu'rat al 'adasa (f)	بؤرة العدسة
to focus	rakkaz	ركّز
sharp, in focus (adj)	wāḍiḥ	واضح
sharpness	wuḍūḥ (m)	وضوح

| contrast | tabāyun (m) | تباين |
| contrast (as adj) | mutabāyin | متباين |

picture (photo)	ṣūra (f)	صورة
negative (n)	ṣūra sāliba (f)	صورة سالبة
film (a roll of ~)	film (m)	فيلم
frame (still)	iṭār (m)	إطار
to print (photos)	ṭaba'	طبع

138. Beach. Swimming

beach	ʃāṭi' (m)	شاطئ
sand	raml (m)	رمل
deserted (beach)	mahʒūr	مهجور

suntan	sumrat al baʃara (f)	سمرة البشرة
to get a tan	taʃammas	تشمّس
tan (adj)	asmar	أسمر
sunscreen	krīm wāqi aʃ ʃams (m)	كريم واقي الشمس

bikini	bikini (m)	بكيني
bathing suit	libās sibāḥa (m)	لباس سباحة
swim trunks	libās sibāḥa riʒāliy (m)	لباس سباحة رجاليّ

swimming pool	masbaḥ (m)	مسبح
to swim (vi)	sabaḥ	سبح
shower	dūʃ (m)	دوش
to change (one's clothes)	ɣayyar libāsuh	غيّر لباسه
towel	fūṭa (f)	فوطة

boat	markab (m)	مركب
motorboat	lanʃ (m)	لنش
water ski	tazalluʒ 'alal mā' (m)	تزلج على الماء

paddle boat	'aʒala mā'iyya (f)	عجلة مائيّة
surfing	rukūb al amwāʒ (m)	ركوب الأمواج
surfer	rākib al amwāʒ (m)	راكب الأمواج
scuba set	ʒihāz at tanaffus (m)	جهاز التنفّس
flippers (swim fins)	za'ānif as sibāḥa (pl)	زعانف السباحة
mask (diving ~)	kimāma (f)	كمامة
diver	ɣawwāṣ (m)	غوّاص
to dive (vi)	ɣāṣ	غاص
underwater (adv)	taḥt al mā'	تحت الماء
beach umbrella	ʃamsiyya (f)	شمسيّة
sunbed (lounger)	kursiy blāʒ (m)	كرسيّ بلاج
sunglasses	nazzārat ʃams (f)	نظّارة شمس
air mattress	martaba hawā'iyya (f)	مرتبة هوائيّة
to play (amuse oneself)	la'ib	لعب
to go for a swim	sabaḥ	سبح
beach ball	kura (f)	كرة
to inflate (vt)	nafaχ	نفخ
inflatable, air (adj)	qābil lin nafχ	قابل للنفخ
wave	mawʒa (f)	موجة
buoy (line of ~s)	ʃamandūra (f)	شمندورة
to drown (ab. person)	ɣariq	غرق
to save, to rescue	anqað	أنقذ
life vest	sutrat naʒāt (f)	سترة نجاة
to observe, to watch	rāqab	راقب
lifeguard	ḥāris ʃāṭi' (m)	حارس شاطئ

TECHNICAL EQUIPMENT. TRANSPORTATION

Technical equipment

139. Computer

computer	kumbyūtir (m)	كمبيوتر
notebook, laptop	kumbyūtir maḥmūl (m)	كمبيوتر محمول
to turn on	ʃayyal	شغّل
to turn off	aylaq	أغلق
keyboard	lawḥat al mafātīḥ (f)	لوحة المفاتيح
key	miftāḥ (m)	مفتاح
mouse	fa'ra (f)	فأرة
mouse pad	wisādat fa'ra (f)	وسادة فأرة
button	zirr (m)	زرّ
cursor	mu'aʃʃir (m)	مؤشّر
monitor	ʃāʃa (f)	شاشة
screen	ʃāʃa (f)	شاشة
hard disk	qurṣ ṣalib (m)	قرص صلب
hard disk capacity	si'at taxzīn (f)	سعة تخزين
memory	ðākira (f)	ذاكرة
random access memory	ðākirat al wuṣūl al 'aʃwā'iy (f)	ذاكرة الوصول العشوائيّ
file	malaff (m)	ملفّ
folder	ḥāfiẓa (m)	حافظة
to open (vt)	fataḥ	فتح
to close (vt)	aylaq	أغلق
to save (vt)	ḥafaẓ	حفظ
to delete (vt)	masaḥ	مسح
to copy (vt)	nasax	نسخ
to sort (vt)	ṣannaf	صنّف
to transfer (copy)	naqal	نقل
program	barnāmaʒ (m)	برنامج
software	barāmiʒ kumbyūtir (pl)	برامج كمبيوتر
programmer	mubarmiʒ (m)	مبرمج
to program (vt)	barmaʒ	برمج
hacker	hākir (m)	هاكر

password	kalimat as sirr (f)	كلمة السرّ
virus	virūs (m)	فيروس
to find, to detect	waʒad	وجد

| byte | bayt (m) | بايت |
| megabyte | miʒabāyt (m) | ميجابايت |

| data | bayānāt (pl) | بيانات |
| database | qaʿidat bayānāt (f) | قاعدة بيانات |

cable (USB, etc.)	kābil (m)	كابل
to disconnect (vt)	faṣal	فصل
to connect (sth to sth)	waṣṣal	وصّل

140. Internet. E-mail

Internet	intirnit (m)	إنترنت
browser	mutaṣaffiḥ (m)	متصفح
search engine	muḥarrik baḥθ (m)	محرّك بحث
provider	ʃarikat al intirnīt (f)	شركة الإنترنيت

webmaster	mudīr al mawqiʿ (m)	مدير الموقع
website	mawqiʿ iliktrūniy (m)	موقع إلكتروني
webpage	ṣafḥat wīb (f)	صفحة ويب

| address (e-mail ~) | ʿunwān (m) | عنوان |
| address book | daftar al ʿanāwīn (m) | دفتر العناوين |

mailbox	ṣundūq al barīd (m)	صندوق البريد
mail	barīd (m)	بريد
full (adj)	mumtaliʾ	ممتلىء

message	risāla iliktrūniyya (f)	رسالة إلكترونيّة
incoming messages	rasaʾil wārida (pl)	رسائل واردة
outgoing messages	rasaʾil ṣādira (pl)	رسائل صادرة
sender	mursil (m)	مرسل
to send (vt)	arsal	أرسل
sending (of mail)	irsāl (m)	إرسال

| receiver | mursal ilayh (m) | مرسل إليه |
| to receive (vt) | istalam | إستلم |

| correspondence | murāsala (f) | مراسلة |
| to correspond (vi) | tarāsal | تراسل |

file	malaff (m)	ملفّ
to download (vt)	ḥammal	حمّل
to create (vt)	anʃaʾ	أنشأ
to delete (vt)	masaḥ	مسح
deleted (adj)	mamsūḥ	ممسوح

connection (ADSL, etc.)	ittiṣāl (m)	إتّصال
speed	sur'a (f)	سرعة
modem	mudim (m)	مودم
access	wuṣūl (m)	وصول
port (e.g., input ~)	maxraʒ (m)	مخرج
connection (make a ~)	ittiṣāl (m)	إتّصال
to connect to … (vi)	ittaṣal	إتّصل
to select (vt)	ixtār	إختار
to search (for …)	baḥaθ	بحث

Transportation

141. Airplane

airplane	ṭā'ira (f)	طائرة
air ticket	taðkirat ṭā'ira (f)	تذكرة طائرة
airline	ʃarikat ṭayarān (f)	شركة طيران
airport	maṭār (m)	مطار
supersonic (adj)	xāriq liṣ ṣawt	خارق للصوت
captain	qā'id aṭ ṭā'ira (m)	قائد الطائرة
crew	ṭāqim (m)	طاقم
pilot	ṭayyār (m)	طيّار
flight attendant (fem.)	muḍīfat ṭayarān (f)	مضيفة طيران
navigator	mallāḥ (m)	ملّاح
wings	aʒniḥa (pl)	أجنحة
tail	ðayl (m)	ذيل
cockpit	kabīna (f)	كابينة
engine	mutūr (m)	موتور
undercarriage (landing gear)	ʿaʒalāt al hubūṭ (pl)	عجلات الهبوط
turbine	turbīna (f)	تربينة
propeller	mirwaḥa (f)	مروحة
black box	musaʒʒil aṭ ṭayarān (m)	مسجّل الطيران
yoke (control column)	ʿaʒalat qiyāda (f)	عجلة قيادة
fuel	wuqūd (m)	وقود
safety card	biṭāqat as salāma (f)	بطاقة السلامة
oxygen mask	qināʿ uksiʒīn (m)	قناع أوكسيجين
uniform	libās muwaḥḥad (m)	لباس موحّد
life vest	sutrat naʒāt (f)	سترة نجاة
parachute	miẓallat hubūṭ (f)	مظلّة هبوط
takeoff	iqlāʿ (m)	إقلاع
to take off (vi)	aqlaʿat	أقلعت
runway	madraʒ aṭ ṭā'irāt (m)	مدرج الطائرات
visibility	ru'ya (f)	رؤية
flight (act of flying)	ṭayarān (m)	طيران
altitude	irtifāʿ (m)	إرتفاع
air pocket	ʒayb hawā'iy (m)	جيب هوائيّ
seat	maqʿad (m)	مقعد
headphones	sammāʿāt ra'siya (pl)	سمّاعات رأسيّة

folding tray (tray table)	ṣīniyya qābila liṭ ṭayy (f)	صينية قابلة للطيّ
airplane window	ʃubbāk aṭ ṭā'ira (m)	شبّاك الطائرة
aisle	mamarr (m)	ممرّ

142. Train

train	qiṭār (m)	قطار
commuter train	qiṭār (m)	قطار
express train	qiṭār sarī' (m)	قطار سريع
diesel locomotive	qāṭirat dīzil (f)	قاطرة ديزل
steam locomotive	qāṭira buxāriyya (f)	قاطرة بخاريّة
passenger car	'araba (f)	عربة
dining car	'arabat al maṭ'am (f)	عربة المطعم
rails	quḍubān (pl)	قضبان
railroad	sikka ḥadīdiyya (f)	سكّة حديديّة
railway tie	'āriḍa (f)	عارضة
platform (railway ~)	raṣīf (m)	رصيف
track (~ 1, 2, etc.)	xaṭṭ (m)	خطّ
semaphore	simafūr (m)	سيمافور
station	maḥaṭṭa (f)	محطّة
engineer (train driver)	sā'iq (m)	سائق
porter (of luggage)	ḥammāl (m)	حمّال
car attendant	mas'ūl 'arabat al qiṭār (m)	مسؤول عربة القطار
passenger	rākib (m)	راكب
conductor (ticket inspector)	kamsariy (m)	كمسريّ
corridor (in train)	mamarr (m)	ممرّ
emergency brake	farāmil aṭ ṭawāri' (pl)	فرامل الطوارئ
compartment	ɣurfa (f)	غرفة
berth	sarīr (m)	سرير
upper berth	sarīr 'ulwiy (m)	سرير علويّ
lower berth	sarīr sufliy (m)	سرير سفليّ
bed linen, bedding	aɣṭiyat as sarīr (pl)	أغطية السرير
ticket	taðkira (f)	تذكرة
schedule	ʒadwal (m)	جدول
information display	lawḥat ma'lūmāt (f)	لوحة معلومات
to leave, to depart	ɣādar	غادر
departure (of train)	muɣādara (f)	مغادرة
to arrive (ab. train)	waṣal	وصل
arrival	wuṣūl (m)	وصول
to arrive by train	waṣal bil qiṭār	وصل بالقطار
to get on the train	rakib al qiṭār	ركب القطار

to get off the train	nazil min al qiṭār	نزل من القطار
train wreck	ḥiṭām qiṭār (m)	حطام قطار
to derail (vi)	xaraʒ 'an xaṭṭ sayrih	خرج عن خطّ سيره
steam locomotive	qāṭira buxāriyya (f)	قاطرة بخاريّة
stoker, fireman	'ataʃʒiy (m)	عطشجيّ
firebox	furn al muḥarrik (m)	فرن المحرّك
coal	faḥm (m)	فحم

143. Ship

ship	safīna (f)	سفينة
vessel	safīna (f)	سفينة
steamship	bāxira (f)	باخرة
riverboat	bāxira nahriyya (f)	باخرة نهريّة
cruise ship	bāxira siyahiyya (f)	باخرة سياحيّة
cruiser	ṭarrād (m)	طرّاد
yacht	yaxt (m)	يخت
tugboat	qāṭira (f)	قاطرة
barge	ṣandal (m)	صندل
ferry	'abbāra (f)	عبّارة
sailing ship	safīna ʃirā'iyya (m)	سفينة شراعيّة
brigantine	markab ʃirā'iy (m)	مركب شراعيّ
ice breaker	muḥaṭṭimat ʒalīd (f)	محطّمة جليد
submarine	ɣawwāṣa (f)	غوّاصة
boat (flat-bottomed ~)	markab (m)	مركب
dinghy	zawraq (m)	زورق
lifeboat	qārib naʒāt (m)	قارب نجاة
motorboat	lanʃ (m)	لنش
captain	qubṭān (m)	قبطان
seaman	baḥḥār (m)	بحّار
sailor	baḥḥār (m)	بحّار
crew	ṭāqim (m)	طاقم
boatswain	ra'īs al baḥḥāra (m)	رئيس البحّارة
ship's boy	ṣabiy as safīna (m)	صبيّ السفينة
cook	ṭabbāx (m)	طبّاخ
ship's doctor	ṭabīb as safīna (m)	طبيب السفينة
deck	saṭḥ as safīna (m)	سطح السفينة
mast	sāriya (f)	سارية
sail	ʃirā' (m)	شراع
hold	'ambar (m)	عنبر
bow (prow)	muqaddama (m)	مقدّمة

stern	mu'axirat as safīna (f)	مؤخّرة السفينة
oar	miʒðāf (m)	مجداف
screw propeller	mirwaḥa (f)	مروحة
cabin	kabīna (f)	كابينة
wardroom	ɣurfat al istirāḥa (f)	غرفة الإستراحة
engine room	qism al 'ālāt (m)	قسم الآلات
bridge	burʒ al qiyāda (m)	برج القيادة
radio room	ɣurfat al lāsilkiyَ (f)	غرفة اللاسلكيَ
wave (radio)	mawʒa (f)	موجة
logbook	siʒil as safīna (m)	سجل السفينة
spyglass	minzār (m)	منظار
bell	ʒaras (m)	جرس
flag	'alam (m)	علم
hawser (mooring ~)	ḥabl (m)	حبل
knot (bowline, etc.)	'uqda (f)	عقدة
deckrails	drabizīn (m)	درابزين
gangway	sullam (m)	سلّم
anchor	mirsāt (f)	مرساة
to weigh anchor	rafa' mirsāt	رفع مرساة
to drop anchor	rasa	رسا
anchor chain	silsilat mirsāt (f)	سلسلة مرساة
port (harbor)	mīnā' (m)	ميناء
quay, wharf	marsa (m)	مرسى
to berth (moor)	rasa	رسا
to cast off	aqla'	أقلع
trip, voyage	riḥla (f)	رحلة
cruise (sea trip)	riḥla baḥriyya (f)	رحلة بحرية
course (route)	masār (m)	مسار
route (itinerary)	ṭarīq (m)	طريق
fairway (safe water channel)	maʒra milāḥiyَ (m)	مجرى ملاحيَ
shallows	miyāh ḍaḥla (f)	مياه ضحلة
to run aground	ʒanaḥ	جنح
storm	'āṣifa (f)	عاصفة
signal	iʃāra (f)	إشارة
to sink (vi)	ɣariq	غرق
Man overboard!	saqaṭ raʒul min as safīna!	سقط رجل من السفينة!
SOS (distress signal)	nidā' iɣāθa (m)	نداء إغاثة
ring buoy	ṭawq naʒāt (m)	طوق نجاة

144. Airport

airport	maṭār (m)	مطار
airplane	ṭā'ira (f)	طائرة
airline	ʃarikat ṭayarān (f)	شركة طيران
air traffic controller	marāqib al ḥaraka al ʒawwiyya (pl)	مراقب الحركة الجوية
departure	muɣādara (f)	مغادرة
arrival	wuṣūl (m)	وصول
to arrive (by plane)	waṣal	وصل
departure time	waqt al muɣādara (m)	وقت المغادرة
arrival time	waqt al wuṣūl (m)	وقت الوصول
to be delayed	ta'axxar	تأخّر
flight delay	ta'axxur ar riḥla (m)	تأخّر الرحلة
information board	lawḥat al maʿlūmāt (f)	لوحة المعلومات
information	istiʿlāmāt (pl)	إستعلامات
to announce (vt)	aʿlan	أعلن
flight (e.g., next ~)	riḥla (f)	رحلة
customs	ʒamārik (pl)	جمارك
customs officer	muwazzaf al ʒamārik (m)	موظّف الجمارك
customs declaration	taṣrīḥ ʒumrukiy (m)	تصريح جمركيّ
to fill out (vt)	mala'	ملأ
to fill out the declaration	mala' at taṣrīḥ	ملأ التصريح
passport control	taftīʃ al ʒawāzāt (m)	تفتيش الجوازات
luggage	aʃ ʃunaṭ (pl)	الشنط
hand luggage	ʃunaṭ al yad (pl)	شنط اليد
luggage cart	ʿarabat ʃunaṭ (f)	عربة شنط
landing	hubūṭ (m)	هبوط
landing strip	mamarr al hubūṭ (m)	ممرّ الهبوط
to land (vi)	habaṭ	هبط
airstairs	sullam aṭ ṭā'ira (m)	سلّم الطائرة
check-in	tasʒīl (m)	تسجيل
check-in counter	makān at tasʒīl (m)	مكان التسجيل
to check-in (vi)	saʒʒal	سجّل
boarding pass	biṭāqat ṣuʿūd (f)	بطاقة صعود
departure gate	bawwābat al muɣādara (f)	بوّابة المغادرة
transit	tranzīt (m)	ترانزيت
to wait (vt)	intazar	إنتظر
departure lounge	qāʿat al muɣādara (f)	قاعة المغادرة
to see off	waddaʿ	ودّع
to say goodbye	waddaʿ	ودّع

145. Bicycle. Motorcycle

bicycle	darrāʒa (f)	درّاجة
scooter	skutir (m)	سكوتر
motorcycle, bike	darrāʒa nāriyya (f)	درّاجة ناريّة
to go by bicycle	rakib ad darrāʒa	ركب الدرّاجة
handlebars	miqwad (m)	مقود
pedal	dawwāsa (f)	دوّاسة
brakes	farāmil (pl)	فرامل
bicycle seat (saddle)	maqʻad (m)	مقعد
pump	ṭulumba (f)	طلمبة
luggage rack	raff al amti'a (m)	رفّ الأمتعة
front lamp	miṣbāḥ (m)	مصباح
helmet	χūða (f)	خوذة
wheel	ʻaʒala (f)	عجلة
fender	rafraf (m)	رفرف
rim	iṭār (m)	إطار
spoke	barmaq al ʻaʒala (m)	برمق العجلة

Cars

146. Types of cars

automobile, car	sayyāra (f)	سيَّارة
sports car	sayyāra riyāḍiyya (f)	سيَّارة رياضيَّة
limousine	limuzīn (m)	ليموزين
off-road vehicle	sayyārat ṭuruq waʿra (f)	سيارة طرق وعرة
convertible (n)	kabriulīh (m)	كابريوليه
minibus	mikrubāṣ (m)	ميكروباص
ambulance	isʿāf (m)	إسعاف
snowplow	ʒarrāfat θalʒ (f)	جرَّافة ثلج
truck	ʃāḥina (f)	شاحنة
tanker truck	nāqilat bitrūl (f)	ناقلة بترول
van (small truck)	ʿarabat naql (f)	عربة نقل
road tractor (trailer truck)	ʒarrār (m)	جرَّار
trailer	maqṭūra (f)	مقطورة
comfortable (adj)	murīḥ	مريح
used (adj)	mustaʿmal	مستعمل

147. Cars. Bodywork

hood	kabbūt (m)	كبُّوت
fender	rafraf (m)	رفرف
roof	saqf (m)	سقف
windshield	zuʒāʒ amāmiy (m)	زجاج أماميّ
rear-view mirror	mirʾāt dāxiliyya (f)	مرآة داخليَّة
windshield washer	munaẓẓif az zuʒāʒ (m)	منظِّف الزجاج
windshield wipers	massāḥāt (pl)	مسَّاحات
side window	zuʒāʒ ʒānibiy (m)	زجاج جانبيّ
window lift (power window)	mākina zuʒāʒ (f)	ماكينة زجاج
antenna	hawāʾiy (m)	هوائيّ
sunroof	nāfiðat as saqf (f)	نافذة السقف
bumper	miṣadd as sayyāra (m)	مصدّ السيارة
trunk	ṣundūq as sayyāra (m)	صندوق السيَّارة
roof luggage rack	raff saqf as sayyāra (m)	رفّ سقف السيَّارة
door	bāb (m)	باب

door handle	ukrat al bāb (f)	أوكرة الباب
door lock	qifl al bāb (m)	قفل الباب
license plate	lawḥat raqm as sayyāra (f)	لوحة رقم السيارة
muffler	kātim aṣ ṣawt (m)	كاتم الصوت
gas tank	χazzān al banzīn (m)	خزّان البنزين
tailpipe	umbūb al ʿādim (m)	أنبوب العادم
gas, accelerator	ɣāz (m)	غاز
pedal	dawwāsa (f)	دوّاسة
gas pedal	dawwāsat al wuqūd (f)	دوّاسة الوقود
brake	farāmil (pl)	فرامل
brake pedal	dawwāsat al farāmil (m)	دوّاسة الفرامل
to brake (use the brake)	farmal	فرمل
parking brake	farmalat al yad (f)	فرملة اليد
clutch	taʿʃīq (m)	تعشيق
clutch pedal	dawwāsat at taʿʃīq (f)	دوّاسة التعشيق
clutch disc	qurṣ at taʿʃīq (m)	قرص التعشيق
shock absorber	mumtaṣṣ liṣ ṣadamāt (m)	ممتصّ الصدمات
wheel	ʿaʒala (f)	عجلة
spare tire	ʿaʒala iḥtiyāṭiyya (f)	عجلة احتياطيّة
tire	iṭār (m)	إطار
hubcap	ɣiṭāʾ miḥwar al ʿaʒala (m)	غطاء محور العجلة
driving wheels	ʿaʒalāt al qiyāda (pl)	عجلات القيادة
front-wheel drive (as adj)	dafʿ amāmiy (m)	دفع أماميّ
rear-wheel drive (as adj)	dafʿ χalfiy (m)	دفع خلفيّ
all-wheel drive (as adj)	dafʿ rubāʿiy (m)	دفع رباعيّ
gearbox	ṣundūq at turūs (m)	صندوق التروس
automatic (adj)	utumatīkiy	أوتوماتيكيّ
mechanical (adj)	yadawiy	يدويّ
gear shift	nāqil as surʿa (m)	ناقل السرعة
headlight	al miṣbāḥ al amāmiy (m)	المصباح الأماميّ
headlights	al maṣābīḥ al amāmiyya (pl)	المصابيح الأماميّة
low beam	al anwār al munχafiḍa (pl)	الأنوار المنخفضة
high beam	al anwār al ʿāliya (m)	الأنوار العالية
brake light	ḍūʾ al farāmil (m)	ضوء الفرامل
parking lights	aḍwāʾ ʒānibiyya (pl)	أضواء جانبيّة
hazard lights	aḍwāʾ at taḥðīr (pl)	أضواء التحذير
fog lights	aḍwāʾ aḍ ḍabāb (pl)	أضواء الضباب
turn signal	iʃārat al inʿiṭāf (f)	إشارة الإنعطاف
back-up light	miṣbāḥ ar ruʒūʿ lil χalf (m)	مصباح الرجوع للخلف

148. Cars. Passenger compartment

car inside (interior)	ṣālūn as sayyāra (m)	صالون السيّارة
leather (as adj)	min al ǧild	من الجلد
velour (as adj)	min al muxmal	من المخمل
upholstery	tanǧīd (m)	تنجيد
instrument (gage)	ǧihāz (m)	جهاز
dashboard	lawḥat at taḥakkum (f)	لوحة التحكم
speedometer	'addād sur'a (m)	عدّاد سرعة
needle (pointer)	mu'aʃʃir (m)	مؤشّر
odometer	'addād al masāfāt (m)	عدّاد المسافات
indicator (sensor)	'addād (m)	عدّاد
level	mustawa (m)	مستوى
warning light	lammbat inðār (f)	لمبة إنذار
steering wheel	miqwad (m)	مقود
horn	zāmūr (m)	زامور
button	zirr (m)	زرّ
switch	nāqil, miftāḥ (m)	ناقل، مفتاح
seat	maq'ad (m)	مقعد
backrest	misnad aẓ ẓahr (m)	مسند الظهر
headrest	masnad ar ra's (m)	مسند الرأس
seat belt	ḥizām al amn (m)	حزام الأمن
to fasten the belt	rabaṭ al ḥizām	ربط الحزام
adjustment (of seats)	ḍabṭ (m)	ضبط
airbag	wisāda hawā'iyya (f)	وسادة هوائيّة
air-conditioner	takyīf (m)	تكييف
radio	iðā'a (f)	إذاعة
CD player	muʃaɣɣil sidi (m)	مشغّل سي دي
to turn on	fataḥ, ʃaɣɣal	فتح، شغّل
antenna	hawā'iy (m)	هوائي
glove box	durǧ (m)	درج
ashtray	ṭaqṭūqa (f)	طقطوقة

149. Cars. Engine

engine	muḥarrik (m)	محرّك
motor	mutūr (m)	موتور
diesel (as adj)	dīzil	ديزل
gasoline (as adj)	'alal banzīn	على البنزين
engine volume	si'at al muḥarrik (f)	سعة المحرّك
power	qudra (f)	قدرة
horsepower	ḥiṣān (m)	حصان

piston	mikbas (m)	مكبس
cylinder	ustuwāna (f)	أسطوانة
valve	simām (m)	صمام

injector	ʒihāz baxxāx (f)	جهاز بخّاخ
generator (alternator)	muwallid (m)	مولّد
carburetor	karburātir (m)	كاريراتير
motor oil	zayt al muharrik (m)	زيت المحرّك

radiator	mubarrid al muharrik (m)	مبرّد المحرّك
coolant	mādda mubarrida (f)	مادّة مبرّدة
cooling fan	mirwaha (f)	مروحة

battery (accumulator)	battāriyya (f)	بطاريّة
starter	miftāh at taʃɣīl (m)	مفتاح التشغيل
ignition	niẓām taʃɣīl (m)	نظام تشغيل
spark plug	ʃamʿat al ihtirāq (f)	شمعة الاحتراق

terminal (of battery)	taraf tawsīl (m)	طرف توصيل
positive terminal	taraf mūʒab (m)	طرف موجب
negative terminal	taraf sālib (m)	طرف سالب
fuse	fāsima (f)	فاصمة

air filter	misfāt al hawā' (f)	مصفاة الهواء
oil filter	misfāt az zayt (f)	مصفاة الزيت
fuel filter	misfāt al banzīn (f)	مصفاة البنزين

150. Cars. Crash. Repair

car crash	hādiθ sayyāra (f)	حادث سيّارة
traffic accident	hādiθ murūriy (m)	حادث مروريّ
to crash (into the wall, etc.)	istadam	إصطدم

to get smashed up	tahattam	تحطّم
damage	xasāra (f)	خسارة
intact (unscathed)	salīm	سليم

| to break down (vi) | taʿattal | تعطّل |
| towrope | habl as sahb (m) | حبل السحب |

puncture	θuqb (m)	ثقب
to be flat	faʃʃ	فشّ
to pump up	nafax	نفخ
pressure	dayt (m)	ضغط
to check (to examine)	ixtabar	إختبر

repair	islāh (m)	إصلاح
auto repair shop	warʃat islāh as sayyārāt (f)	ورشة إصلاح السيّارات
spare part	qitʿat ɣiyār (f)	قطعة غيار
part	qitʿa (f)	قطعة

bolt (with nut)	mismār qalāwūz (m)	مسمار قلاووظ
screw (fastener)	burɣiy (m)	برغيّ
nut	ṣamūla (f)	صامولة
washer	ḥalqa (f)	حلقة
bearing	maḥmal (m)	محمل
tube	umbūba (f)	أنبوبة
gasket (head ~)	ʿazaqa (f)	عزقة
cable, wire	silk (m)	سلك
jack	rāfiʿat sayyāra (f)	رافعة سيّارة
wrench	miftāḥ aṣ ṣawāmīl (m)	مفتاح الصواميل
hammer	miṭraqa (f)	مطرقة
pump	ṭulumba (f)	طلمبة
screwdriver	mifakk (m)	مفكّ
fire extinguisher	miṭfaʾat ḥarīq (f)	مطفأة حريق
warning triangle	muθallaθ taḥðīr (m)	مثلّث تحذير
to stall (vi)	tawaqqaf	توقّف
stall (n)	tawaqquf (m)	توقّف
to be broken	kān maksūran	كان مكسورًا
to overheat (vi)	saχan bi ʃidda	سخن بشدّة
to be clogged up	kān masdūdan	كان مسدودًا
to freeze up (pipes, etc.)	taʒammad	تجمّد
to burst (vi, ab. tube)	infaʒar	إنفجر
pressure	ḍaɣt (m)	ضغط
level	mustawa (m)	مستوى
slack (~ belt)	ḍaʿīf	ضعيف
dent	baʿʒa (f)	بعجة
knocking noise (engine)	daqq (m)	دقّ
crack	ʃaqq (m)	شقّ
scratch	χadʃ (m)	خدش

151. Cars. Road

road	ṭarīq (m)	طريق
highway	ṭarīq sarīʿ (m)	طريق سريع
freeway	ṭarīq sarīʿ (m)	طريق سريع
direction (way)	ittiʒāh (m)	إتّجاه
distance	masāfa (f)	مسافة
bridge	ʒisr (m)	جسر
parking lot	mawqif as sayyārāt (m)	موقف السيّارات
square	maydān (m)	ميدان
interchange	taqāṭuʿ ṭuruq (m)	تقاطع طرق
tunnel	nafaq (m)	نفق

gas station	maḥaṭṭat banzīn (f)	محطّة بنزين
parking lot	mawqif as sayyārāt (m)	موقف السيّارات
gas pump (fuel dispenser)	midaxxat banzīn (f)	مضخّة بنزين
auto repair shop	warʃat iṣlāḥ as sayyārāt (f)	ورشة إصلاح السيّارات
to get gas (to fill up)	mala' bil wuqūd	ملأ بالوقود
fuel	wuqūd (m)	وقود
jerrycan	ʒirikan (m)	جركن
asphalt	asfalt (m)	أسفلت
road markings	'alāmāt aṭ ṭarīq (pl)	علامات الطريق
curb	ḥāffat ar raṣīf (f)	حافة الرصيف
guardrail	sūr (m)	سور
ditch	qanāt (f)	قناة
roadside (shoulder)	ḥāffat aṭ ṭarīq (f)	حافة الطريق
lamppost	'amūd nūr (m)	عمود نور
to drive (a car)	sāq	ساق
to turn (e.g., ~ left)	in'aṭaf	إنعطف
to make a U-turn	istadār lil xalf	إستدار للخلف
reverse (~ gear)	ḥaraka ilal warā' (f)	حركة إلى الوراء
to honk (vi)	zammar	زمّر
honk (sound)	ṣawṭ az zāmūr (m)	صوت الزامور
to get stuck (in the mud, etc.)	waḥil	وحل
to spin the wheels	dawwar al 'aʒala	دوّر العجلة
to cut, to turn off (vt)	awqaf	أوقف
speed	sur'a (f)	سرعة
to exceed the speed limit	taʒāwaz as sur'a al quṣwa	تجاوز السرعة القصوى
to give a ticket	faraḍ ɣarāma	فرض غرامة
traffic lights	iʃārāt al murūr (pl)	إشارات المرور
driver's license	ruxṣat al qiyāda (f)	رخصة قيادة
grade crossing	ma'bar (m)	معبر
intersection	taqāṭu' (m)	تقاطع
crosswalk	ma'bar al muʃāt (m)	معبر المشاة
bend, curve	mun'aṭif (m)	منعطف
pedestrian zone	makān muxaṣṣaṣ lil muʃāt (f)	مكان مخصّص للمشاة

PEOPLE. LIFE EVENTS

Life events

152. Holidays. Event

celebration, holiday	ʿīd (m)	عيد
national day	ʿīd waṭaniy (m)	عيد وطنيّ
public holiday	yawm al ʿuṭla ar rasmiyya (m)	يوم العطلة الرسمية
to commemorate (vt)	iḥtafal	إحتفل
event (happening)	ḥadaθ (m)	حدث
event (organized activity)	munasaba (f)	مناسبة
banquet (party)	walīma (f)	وليمة
reception (formal party)	ḥaflat istiqbāl (f)	حفلة إستقبال
feast	walīma (f)	وليمة
anniversary	ðikra sanawiyya (f)	ذكرى سنويّة
jubilee	yubīl (m)	يوبيل
to celebrate (vt)	iḥtafal	إحتفل
New Year	ra's as sana (m)	رأس السنة
Happy New Year!	kull sana wa anta ṭayyib!	كلّ سنة وأنت طيّب!
Santa Claus	baba nuwīl (m)	بابا نويل
Christmas	ʿīd al mīlād (m)	عيد الميلاد
Merry Christmas!	ʿīd mīlād saʿīd!	عيد ميلاد سعيد!
Christmas tree	ʃaʒarat ra's as sana (f)	شجرة رأس السنة
fireworks (fireworks show)	alʿāb nāriyya (pl)	ألعاب ناريّة
wedding	zifāf (m)	زفاف
groom	ʿarīs (m)	عريس
bride	ʿarūsa (f)	عروسة
to invite (vt)	daʿa	دعا
invitation card	biṭāqat daʿwa (f)	بطاقة دعوة
guest	ḍayf (m)	ضيف
to visit (~ your parents, etc.)	zār	زار
to meet the guests	istaqbal aḍ ḍuyūf	إستقبل الضيوف
gift, present	hadiyya (f)	هديّة
to give (sth as present)	qaddam	قدّم

to receive gifts	istalam al hadāya	إستلم الهدايا
bouquet (of flowers)	bāqat zuhūr (f)	باقة زهور
congratulations	tahnī'a (f)	تهنئة
to congratulate (vt)	hanna'	هنّأ
greeting card	biṭāqat tahnī'a (f)	بطاقة تهنئة
to send a postcard	arsal biṭāqat tahni'a	أرسل بطاقة تهنئة
to get a postcard	istalam biṭāqat tahnī'a	إستلم بطاقة تهنئة
toast	naχb (m)	نخب
to offer (a drink, etc.)	ḍayyaf	ضيّف
champagne	ʃambāniya (f)	شمبانيا
to enjoy oneself	istamta'	إستمتع
merriment (gaiety)	faraḥ (m)	فرح
joy (emotion)	sa'āda (f)	سعادة
dance	rāqiṣa (f)	رقصة
to dance (vi, vt)	raqaṣ	رقص
waltz	vāls (m)	فالس
tango	tāngu (m)	تانجو

153. Funerals. Burial

cemetery	maqbara (f)	مقبرة
grave, tomb	qabr (m)	قبر
cross	ṣalīb (m)	صليب
gravestone	ʃāhid al qabr (m)	شاهد القبر
fence	sūr (m)	سور
chapel	kanīsa saɣīra (f)	كنيسة صغيرة
death	mawt (m)	موت
to die (vi)	māt	مات
the deceased	al mutawaffi (m)	المتوفّي
mourning	ḥidād (m)	حداد
to bury (vt)	dafan	دفن
funeral home	bayt al ʒanāzāt (m)	بيت الجنازات
funeral	ʒanāza (f)	جنازة
wreath	iklīl (m)	إكليل
casket, coffin	tābūt (m)	تابوت
hearse	sayyārat naql al mawta (f)	سيّارة نقل الموتى
shroud	kafan (m)	كفن
funeral procession	ʒanāza (f)	جنازة
funerary urn	qārūra li ḥifẓ ramād al mawta (f)	قارورة لحفظ رماد الموتى

crematory	maḥraqat ʒuθaθ al mawta (f)	محرقة جثث الموتى
obituary	naʿiy (m)	نعي
to cry (weep)	baka	بكى
to sob (vi)	naḥab	نحب

154. War. Soldiers

platoon	faṣīla (f)	فصيلة
company	sariyya (f)	سرية
regiment	fawʒ (m)	فوج
army	ʒayʃ (m)	جيش
division	firqa (f)	فرقة
section, squad	waḥda (f)	وحدة
host (army)	ʒayʃ (m)	جيش
soldier	ʒundiy (m)	جندي
officer	ḍābiṭ (m)	ضابط
private	ʒundiy (m)	جندي
sergeant	raqīb (m)	رقيب
lieutenant	mulāzim (m)	ملازم
captain	naqīb (m)	نقيب
major	rā'id (m)	رائد
colonel	ʿaqīd (m)	عقيد
general	ʒinirāl (m)	جنرال
sailor	baḥḥār (m)	بحّار
captain	qubṭān (m)	قبطان
boatswain	ra'īs al baḥḥāra (m)	رئيس البحّارة
artilleryman	madfaʿiy (m)	مدفعي
paratrooper	ʒundiy al maẓallāt (m)	جندي المظلّات
pilot	ṭayyār (m)	طيّار
navigator	mallāḥ (m)	ملّاح
mechanic	mikanīkiy (m)	ميكانيكي
pioneer (sapper)	muhandis ʿaskariy (m)	مهندس عسكري
parachutist	miẓalliy (m)	مظلّي
reconnaissance scout	mustakʃif (m)	مستكشف
sniper	qannāṣ (m)	قنّاص
patrol (group)	dawriyya (f)	دورية
to patrol (vt)	qām bi dawriyya	قام بدورية
sentry, guard	ḥāris (m)	حارس
warrior	muḥārib (m)	محارب
patriot	waṭaniy (m)	وطني
hero	baṭal (m)	بطل

heroine	baṭala (f)	بطلة
traitor	χā'in (m)	خائن
to betray (vt)	χān	خان
deserter	hārib min al ʒayʃ (m)	هارب من الجيش
to desert (vi)	harab min al ʒayʃ	هرب من الجيش
mercenary	ma'ʒūr (m)	مأجور
recruit	ʒundiy ʒadīd (m)	جنديّ جديد
volunteer	mutaṭawwi' (m)	متطوّع
dead (n)	qatīl (m)	قتيل
wounded (n)	ʒarīḥ (m)	جريح
prisoner of war	asīr (m)	أسير

155. War. Military actions. Part 1

war	ḥarb (f)	حرب
to be at war	ḥārab	حارب
civil war	ḥarb ahliyya (f)	حرب أهليّة
treacherously (adv)	yadran	غدرًا
declaration of war	i'lān ḥarb (m)	إعلان حرب
to declare (~ war)	a'lan	أعلن
aggression	'udwān (m)	عدوان
to attack (invade)	haʒam	هجم
to invade (vt)	iḥtall	إحتلّ
invader	muḥtall (m)	محتلّ
conqueror	fātiḥ (m)	فاتح
defense	difā' (m)	دفاع
to defend (a country, etc.)	dāfa'	دافع
to defend (against ...)	dāfa' 'an nafsih	دافع عن نفسه
enemy	'aduww (m)	عدوّ
foe, adversary	χaṣm (m)	خصم
enemy (as adj)	'aduww	عدوّ
strategy	istratiʒiyya (f)	إستراتيجيّة
tactics	taktīk (m)	تكتيك
order	amr (m)	أمر
command (order)	amr (m)	أمر
to order (vt)	amar	أمر
mission	muhimma (f)	مهمّة
secret (adj)	sirriy	سرّيّ
battle	ma'raka (f)	معركة
combat	qitāl (m)	قتال
attack	huʒūm (m)	هجوم

charge (assault)	inqiḍāḍ (m)	إنقضاض
to storm (vt)	inqaḍḍ	إنقضّ
siege (to be under ~)	ḥiṣār (m)	حصار
offensive (n)	huʒūm (m)	هجوم
to go on the offensive	haʒam	هجم
retreat	insiḥāb (m)	إنسحاب
to retreat (vi)	insaḥab	إنسحب
encirclement	iḥāṭa (f)	إحاطة
to encircle (vt)	aḥāṭ	أحاط
bombing (by aircraft)	qaṣf (m)	قصف
to drop a bomb	asqaṭ qumbula	أسقط قنبلة
to bomb (vt)	qaṣaf	قصف
explosion	infiʒār (m)	إنفجار
shot	ṭalaqa (f)	طلقة
to fire (~ a shot)	aṭlaq an nār	أطلق النار
firing (burst of ~)	iṭlāq an nār (m)	إطلاق النار
to aim (to point a weapon)	ṣawwab	صوّب
to point (a gun)	ṣawwab	صوّب
to hit (the target)	aṣāb al hadaf	أصاب الهدف
to sink (~ a ship)	aɣraq	أغرق
hole (in a ship)	θuqb (m)	ثقب
to founder, to sink (vi)	ɣariq	غرق
front (war ~)	ʒabha (f)	جبهة
evacuation	iχlāʼ aṭ ṭawāriʼ (m)	إخلاء الطوارئ
to evacuate (vt)	aχla	أخلى
trench	χandaq (m)	خندق
barbwire	aslāk ʃāʼika (pl)	أسلاك شائكة
barrier (anti tank ~)	ḥāʒiz (m)	حاجز
watchtower	burʒ muraqaba (m)	برج مراقبة
military hospital	mustaʃfa ʿaskariy (m)	مستشفى عسكريّ
to wound (vt)	ʒaraḥ	جرح
wound	ʒurḥ (m)	جرح
wounded (n)	ʒarīḥ (m)	جريح
to be wounded	uṣīb bil ʒirāḥ	أصيب بالجراح
serious (wound)	χaṭīr	خطير

156. Weapons

weapons	asliḥa (pl)	أسلحة
firearms	asliḥa nāriyya (pl)	أسلحة ناريّة

cold weapons (knives, etc.)	asliḥa bayḍā' (pl)	أسلحة بيضاء
chemical weapons	asliḥa kīmyā'iyya (pl)	أسلحة كيميائيّة
nuclear (adj)	nawawiy	نوويّ
nuclear weapons	asliḥa nawawiyya (pl)	أسلحة نوويّة
bomb	qumbula (f)	قنبلة
atomic bomb	qumbula nawawiyya (f)	قنبلة نوويّة
pistol (gun)	musaddas (m)	مسدّس
rifle	bunduqiyya (f)	بندقيّة
submachine gun	bunduqiyya huȝūmiyya (f)	بندقيّة هجوميّة
machine gun	raʃʃāʃ (m)	رشّاش
muzzle	fūha (f)	فوهة
barrel	sabṭāna (f)	سبطانة
caliber	ʿiyār (m)	عيار
trigger	zinād (m)	زناد
sight (aiming device)	muṣawwib (m)	مصوّب
magazine	maxzan (m)	مخزن
butt (shoulder stock)	ʿaqab al bunduqiyya (m)	عقب البندقيّة
hand grenade	qumbula yadawiyya (f)	قنبلة يدويّة
explosive	mawādd mutafaȝȝira (pl)	موادّ متفجّرة
bullet	ruṣāṣa (f)	رصاصة
cartridge	xarṭūʃa (f)	خرطوشة
charge	ḥaʃwa (f)	حشوة
ammunition	ðaxā'ir (pl)	ذخائر
bomber (aircraft)	qāðifat qanābil (f)	قاذفة قنابل
fighter	ṭā'ira muqātila (f)	طائرة مقاتلة
helicopter	hiliukūbtir (m)	هليكوبتر
anti-aircraft gun	madfaθ muḍādd liṭ ṭa'irāṭ (m)	مدفع مضادّ للطائرات
tank	dabbāba (f)	دبّابة
tank gun	madfaʿ ad dabbāba (m)	مدفع الدبّابة
artillery	madfaʿiyya (f)	مدفعيّة
gun (cannon, howitzer)	madfaʿ (m)	مدفع
to lay (a gun)	ṣawwab	صوّب
shell (projectile)	qaðīfa (f)	قذيفة
mortar bomb	qumbula hāwun (f)	قنبلة هاون
mortar	hāwun (m)	هاون
splinter (shell fragment)	ʃaẓiyya (f)	شظيّة
submarine	ɣawwāṣa (f)	غوّاصة
torpedo	ṭurbīd (m)	طوربيد
missile	ṣārūx (m)	صاروخ

to load (gun)	ḥaʃa	حشا
to shoot (vi)	aṭlaq an nār	أطلق النار
to point at (the cannon)	ṣawwab	صوّب
bayonet	ḥarba (f)	حربة

rapier	ʃīʃ (m)	شيش
saber (e.g., cavalry ~)	sayf munḥani (m)	سيف منحن
spear (weapon)	rumḥ (m)	رمح
bow	qaws (m)	قوس
arrow	sahm (m)	سهم
musket	muskīt (m)	مسكيت
crossbow	qaws mustaʿraḍ (m)	قوس مستعرض

157. Ancient people

primitive (prehistoric)	bidāʼiy	بدائيّ
prehistoric (adj)	ma qabl at tarīχ	ما قبل التاريخ
ancient (~ civilization)	qadīm	قديم

Stone Age	al ʿaṣr al ḥaʒariy (m)	العصر الحجريّ
Bronze Age	al ʿaṣr al brunziy (m)	العصر البرونزيّ
Ice Age	al ʿaṣr al ʒalīdiy (m)	العصر الجليديّ

tribe	qabīla (f)	قبيلة
cannibal	ʼākil laḥm al baʃar (m)	آكل لحم البشر
hunter	ṣayyād (m)	صيّاد
to hunt (vi, vt)	iṣṭād	إصطاد
mammoth	mamūθ (m)	ماموث

cave	kahf (m)	كهف
fire	nār (f)	نار
campfire	nār muχayyam (m)	نار مخيّم
cave painting	rasm fil kahf (m)	رسم في الكهف

tool (e.g., stone ax)	adāt (f)	أداة
spear	rumḥ (m)	رمح
stone ax	faʼs ḥaʒariy (m)	فأس حجريّ
to be at war	ḥārab	حارب
to domesticate (vt)	daʒʒan	دجّن

idol	ṣanam (m)	صنم
to worship (vt)	ʿabad	عبد
superstition	χurāfa (f)	خرافة
rite	mansak (m)	منسك

evolution	taṭawwur (m)	تطوّر
development	numuww (m)	نمو
disappearance (extinction)	iχtifāʼ (m)	إختفاء
to adapt oneself	takayyaf	تكيّف
archeology	ʿilm al ʼāθār (m)	علم الآثار

| archeologist | ʿālim ʾāθār (m) | عالم آثار |
| archeological (adj) | aθariy | أثريّ |

excavation site	mawqiʿ ḥafr (m)	موقع حفر
excavations	tanqīb (m)	تنقيب
find (object)	iktiʃāf (m)	إكتشاف
fragment	qiṭʿa (f)	قطعة

158. Middle Ages

people (ethnic group)	ʃaʿb (m)	شعب
peoples	ʃuʿūb (pl)	شعوب
tribe	qabīla (f)	قبيلة
tribes	qabāʾil (pl)	قبائل

barbarians	al barābira (pl)	البرابرة
Gauls	al ɣalyūn (pl)	الغاليون
Goths	al qūṭiyyūn (pl)	القوطيّون
Slavs	as silāf (pl)	السلاف
Vikings	al vaykinɣ (pl)	الفايكينغ

| Romans | ar rūmān (pl) | الرومان |
| Roman (adj) | rumāniy | رومانيّ |

Byzantines	bizanṭiyyūn (pl)	بيزنطيّون
Byzantium	bīzanṭa (f)	بيزنطة
Byzantine (adj)	bizanṭiy	بيزنطيّ

emperor	imbiraṭūr (m)	إمبراطور
leader, chief (tribal ~)	zaʿīm (m)	زعيم
powerful (~ king)	qawiy	قويّ
king	malik (m)	ملك
ruler (sovereign)	ḥākim (m)	حاكم

knight	fāris (m)	فارس
feudal lord	iqṭāʿiy (m)	إقطاعيّ
feudal (adj)	iqṭāʿiy	إقطاعيّ
vassal	muqtaʿ (m)	مقطع

duke	dūq (m)	دوق
earl	īrl (m)	إيرل
baron	barūn (m)	بارون
bishop	usquf (m)	أسقف

armor	dirʿ (m)	درع
shield	turs (m)	ترس
sword	sayf (m)	سيف
visor	ḥāffa amāmiyya lil χūða (f)	حافة أماميّة للخوذة
chainmail	dirʿ az zarad (m)	درع الزرد
Crusade	ḥamla ṣalībiyya (f)	حملة صليبيّة

crusader	ṣalībiy (m)	صليبيّ
territory	arḍ (f)	أرض
to attack (invade)	haʒam	هجم
to conquer (vt)	fataḥ	فتح
to occupy (invade)	iḥtall	إحتلّ

siege (to be under ~)	ḥiṣār (m)	حصار
besieged (adj)	muḥāṣar	محاصر
to besiege (vt)	ḥāṣar	حاصر

inquisition	maḥākim at taftīʃ (pl)	محاكم التفتيش
inquisitor	mufattiʃ (m)	مفتّش
torture	taʕðīb (m)	تعذيب
cruel (adj)	qās	قاس
heretic	harṭūqiy (m)	هرطوقيّ
heresy	harṭaqa (f)	هرطقة

seafaring	as safar bil baḥr (m)	السفر بالبحر
pirate	qurṣān (m)	قرصان
piracy	qarṣana (f)	قرصنة
boarding (attack)	muhāʒmat safīna (f)	مهاجمة سفينة
loot, booty	ɣanīma (f)	غنيمة
treasures	kunūz (pl)	كنوز

discovery	iktiʃāf (m)	إكتشاف
to discover (new land, etc.)	iktaʃaf	إكتشف
expedition	baʕθa (f)	بعثة

musketeer	fāris (m)	فارس
cardinal	kardināl (m)	كاردينال
heraldry	ʃiʕārāt an nabāla (pl)	شعارات النبالة
heraldic (adj)	χāṣṣ bi ʃiʕārāt an nabāla	خاصّ بشعارات النبالة

159. Leader. Chief. Authorities

king	malik (m)	ملك
queen	malika (f)	ملكة
royal (adj)	malakiy	ملكيّ
kingdom	mamlaka (f)	مملكة

| prince | amīr (m) | أمير |
| princess | amīra (f) | أميرة |

president	raʔīs (m)	رئيس
vice-president	nāʔib ar raʔīs (m)	نائب الرئيس
senator	ʕuḍw maʒlis aʃ ʃuyūχ (m)	عضو مجلس الشيوخ

monarch	ʕāhil (m)	عاهل
ruler (sovereign)	ḥākim (m)	حاكم
dictator	diktatūr (m)	ديكتاتور

tyrant	ṭāɣiya (f)	طاغية
magnate	ra'smāliy kabīr (m)	رأسمالي كبير
director	mudīr (m)	مدير
chief	ra'īs (m)	رئيس
manager (director)	mudīr (m)	مدير
boss	ra'īs (m), mudīr (m)	رئيس, مدير
owner	ṣāḥib (m)	صاحب
leader	za'īm (m)	زعيم
head (~ of delegation)	ra'īs (m)	رئيس
authorities	suluṭāt (pl)	سلطات
superiors	ru'asā' (pl)	رؤساء
governor	muḥāfiẓ (m)	محافظ
consul	qunṣul (m)	قنصل
diplomat	diblumāsiy (m)	دبلوماسيّ
mayor	ra'īs al baladiyya (m)	رئيس البلديّة
sheriff	ʃarīf (m)	شريف
emperor	imbiraṭūr (m)	إمبراطور
tsar, czar	qayṣar (m)	قيصر
pharaoh	fir'awn (m)	فرعون
khan	χān (m)	خان

160. Breaking the law. Criminals. Part 1

bandit	qāṭi' ṭarīq (m)	قاطع طريق
crime	ʒarīma (f)	جريمة
criminal (person)	muʒrim (m)	مجرم
thief	sāriq (m)	سارق
to steal (vi, vt)	saraq	سرق
stealing, theft	sirqa (f)	سرقة
to kidnap (vt)	χaṭaf	خطف
kidnapping	χaṭf (m)	خطف
kidnapper	χāṭif (m)	خاطف
ransom	fidya (f)	فدية
to demand ransom	ṭalab fidya	طلب فدية
to rob (vt)	nahab	نهب
robbery	nahb (m)	نهب
robber	nahhāb (m)	نهّاب
to extort (vt)	balṭaʒ	بلطج
extortionist	balṭaʒiy (m)	بلطجيّ
extortion	balṭaʒa (f)	بلطجة
to murder, to kill	qatal	قتل

| murder | qatl (m) | قتل |
| murderer | qātil (m) | قاتل |

gunshot	ṭalaqat nār (f)	طلقة نار
to fire (~ a shot)	aṭlaq an nār	أطلق النار
to shoot to death	qatal bir ruṣāṣ	قتل بالرصاص
to shoot (vi)	aṭlaq an nār	أطلق النار
shooting	iṭlāq an nār (m)	إطلاق النار

incident (fight, etc.)	ḥādiθ (m)	حادث
fight, brawl	ʿirāk (m)	عراك
Help!	sāʿidni	ساعدني!
victim	ḍaḥiyya (f)	ضحيّة

to damage (vt)	atlaf	أتلف
damage	χasāra (f)	خسارة
dead body, corpse	ʒuθθa (f)	جثّة
grave (~ crime)	ʿanīf	عنيف

to attack (vt)	haʒam	هجم
to beat (to hit)	ḍarab	ضرب
to beat up	ḍarab	ضرب
to take (rob of sth)	salab	سلب
to stab to death	ṭaʿan ḥatta al mawt	طعن حتّى الموت
to maim (vt)	ʃawwah	شوّه
to wound (vt)	ʒaraḥ	جرح

blackmail	balṭaʒa (f)	بلطجة
to blackmail (vt)	ibtazz	إبتزّ
blackmailer	mubtazz (m)	مبتزّ

protection racket	naṣb (m)	نصب
racketeer	naṣṣāb (m)	نصّاب
gangster	raʒul ʿiṣāba (m)	رجل عصابة
mafia, Mob	māfia (f)	مافيا

pickpocket	naʃʃāl (m)	نشّال
burglar	liṣṣ buyūt (m)	لصّ بيوت
smuggling	tahrīb (m)	تهريب
smuggler	muharrib (m)	مهرّب

forgery	tazwīr (m)	تزوير
to forge (counterfeit)	zawwar	زوّر
fake (forged)	muzawwar	مزوّر

161. Breaking the law. Criminals. Part 2

rape	iɣtiṣāb (m)	إغتصاب
to rape (vt)	iɣtaṣab	إغتصب
rapist	muɣtaṣib (m)	مغتصب

maniac	mahwūs (m)	مهووس
prostitute (fem.)	'āhira (f)	عاهرة
prostitution	da'āra (f)	دعارة
pimp	qawwād (m)	قوّاد
drug addict	mudmin muxaddirāt (m)	مدمن مخدّرات
drug dealer	tāʒir muxaddirāt (m)	تاجر مخدّرات
to blow up (bomb)	faʒʒar	فجّر
explosion	infiʒār (m)	إنفجار
to set fire	aʃal an nār	أشعل النار
arsonist	muʃil ḥarīq (m)	مشعل حريق
terrorism	irhāb (m)	إرهاب
terrorist	irhābiy (m)	إرهابيّ
hostage	rahīna (m)	رهينة
to swindle (deceive)	iḥtāl	إحتال
swindle, deception	iḥtiyāl (m)	إحتيال
swindler	muḥtāl (m)	محتال
to bribe (vt)	raʃa	رشا
bribery	irtiʃā' (m)	إرتشاء
bribe	raʃwa (f)	رشوة
poison	samm (m)	سمّ
to poison (vt)	sammam	سمّم
to poison oneself	sammam nafsahu	سمّم نفسه
suicide (act)	intiḥār (m)	إنتحار
suicide (person)	muntaḥir (m)	منتحر
to threaten (vt)	haddad	هدّد
threat	tahdīd (m)	تهديد
to make an attempt	ḥāwal iɣtiyāl	حاول الإغتيال
attempt (attack)	muḥāwalat iɣtiyāl (f)	محاولة إغتيال
to steal (a car)	saraq	سرق
to hijack (a plane)	ixtaṭaf	إختطف
revenge	intiqām (m)	إنتقام
to avenge (get revenge)	intaqam	إنتقم
to torture (vt)	'aððab	عذّب
torture	ta'ðīb (m)	تعذيب
to torment (vt)	'aððab	عذّب
pirate	qurṣān (m)	قرصان
hooligan	wabaʃ (m)	وبش
armed (adj)	musallaḥ	مسلّح
violence	'unf (m)	عنف
illegal (unlawful)	ɣayr qānūniy	غير قانونيّ

| spying (espionage) | taʒassas (m) | تجسّس |
| to spy (vi) | taʒassas | تجسّس |

162. Police. Law. Part 1

justice	qaḍā' (m)	قضاء
court (see you in ~)	maḥkama (f)	محكمة
judge	qāḍi (m)	قاض
jurors	muḥallafūn (pl)	محلّفون
jury trial	qaḍā' al muḥallafīn (m)	قضاء المحلّفين
to judge (vt)	ḥakam	حكم
lawyer, attorney	muḥāmi (m)	محام
defendant	mudda'a 'alayh (m)	مدّعى عليه
dock	qafṣ al ittihām (m)	قفص الإتّهام
charge	ittihām (m)	إتّهام
accused	muttaham (m)	متّهم
sentence	ḥukm (m)	حكم
to sentence (vt)	ḥakam	حكم
guilty (culprit)	muðnib (m)	مذنب
to punish (vt)	'āqab	عاقب
punishment	'uqūba (f), 'iqāb (m)	عقوبة, عقاب
fine (penalty)	ɣarāma (f)	غرامة
life imprisonment	siʒn mada al ḥayāt (m)	سجن مدى الحياة
death penalty	'uqūbat 'i'dām (f)	عقوبة إعدام
electric chair	kursiy kaharabā'iy (m)	كرسيّ كهربائيّ
gallows	maʃnaqa (f)	مشنقة
to execute (vt)	a'dam	أعدم
execution	i'dām (m)	إعدام
prison, jail	siʒn (m)	سجن
cell	zinzāna (f)	زنزانة
escort	ḥirāsa (f)	حراسة
prison guard	ḥāris siʒn (m)	حارس سجن
prisoner	saʒīn (m)	سجين
handcuffs	aṣfād (pl)	أصفاد
to handcuff (vt)	ṣaffad	صفّد
prison break	hurūb min as siʒn (m)	هروب من السجن
to break out (vi)	harab	هرب
to disappear (vi)	iχtafa	إختفى
to release (from prison)	aχla sabīl	أخلى سبيل

amnesty	ʻafw ʻāmm (m)	عفو عامّ
police	ʃurṭa (f)	شرطة
police officer	ʃurṭiy (m)	شرطيّ
police station	qism ʃurṭa (m)	قسم شرطة
billy club	hirāwat aʃ ʃurṭiy (f)	هراوة الشرطيّ
bullhorn	būq (m)	بوق

patrol car	sayyārat dawrīyyāt (f)	سيّارة دوريّات
siren	ṣaffārat inðār (f)	صفّارة إنذار
to turn on the siren	aṭlaq sirīna	أطلق سرينة
siren call	ṣawt sirīna (m)	صوت سرينة

crime scene	masraḥ al ʒarīma (m)	مسرح الجريمة
witness	ʃāhid (m)	شاهد
freedom	ḥurriyya (f)	حرّيّة
accomplice	ʃarīk fil ʒarīma (m)	شريك في الجريمة
to flee (vi)	harab	هرب
trace (to leave a ~)	aθar (m)	أثر

163. Police. Law. Part 2

search (investigation)	baḥθ (m)	بحث
to look for ...	baḥaθ	بحث
suspicion	ʃubha (f)	شبهة
suspicious (e.g., ~ vehicle)	maʃbūh	مشبوه
to stop (cause to halt)	awqaf	أوقف
to detain (keep in custody)	iʻtaqal	إعتقل

case (lawsuit)	qaḍiyya (f)	قضيّة
investigation	taḥqīq (m)	تحقيق
detective	muḥaqqiq (m)	محقّق
investigator	mufattiʃ (m)	مفتّش
hypothesis	riwāya (f)	رواية

motive	dāfiʻ (m)	دافع
interrogation	istiʒwāb (m)	إستجواب
to interrogate (vt)	istaʒwab	إستجوب
to question (~ neighbors, etc.)	istanṭaq	إستنطق
check (identity ~)	faḥṣ (m)	فحص

round-up	ʒamʻ (m)	جمع
search (~ warrant)	taftīʃ (m)	تفتيش
chase (pursuit)	muṭārada (f)	مطاردة
to pursue, to chase	ṭārad	طارد
to track (a criminal)	tābaʻ	تابع

arrest	iʻtiqāl (m)	إعتقال
to arrest (sb)	iʻtaqal	إعتقل
to catch (thief, etc.)	qabaḍ	قبض

capture	qabḍ (m)	قبض
document	waθīqa (f)	وثيقة
proof (evidence)	dalīl (m)	دليل
to prove (vt)	aθbat	أثبت
footprint	baṣma (f)	بصمة
fingerprints	baṣamāt al aṣābi' (pl)	بصمات الأصابع
piece of evidence	dalīl (m)	دليل

alibi	daf' bil ɣayba (f)	دفع بالغيبة
innocent (not guilty)	barī'	بريء
injustice	ẓulm (m)	ظلم
unjust, unfair (adj)	ɣayr 'ādil	غير عادل

criminal (adj)	iʒrāmiy	إجراميّ
to confiscate (vt)	ṣādar	صادر
drug (illegal substance)	muxaddirāt (pl)	مخدّرات
weapon, gun	silāḥ (m)	سلاح
to disarm (vt)	ʒarrad min as silāḥ	جرّد من السلاح
to order (command)	amar	أمر
to disappear (vi)	ixtafa	إختفى

law	qānūn (m)	قانون
legal, lawful (adj)	qānūniy, ʃar'iy	قانونيّ، شرعيّ
illegal, illicit (adj)	ɣayr qanūny, ɣayr ʃar'i	غير قانونيّ، غير شرعيّ

| responsibility (blame) | mas'ūliyya (f) | مسؤوليّة |
| responsible (adj) | mas'ūl (m) | مسؤول |

NATURE

The Earth. Part 1

164. Outer space

space	faḍā' (m)	فضاء
space (as adj)	faḍā'iy	فضائيّ
outer space	faḍā' (m)	فضاء
world	'ālam (m)	عالم
universe	al kawn (m)	الكون
galaxy	al maʒarra (f)	المجرّة
star	naʒm (m)	نجم
constellation	burʒ (m)	برج
planet	kawkab (m)	كوكب
satellite	qamar ṣinā'iy (m)	قمر صناعيّ
meteorite	ḥaʒar nayzakiy (m)	حجر نيزكيّ
comet	muðannab (m)	مذنّب
asteroid	kuwaykib (m)	كويكب
orbit	madār (m)	مدار
to revolve (~ around the Earth)	dār	دار
atmosphere	al ɣilāf al ʒawwiy (m)	الغلاف الجوّيّ
the Sun	aʃ ʃams (f)	الشمس
solar system	al maʒmū'a aʃ ʃamsiyya (f)	المجموعة الشمسيّة
solar eclipse	kusūf aʃ ʃams (m)	كسوف الشمس
the Earth	al arḍ (f)	الأرض
the Moon	al qamar (m)	القمر
Mars	al mirrīχ (m)	المرّيخ
Venus	az zahra (f)	الزهرة
Jupiter	al muʃtari (m)	المشتري
Saturn	zuḥal (m)	زحل
Mercury	'aṭārid (m)	عطارد
Uranus	urānus (m)	اورانوس
Neptune	nibtūn (m)	نبتون
Pluto	blūtu (m)	بلوتو
Milky Way	darb at tabbāna (m)	درب التبّانة
Great Bear (Ursa Major)	ad dubb al akbar (m)	الدبّ الأكبر

North Star	naʒm al ʾqutb (m)	نجم القطب
Martian	sākin al mirrīχ (m)	ساكن المرّيخ
extraterrestrial (n)	faḍāʾiy (m)	فضائيّ
alien	faḍāʾiy (m)	فضائيّ
flying saucer	ṭabaq ṭāʾir (m)	طبق طائر
spaceship	markaba faḍāʾiyya (f)	مركبة فضائيّة
space station	maḥaṭṭat faḍāʾ (f)	محطّة فضاء
blast-off	intilāq (m)	إنطلاق
engine	mutūr (m)	موتور
nozzle	manfaθ (m)	منفث
fuel	wuqūd (m)	وقود
cockpit, flight deck	kabīna (f)	كابينة
antenna	hawāʾiy (m)	هوائيّ
porthole	kuwwa mustadīra (f)	كوّة مستديرة
solar panel	lawḥ ʃamsiy (m)	لوح شمسيّ
spacesuit	baðlat al faḍāʾ (f)	بذلة الفضاء
weightlessness	inʿidām al wazn (m)	إنعدام الوزن
oxygen	uksiʒīn (m)	أكسجين
docking (in space)	rasw (m)	رسو
to dock (vi, vt)	rasa	رسا
observatory	marṣad (m)	مرصد
telescope	tiliskūp (m)	تلسكوب
to observe (vt)	rāqab	راقب
to explore (vt)	istakʃaf	إستكشف

165. The Earth

the Earth	al arḍ (f)	الأرض
the globe (the Earth)	al kura al arḍiyya (f)	الكرة الأرضيّة
planet	kawkab (m)	كوكب
atmosphere	al ɣilāf al ʒawwiy (m)	الغلاف الجوّيّ
geography	ʒuɣrāfiya (f)	جغرافيا
nature	ṭabīʿa (f)	طبيعة
globe (table ~)	namūðaʒ lil kura al arḍiyya (m)	نموذج للكرة الأرضيّة
map	χarīṭa (f)	خريطة
atlas	aṭlas (m)	أطلس
Europe	urūbba (f)	أوروبّا
Asia	ʾāsiya (f)	آسيا
Africa	afrīqiya (f)	أفريقيا
Australia	usturāliya (f)	أستراليا

America	amrīka (f)	أمريكا
North America	amrīka aʃ ʃimāliyya (f)	أمريكا الشماليّة
South America	amrīka al ʒanūbiyya (f)	أمريكا الجنوبيّة

| Antarctica | al quṭb al ʒanūbiyy (m) | القطب الجنوبيّ |
| the Arctic | al quṭb aʃ ʃimāliy (m) | القطب الشماليّ |

166. Cardinal directions

north	ʃimāl (m)	شمال
to the north	ilaʃ ʃimāl	إلى الشمال
in the north	fiʃ ʃimāl	في الشمال
northern (adj)	ʃimāliy	شماليّ

south	ʒanūb (m)	جنوب
to the south	ilal ʒanūb	إلى الجنوب
in the south	fil ʒanūb	في الجنوب
southern (adj)	ʒanūbiy	جنوبيّ

west	ɣarb (m)	غرب
to the west	ilal ɣarb	إلى الغرب
in the west	fil ɣarb	في الغرب
western (adj)	ɣarbiy	غربيّ

east	ʃarq (m)	شرق
to the east	ilaʃ ʃarq	إلى الشرق
in the east	fiʃ ʃarq	في الشرق
eastern (adj)	ʃarqiy	شرقيّ

167. Sea. Ocean

sea	baḥr (m)	بحر
ocean	muḥīṭ (m)	محيط
gulf (bay)	xalīʒ (m)	خليج
straits	maḍīq (m)	مضيق

land (solid ground)	barr (m)	برّ
continent (mainland)	qārra (f)	قارّة
island	ʒazīra (f)	جزيرة
peninsula	ʃibh ʒazīra (f)	شبه جزيرة
archipelago	maʒmūʕat ʒuzur (f)	مجموعة جزر

bay, cove	xalīʒ (m)	خليج
harbor	mīnā' (m)	ميناء
lagoon	buḥayra ʃāṭi'a (f)	بحيرة شاطئة
cape	ra's (m)	رأس
atoll	ʒazīra marʒāniyya istiwā'iyya (f)	جزيرة مرجانيّة إستوائيّة

reef	ʃiʿāb (pl)	شعاب
coral	murʒān (m)	مرجان
coral reef	ʃiʿāb marʒāniyya (pl)	شعاب مرجانيّة
deep (adj)	ʿamīq	عميق
depth (deep water)	ʿumq (m)	عمق
abyss	mahwāt (f)	مهواة
trench (e.g., Mariana ~)	χandaq (m)	خندق
current (Ocean ~)	tayyār (m)	تيّار
to surround (bathe)	aḥāṭ	أحاط
shore	sāḥil (m)	ساحل
coast	sāḥil (m)	ساحل
flow (flood tide)	madd (m)	مدّ
ebb (ebb tide)	ʒazr (m)	جزر
shoal	miyāh ḍaḥla (f)	مياه ضحلة
bottom (~ of the sea)	qāʿ (m)	قاع
wave	mawʒa (f)	موجة
crest (~ of a wave)	qimmat mawʒa (f)	قمّة موجة
spume (sea foam)	zabad al baḥr (m)	زبد البحر
storm (sea storm)	ʿāṣifa (f)	عاصفة
hurricane	iʿṣār (m)	إعصار
tsunami	tsunāmi (m)	تسونامي
calm (dead ~)	hudū' (m)	هدوء
quiet, calm (adj)	hādi'	هادئ
pole	quṭb (m)	قطب
polar (adj)	quṭby	قطبيّ
latitude	ʿarḍ (m)	عرض
longitude	ṭūl (m)	طول
parallel	mutawāzi (m)	متواز
equator	χaṭṭ al istiwā' (m)	خط الإستواء
sky	samā' (f)	سماء
horizon	ufuq (m)	أفق
air	hawā' (m)	هواء
lighthouse	manāra (f)	منارة
to dive (vi)	ɣāṣ	غاص
to sink (ab. boat)	ɣariq	غرق
treasures	kunūz (pl)	كنوز

168. Mountains

mountain	ʒabal (m)	جبل
mountain range	silsilat ʒibāl (f)	سلسلة جبال

mountain ridge	qimam ʒabaliyya (pl)	قمم جبليّة
summit, top	qimma (f)	قمّة
peak	qimma (f)	قمّة
foot (~ of the mountain)	asfal (m)	أسفل
slope (mountainside)	munḥadar (m)	منحدر
volcano	burkān (m)	بركان
active volcano	burkān naʃiṭ (m)	بركان نشط
dormant volcano	burkān xāmid (m)	بركان خامد
eruption	θawrān (m)	ثوران
crater	fūhat al burkān (f)	فوهة البركان
magma	māɣma (f)	ماغما
lava	ḥumam burkāniyya (pl)	حمم بركانيّة
molten (~ lava)	munṣahira	منصهرة
canyon	talʿa (m)	تلعة
gorge	wādi ḍayyiq (m)	واد ضيّق
crevice	ʃaqq (m)	شقّ
abyss (chasm)	hāwiya (f)	هاوية
pass, col	mamarr ʒabaliy (m)	ممرّ جبليّ
plateau	haḍba (f)	هضبة
cliff	ʒurf (m)	جرف
hill	tall (m)	تلّ
glacier	nahr ʒalīdiy (m)	نهر جليديّ
waterfall	ʃallāl (m)	شلّال
geyser	fawwāra ḥārra (m)	فوّارة حارّة
lake	buḥayra (f)	بحيرة
plain	sahl (m)	سهل
landscape	manẓar ṭabīʿiy (m)	منظر طبيعيّ
echo	ṣada (m)	صدى
alpinist	mutasalliq al ʒibāl (m)	متسلّق الجبال
rock climber	mutasalliq ṣuxūr (m)	متسلّق صخور
to conquer (in climbing)	taɣallab ʿala	تغلّب على
climb (an easy ~)	tasalluq (m)	تسلّق

169. Rivers

river	nahr (m)	نهر
spring (natural source)	ʿayn (m)	عين
riverbed (river channel)	maʒra an nahr (m)	مجرى النهر
basin (river valley)	ḥawḍ (m)	حوض
to flow into ...	ṣabb fi ...	صبّ في...
tributary	rāfid (m)	رافد
bank (of river)	ḍiffa (f)	ضفّة

current (stream)	tayyār (m)	تيّار
downstream (adv)	f ittiʒāh maʒra an nahr	في إتجاه مجرى النهر
upstream (adv)	ḍidd at tayyār	ضد التيّار
inundation	ɣamr (m)	غمر
flooding	fayaḍān (m)	فيضان
to overflow (vi)	fāḍ	فاض
to flood (vt)	ɣamar	غمر
shallow (shoal)	miyāh ḍaḥla (f)	مياه ضحلة
rapids	munḥadar an nahr (m)	منحدر النهر
dam	sadd (m)	سدّ
canal	qanāt (f)	قناة
reservoir (artificial lake)	xazzān māʼiy (m)	خزّان مائيّ
sluice, lock	hawīs (m)	هويس
water body (pond, etc.)	masṭaḥ māʼiy (m)	مسطح مائيّ
swamp (marshland)	mustanqaʻ (m)	مستنقع
bog, marsh	mustanqaʻ (m)	مستنقع
whirlpool	dawwāma (f)	دوّامة
stream (brook)	ʒadwal māʼiy (m)	جدول مائيّ
drinking (ab. water)	aʃ ʃurb	الشرب
fresh (~ water)	ʻaðb	عذب
ice	ʒalīd (m)	جليد
to freeze over	taʒammad	تجمّد
(ab. river, etc.)		

170. Forest

forest, wood	ɣāba (f)	غابة
forest (as adj)	ɣāba	غابة
thick forest	ɣāba kaθīfa (f)	غابة كثيفة
grove	ɣāba ṣaɣīra (f)	غابة صغيرة
forest clearing	minṭaqa uzīlat minha al aʃʒār (f)	منطقة أزيلت منها الأشجار
thicket	aʒama (f)	أجمة
scrubland	ʃuʒayrāt (pl)	شجيرات
footpath (troddenpath)	mamarr (m)	ممرّ
gully	wādi ḍayyiq (m)	واد ضيّق
tree	ʃaʒara (f)	شجرة
leaf	waraqa (f)	ورقة
leaves (foliage)	waraq (m)	ورق
fall of leaves	tasāquṭ al awrāq (m)	تساقط الأوراق

| to fall (ab. leaves) | saqaṭ | سقط |
| top (of the tree) | ra's (m) | رأس |

branch	ɣuṣn (m)	غصن
bough	ɣuṣn (m)	غصن
bud (on shrub, tree)	bur'um (m)	برعم
needle (of pine tree)	ʃawka (f)	شوكة
pine cone	kūz aṣ ṣanawbar (m)	كوز الصنوبر

hollow (in a tree)	ʒawf (m)	جوف
nest	'uʃʃ (m)	عشّ
burrow (animal hole)	ʒuḥr (m)	جحر

trunk	ʒiðʻ (m)	جذع
root	ʒiðr (m)	جذر
bark	liḥā' (m)	لحاء
moss	ṭuḥlub (m)	طحلب

to uproot (remove trees or tree stumps)	iqtalaʻ	إقتلع
to chop down	qaṭaʻ	قطع
to deforest (vt)	azāl al ɣābāt	أزال الغابات
tree stump	ʒiðʻ aʃ ʃaʒara (m)	جذع الشجرة

campfire	nār muxayyam (m)	نار مخيّم
forest fire	ḥarīq ɣāba (m)	حريق غابة
to extinguish (vt)	aṭfa'	أطفأ

forest ranger	ḥāris al ɣāba (m)	حارس الغابة
protection	ḥimāya (f)	حماية
to protect (~ nature)	ḥama	حمى
poacher	sāriq aṣ ṣayd (m)	سارق الصيد
steel trap	maṣyada (f)	مصيدة

| to gather, to pick (vt) | ʒamaʻ | جمع |
| to lose one's way | tāh | تاه |

171. Natural resources

natural resources	θarawāt ṭabīʻiyya (pl)	ثروات طبيعيّة
minerals	maʻādin (pl)	معادن
deposits	makāmin (pl)	مكامن
field (e.g., oilfield)	ḥaql (m)	حقل

to mine (extract)	istaxraʒ	إستخرج
mining (extraction)	istixrāʒ (m)	إستخراج
ore	xām (m)	خام
mine (e.g., for coal)	manʒam (m)	منجم
shaft (mine ~)	manʒam (m)	منجم
miner	'āmil manʒam (m)	عامل منجم

gas (natural ~)	ɣāz (m)	غاز
gas pipeline	χaṭṭ anābīb ɣāz (m)	خط أنابيب غاز
oil (petroleum)	naft (m)	نفط
oil pipeline	anābīb an naft (pl)	أنابيب النفط
oil well	bi'r an naft (m)	بئر النفط
derrick (tower)	ḥaffāra (f)	حفّارة
tanker	nāqilat an naft (f)	ناقلة النفط
sand	raml (m)	رمل
limestone	ḥaʒar kalsiy (m)	حجر كلسيّ
gravel	ḥaṣa (m)	حصى
peat	χaθθ faḥm nabātiy (m)	خثّ فحم نباتيّ
clay	ṭīn (m)	طين
coal	faḥm (m)	فحم
iron (ore)	ḥadīd (m)	حديد
gold	ðahab (m)	ذهب
silver	fiḍḍa (f)	فضّة
nickel	nikil (m)	نيكل
copper	nuḥās (m)	نحاس
zinc	zink (m)	زنك
manganese	manɣanīz (m)	منغنيز
mercury	zi'baq (m)	زئبق
lead	ruṣāṣ (m)	رصاص
mineral	maʿdan (m)	معدن
crystal	ballūra (f)	بلّورة
marble	ruχām (m)	رخام
uranium	yurānuim (m)	يورانيوم

The Earth. Part 2

172. Weather

weather	ṭaqs (m)	طقس
weather forecast	naʃra ʒawwiyya (f)	نشرة جوّيّة
temperature	ḥarāra (f)	حرارة
thermometer	tirmūmitr (m)	ترمومتر
barometer	barūmitr (m)	بارومتر
humid (adj)	raṭib	رطب
humidity	ruṭūba (f)	رطوبة
heat (extreme ~)	ḥarāra (f)	حرارة
hot (torrid)	ḥārr	حارّ
it's hot	al ʒaww ḥārr	الجوّ حارّ
it's warm	al ʒaww dāfi'	الجوّ دافئ
warm (moderately hot)	dāfi'	دافئ
it's cold	al ʒaww bārid	الجوّ بارد
cold (adj)	bārid	بارد
sun	ʃams (f)	شمس
to shine (vi)	aḍā'	أضاء
sunny (day)	muʃmis	مشمس
to come up (vi)	ʃaraq	شرق
to set (vi)	ɣarab	غرب
cloud	saḥāba (f)	سحابة
cloudy (adj)	ɣā'im	غائم
rain cloud	saḥābat maṭar (f)	سحابة مطر
somber (gloomy)	ɣā'im	غائم
rain	maṭar (m)	مطر
it's raining	innaha tamṭur	إنّها تمطر
rainy (~ day, weather)	mumṭir	ممطر
to drizzle (vi)	raðð	رذّ
pouring rain	maṭar munhamir (f)	مطر منهمر
downpour	maṭar ɣazīr (m)	مطر غزير
heavy (e.g., ~ rain)	ʃadīd	شديد
puddle	birka (f)	بركة
to get wet (in rain)	ibtall	إبتلّ
fog (mist)	ḍabāb (m)	ضباب
foggy	muḍabbab	مضبّب

| snow | θalʒ (m) | ثلج |
| it's snowing | innaha taθluʒ | إنّها تثلج |

173. Severe weather. Natural disasters

thunderstorm	'āṣifa ra'diyya (f)	عاصفة رعديّة
lightning (~ strike)	barq (m)	برق
to flash (vi)	baraq	برق

thunder	ra'd (m)	رعد
to thunder (vi)	ra'ad	رعد
it's thundering	tar'ad as samā'	ترعد السماء

| hail | maṭar bard (m) | مطر برد |
| it's hailing | tamṭur as samā' bardan | تمطر السماء بردًا |

| to flood (vt) | ɣamar | غمر |
| flood, inundation | fayaḍān (m) | فيضان |

earthquake	zilzāl (m)	زلزال
tremor, quake	hazza arḍiyya (f)	هزّة أرضيّة
epicenter	markaz az zilzāl (m)	مركز الزلزال

| eruption | θawrān (m) | ثوران |
| lava | ḥumam burkāniyya (pl) | حمم بركانيّة |

| twister, tornado | i'ṣār (m) | إعصار |
| typhoon | ṭūfān (m) | طوفان |

hurricane	i'ṣār (m)	إعصار
storm	'āṣifa (f)	عاصفة
tsunami	tsunāmi (m)	تسونامي

cyclone	i'ṣār (m)	إعصار
bad weather	ṭaqs sayyi' (m)	طقس سيّء
fire (accident)	ḥarīq (m)	حريق
disaster	kāriθa (f)	كارثة
meteorite	ḥaʒar nayzakiy (m)	حجر نيزكيّ

avalanche	inhiyār θalʒiy (m)	إنهيار ثلجيّ
snowslide	inhiyār θalʒiy (m)	إنهيار ثلجيّ
blizzard	'āṣifa θalʒiyya (f)	عاصفة ثلجيّة
snowstorm	'āṣifa θalʒiyya (f)	عاصفة ثلجيّة

Fauna

174. Mammals. Predators

predator	ḥayawān muftaris (m)	حيوان مفترس
tiger	namir (m)	نمر
lion	asad (m)	أسد
wolf	ði'b (m)	ذئب
fox	θaʻlab (m)	ثعلب
jaguar	namir amrīkiy (m)	نمر أمريكيّ
leopard	fahd (m)	فهد
cheetah	namir ṣayyād (m)	نمر صيّاد
black panther	namir aswad (m)	نمر أسود
puma	būma (m)	بوما
snow leopard	namir aθ θulūʒ (m)	نمر الثلوج
lynx	waʃaq (m)	وشق
coyote	qayūṭ (m)	قيوط
jackal	ibn 'āwa (m)	ابن آوى
hyena	ḍabuʻ (m)	ضبع

175. Wild animals

animal	ḥayawān (m)	حيوان
beast (animal)	ḥayawān (m)	حيوان
squirrel	sinʒāb (m)	سنجاب
hedgehog	qumfuð (m)	قنفذ
hare	arnab barriy (m)	أرنب بريّ
rabbit	arnab (m)	أرنب
badger	ɣarīr (m)	غرير
raccoon	rākūn (m)	راكون
hamster	qidād (m)	قداد
marmot	marmuṭ (m)	مرموط
mole	xuld (m)	خلد
mouse	fa'r (m)	فأر
rat	ʒurað (m)	جرذ
bat	xuffāʃ (m)	خفّاش
ermine	qāqum (m)	قاقم
sable	sammūr (m)	سمّور

marten	dalaq (m)	دلق
weasel	ibn 'irs (m)	إبن عرس
mink	mink (m)	منك
beaver	qundus (m)	قندس
otter	quḍā'a (f)	قضاعة
horse	ḥiṣān (m)	حصان
moose	mūz (m)	موظ
deer	ayyil (m)	أيّل
camel	ʒamal (m)	جمل
bison	bisūn (m)	بيسون
aurochs	θawr barriy (m)	ثور برّيَ
buffalo	ʒāmūs (m)	جاموس
zebra	ḥimār zarad (m)	حمار زرد
antelope	ẓabiy (m)	ظبي
roe deer	yaḥmūr (m)	يحمور
fallow deer	ayyil asmar urubbiy (m)	أيّل أسمر أوروبّيَ
chamois	ʃamwāh (f)	شامواه
wild boar	xinzīr barriy (m)	خنزير برّيَ
whale	ḥūt (m)	حوت
seal	fuqma (f)	فقمة
walrus	fazẓ (m)	فظّ
fur seal	fuqmat al firā' (f)	فقمة الفراء
dolphin	dilfīn (m)	دلفين
bear	dubb (m)	دبّ
polar bear	dubb quṭbiy (m)	دبّ قطبيّ
panda	bānda (m)	باندا
monkey	qird (m)	قرد
chimpanzee	ʃimbanzi (m)	شيمبانزي
orangutan	urangutān (m)	أورنغوتان
gorilla	ɣurīlla (f)	غوريلا
macaque	qird al makāk (m)	قرد المكاك
gibbon	ʒibbūn (m)	جببون
elephant	fīl (m)	فيل
rhinoceros	xartīt (m)	خرتيت
giraffe	zarāfa (f)	زرافة
hippopotamus	faras an nahr (m)	فرس النهر
kangaroo	kanɣar (m)	كنغر
koala (bear)	kuala (m)	كوالا
mongoose	nims (m)	نمس
chinchilla	ʃinʃila (f)	شنشيلة
skunk	ẓaribān (m)	ظربان
porcupine	nīṣ (m)	نيص

176. Domestic animals

cat	qiṭṭa (f)	قِطَة
tomcat	ðakar al qiṭṭ (m)	ذكر القطّ
dog	kalb (m)	كلب
horse	ḥiṣān (m)	حصان
stallion (male horse)	faḥl al xayl (m)	فحل الخيل
mare	unθa al faras (f)	أنثى الفرس
cow	baqara (f)	بقرة
bull	θawr (m)	ثور
ox	θawr (m)	ثور
sheep (ewe)	xarūf (f)	خروف
ram	kabʃ (m)	كبش
goat	māʿiz (m)	ماعز
billy goat, he-goat	ðakar al māʿið (m)	ذكر الماعز
donkey	ḥimār (m)	حمار
mule	baɣl (m)	بغل
pig, hog	xinzīr (m)	خنزير
piglet	xannūṣ (m)	خنّوص
rabbit	arnab (m)	أرنب
hen (chicken)	daʒāʒa (f)	دجاجة
rooster	dīk (m)	ديك
duck	baṭṭa (f)	بطّة
drake	ðakar al baṭṭ (m)	ذكر البطّ
goose	iwazza (f)	إوزّة
tom turkey, gobbler	dīk rūmiy (m)	ديك رومّي
turkey (hen)	daʒāʒ rūmiy (m)	دجاج رومّي
domestic animals	ḥayawānāt dawāʒin (pl)	حيوانات دواجن
tame (e.g., ~ hamster)	alīf	أليف
to tame (vt)	allaf	ألّف
to breed (vt)	rabba	ربّى
farm	mazraʿa (f)	مزرعة
poultry	ṭuyūr dāʒina (pl)	طيور داجنة
cattle	māʃiya (f)	ماشية
herd (cattle)	qaṭīʿ (m)	قطيع
stable	isṭabl xayl (m)	إسطبل خيل
pigpen	ḥazīrat al xanāzīr (f)	حظيرة الخنازير
cowshed	zirībat al baqar (f)	زريبة البقر
rabbit hutch	qunn al arānib (m)	قنّ الأرانب
hen house	qunn ad daʒāʒ (m)	قن الدجاج

177. Dogs. Dog breeds

dog	kalb (m)	كلب
sheepdog	kalb ra'y (m)	كلب رعي
German shepherd	kalb ar rā'i al almāniy (m)	كلب الراعي الألمانيّ
poodle	būdli (m)	بودل
dachshund	daʃhund (m)	دشهند
bulldog	bulduɣ (m)	بلدغ
boxer	buksir (m)	بوكسر
mastiff	mastīf (m)	ماستيف
Rottweiler	rut vāylir (m)	روت فايلر
Doberman	dubirmān (m)	دوبرمان
basset	bāsit (m)	باسيت
bobtail	bubteyl (m)	بوبتيل
Dalmatian	kalb dalmāsiy (m)	كلب دلماسي
cocker spaniel	kukkir spaniil (m)	كوكر سبانييل
Newfoundland	nyu faundland (m)	نيوفاوندلاند
Saint Bernard	san birnār (m)	سنبرنار
husky	haski (m)	هاسكي
Chow Chow	tʃaw tʃaw (m)	تشاوتشاو
spitz	ʃbītz (m)	شبيتز
pug	bāk (m)	باك

178. Sounds made by animals

barking (n)	nubāḥ (m)	نباح
to bark (vi)	nabaḥ	نبح
to meow (vi)	mā'	ماء
to purr (vi)	ɣarɣar	خرخر
to moo (vi)	ɣār	خار
to bellow (bull)	ɣār	خار
to growl (vi)	damdam	دمدم
howl (n)	'uwā' (m)	عواء
to howl (vi)	'awa	عوى
to whine (vi)	'awa	عوى
to bleat (sheep)	ma'ma'	مأمأ
to oink, to grunt (pig)	qaba'	قبع
to squeal (vi)	ṣāḥ	صاح
to croak (vi)	naqq	نقّ
to buzz (insect)	ṭann	طنّ
to chirp (crickets, grasshopper)	zaqzaq	زقزق

179. Birds

bird	ṭā'ir (m)	طائر
pigeon	ḥamāma (f)	حمامة
sparrow	'uṣfūr (m)	عصفور
tit (great tit)	qurquf (m)	قرقف
magpie	'aq'aq (m)	عقعق
raven	ɣurāb aswad (m)	غراب أسود
crow	ɣurāb (m)	غراب
jackdaw	zāɣ (m)	زاغ
rook	ɣurāb al qayẓ (m)	غراب القيظ
duck	baṭṭa (f)	بطة
goose	iwazza (f)	إوزة
pheasant	tadarruʒ (m)	تدرج
eagle	nasr (m)	نسر
hawk	bāz (m)	باز
falcon	ṣaqr (m)	صقر
vulture	raχam (m)	رخم
condor (Andean ~)	kundūr (m)	كندور
swan	timma (m)	تمّة
crane	kurkiy (m)	كركي
stork	laqlaq (m)	لقلق
parrot	babaɣā' (m)	ببغاء
hummingbird	ṭannān (m)	طنّان
peacock	ṭāwūs (m)	طاووس
ostrich	na'āma (f)	نعامة
heron	balaʃūn (m)	بلشون
flamingo	nuḥām wardiy (m)	نحام وردي
pelican	baʒa'a (f)	بجعة
nightingale	bulbul (m)	بلبل
swallow	sunūnū (m)	سنونو
thrush	sumna (m)	سمنة
song thrush	summuna muɣarrida (m)	سمنة مغرّدة
blackbird	ʃaḥrūr aswad (m)	شحرور أسود
swift	samāma (m)	سمامة
lark	qubbara (f)	قبّرة
quail	sammān (m)	سمّان
woodpecker	naqqār al χaʃab (m)	نقّار الخشب
cuckoo	waqwāq (m)	وقواق
owl	būma (f)	بومة
eagle owl	būm urāsiy (m)	بوم أوراسي

wood grouse	dīk il χalanʒ (m)	ديك الخلنج
black grouse	ṭayhūʒ aswad (m)	طيهوج أسود
partridge	ḥaʒal (m)	حجل

starling	zurzūr (m)	زرزور
canary	kanāriy (m)	كناريّ
hazel grouse	ṭayhūʒ il bunduq (m)	طيهوج البندق
chaffinch	ʃurʃūr (m)	شرشور
bullfinch	diɣnāʃ (m)	دغناش

seagull	nawras (m)	نورس
albatross	al qaṭras (m)	القطرس
penguin	biṭrīq (m)	بطريق

180. Birds. Singing and sounds

to sing (vi)	ɣanna	غنّى
to call (animal, bird)	nāda	نادى
to crow (rooster)	ṣāḥ	صاح
cock-a-doodle-doo	kukukuku	كوكوكوكوكو

to cluck (hen)	qaraq	قرق
to caw (vi)	na'aq	نعق
to quack (duck)	baṭbaṭ	بطبط
to cheep (vi)	ṣa'ṣa'	صأصأ
to chirp, to twitter	zaqzaq	زقزق

181. Fish. Marine animals

bream	abramīs (m)	أبراميس
carp	ʃabbūṭ (m)	شبّوط
perch	farχ (m)	فرخ
catfish	qarmūṭ (m)	قرموط
pike	samak al karāki (m)	سمك الكراكي

| salmon | salmūn (m) | سلمون |
| sturgeon | ḥaʃʃ (m) | حفش |

herring	rinʒa (f)	رنجة
Atlantic salmon	salmūn aṭlasiy (m)	سلمون أطلسيّ
mackerel	usqumriy (m)	أسقمريّ
flatfish	samak mufalṭaḥ (f)	سمك مفلطح

zander, pike perch	samak sandar (m)	سمك سندر
cod	qudd (m)	قدّ
tuna	tūna (f)	تونة
trout	salmūn muraqqaṭ (m)	سلمون مرقّط
eel	ḥankalīs (m)	حنكليس

electric ray	ra''ād (m)	رعّاد
moray eel	murāy (m)	موراي
piranha	birāna (f)	بيرانا

shark	qirʃ (m)	قرش
dolphin	dilfīn (m)	دلفين
whale	ḥūt (m)	حوت

crab	salṭaʿūn (m)	سلطعون
jellyfish	qindīl al baḥr (m)	قنديل البحر
octopus	uxṭubūṭ (m)	أخطبوط

starfish	naʒmat al baḥr (f)	نجمة البحر
sea urchin	qumfuð al baḥr (m)	قنفذ البحر
seahorse	ḥiṣān al baḥr (m)	فرس البحر

oyster	maḥār (m)	محار
shrimp	ʒambari (m)	جمبريَ
lobster	istakūza (f)	إستكوزا
spiny lobster	karkand ʃāik (m)	كركند شائك

182. Amphibians. Reptiles

| snake | θuʿbān (m) | ثعبان |
| venomous (snake) | sāmm | سامّ |

| viper | afʿa (f) | أفعى |
| cobra | kūbra (m) | كوبرا |

| python | biθūn (m) | بيثون |
| boa | buwā' (f) | بواء |

grass snake	θuʿbān al ʿuʃb (m)	ثعبان العشب
rattle snake	afʿa al ʒalʒala (f)	أفعى الجلجلة
anaconda	anakūnda (f)	أناكوندا

| lizard | siḥliyya (f) | سحليّة |
| iguana | iɣwāna (f) | إغوانة |

| monitor lizard | waral (m) | ورل |
| salamander | samandar (m) | سمندر |

| chameleon | ḥirbā' (f) | حرباء |
| scorpion | ʿaqrab (m) | عقرب |

| turtle | sulaḥfāt (f) | سلحفاة |
| frog | ḍifḍaʿ (m) | ضفدع |

| toad | ḍifḍaʿ aṭ ṭīn (m) | ضفدع الطين |
| crocodile | timsāḥ (m) | تمساح |

183. Insects

insect, bug	ḥaʃara (f)	حشرة
butterfly	farāʃa (f)	فراشة
ant	namla (f)	نملة
fly	ðubāba (f)	ذبابة
mosquito	namūsa (f)	ناموسة
beetle	xunfusa (f)	خنفسة
wasp	dabbūr (m)	دبّور
bee	naḥla (f)	نحلة
bumblebee	naḥla ṭannāna (f)	نحلة طنّانة
gadfly (botfly)	naʿra (f)	نعرة
spider	ʿankabūt (m)	عنكبوت
spiderweb	nasīʒ ʿankabūt (m)	نسيج عنكبوت
dragonfly	yaʿsūb (m)	يعسوب
grasshopper	ʒarād (m)	جراد
moth (night butterfly)	ʿitta (f)	عتّة
cockroach	ṣurṣūr (m)	صرصور
tick	qurāda (f)	قرادة
flea	burxūθ (m)	برغوث
midge	baʿūḍa (f)	بعوضة
locust	ʒarād (m)	جراد
snail	ḥalzūn (m)	حلزون
cricket	ṣarrār al layl (m)	صرّار الليل
lightning bug	yarāʿa muḍīʿa (f)	يراعة مضيئة
ladybug	daʿsūqa (f)	دعسوقة
cockchafer	xunfusa kabīra (f)	خنفسة كبيرة
leech	ʿalaqa (f)	علقة
caterpillar	yasrūʿ (m)	يسروع
earthworm	dūda (f)	دودة
larva	yaraqa (f)	يرقة

184. Animals. Body parts

beak	minqār (m)	منقار
wings	aʒniḥa (pl)	أجنحة
foot (of bird)	riʒl (f)	رجل
feathers (plumage)	rīʃ (m)	ريش
feather	rīʃa (f)	ريشة
crest	tāʒ (m)	تاج
gills	xayāʃīm (pl)	خياشيم
spawn	bayḍ as samak (pl)	بيض السمك

larva	yaraqa (f)	يرقة
fin	zi'nifa (f)	زعنفة
scales (of fish, reptile)	ḥarãfiʃ (pl)	حرافش
fang (canine)	nãb (m)	ناب
paw (e.g., cat's ~)	qadam (f)	قدم
muzzle (snout)	χaṭm (m)	خطم
mouth (of cat, dog)	fam (m)	فم
tail	ðayl (m)	ذيل
whiskers	ʃawãrib (pl)	شوارب
hoof	ḥãfir (m)	حافر
horn	qarn (m)	قرن
carapace	dir' (m)	درع
shell (of mollusk)	maḥãra (f)	محارة
eggshell	qiʃrat bayḍa (f)	قشرة بيضة
animal's hair (pelage)	ʃa'r (m)	شعر
pelt (hide)	ʒild (m)	جلد

185. Animals. Habitats

habitat	mawṭin (m)	موطن
migration	hiʒra (f)	هجرة
mountain	ʒabal (m)	جبل
reef	ʃi'ãb (pl)	شعاب
cliff	ʒurf (m)	جرف
forest	ɣãba (f)	غابة
jungle	adɣãl (pl)	أدغال
savanna	savãnna (f)	سافانّا
tundra	tundra (f)	تندرا
steppe	sahb (m)	سهب
desert	ṣaḥrã' (f)	صحراء
oasis	wãḥa (f)	واحة
sea	baḥr (m)	بحر
lake	buḥayra (f)	بحيرة
ocean	muḥīṭ (m)	محيط
swamp (marshland)	mustanqa' (m)	مستنقع
freshwater (adj)	al miyãh al 'aðba	المياه العذبة
pond	birka (f)	بركة
river	nahr (m)	نهر
den (bear's ~)	wakr (m)	وكر
nest	'uʃʃ (m)	عشّ

hollow (in a tree)	ʒawf (m)	جوف
burrow (animal hole)	ʒuḥr (m)	جحر
anthill	ʿuʃʃ naml (m)	عشّ نمل

Flora

186. Trees

tree	ʃaʒara (f)	شجرة
deciduous (adj)	nafḍiyya	نفضيّة
coniferous (adj)	ṣanawbariyya	صنوبريّة
evergreen (adj)	dā'imat al xuḍra	دائمة الخضرة
apple tree	ʃaʒarat tuffāḥ (f)	شجرة تفّاح
pear tree	ʃaʒarat kummaθra (f)	شجرة كمّثرى
cherry tree	ʃaʒarat karaz (f)	شجرة كرز
plum tree	ʃaʒarat barqūq (f)	شجرة برقوق
birch	batūla (f)	بتولا
oak	ballūṭ (f)	بلّوط
linden tree	ʃaʒarat zayzafūn (f)	شجرة زيزفون
aspen	ḥawr raʒrāʒ (m)	حور رجراج
maple	qayqab (f)	قيقب
spruce	ratinaʒ (f)	راتينج
pine	ṣanawbar (f)	صنوبر
larch	arziyya (f)	أرزيّة
fir tree	tannūb (f)	تنّوب
cedar	arz (f)	أرز
poplar	ḥawr (f)	حور
rowan	ɣubayrā' (f)	غبيراء
willow	ṣafṣāf (f)	صفصاف
alder	ʒār il mā' (m)	جار الماء
beech	zān (m)	زان
elm	dardār (f)	دردار
ash (tree)	marān (f)	مران
chestnut	kastanā' (f)	كستناء
magnolia	maɣnūliya (f)	مغنوليا
palm tree	naxla (f)	نخلة
cypress	sarw (f)	سرو
mangrove	ayka sāḥiliyya (f)	أيكة ساحليّة
baobab	bāubāb (f)	باوباب
eucalyptus	ukaliptus (f)	أوكالبتوس
sequoia	siqūya (f)	سيكويا

187. Shrubs

bush	ʃuʒayra (f)	شجيرة
shrub	ʃuʒayrāt (pl)	شجيرات
grapevine	karma (f)	كرمة
vineyard	karam (m)	كرم
raspberry bush	tūt al ʿullayq al aḥmar (m)	توت العُليق الأحمر
redcurrant bush	kiʃmiʃ aḥmar (m)	كشمش أحمر
gooseberry bush	ʿinab aθ θaʿlab (m)	عنب الثعلب
acacia	sanṭ (f)	سنط
barberry	amīr barīs (m)	أمير باريس
jasmine	yāsmīn (m)	ياسمين
juniper	ʿarʿar (m)	عرعر
rosebush	ʃuʒayrat ward (f)	شجيرة ورد
dog rose	ward ʒabaliy (m)	ورد جبليّ

188. Mushrooms

mushroom	fuṭr (f)	فطر
edible mushroom	fuṭr ṣāliḥ lil akl (m)	فطر صالح للأكل
poisonous mushroom	fuṭr sāmm (m)	فطر سامّ
cap (of mushroom)	ṭarbūʃ al fuṭr (m)	طربوش الفطر
stipe (of mushroom)	sāq al fuṭr (m)	ساق الفطر
cep (Boletus edulis)	fuṭr bulīt maʾkūl (m)	فطر بوليط مأكول
orange-cap boletus	fuṭr aḥmar (m)	فطر أحمر
birch bolete	fuṭr bulīt (m)	فطر بوليط
chanterelle	fuṭr kwīzi (m)	فطر كويزي
russula	fuṭr russūla (m)	فطر روسولا
morel	fuṭr al ɣūʃna (m)	فطر الغوشنة
fly agaric	fuṭr amānīt aṭ ṭāʾir as sāmm (m)	فطر أمانيت الطائر السامّ
death cap	fuṭr amānīt falusyāniy as sāmm (m)	فطر أمانيت فالوسياني السامّ

189. Fruits. Berries

fruit	θamra (f)	ثمرة
fruits	θamr (m)	ثمر
apple	tuffāḥa (f)	تفّاحة
pear	kummaθra (f)	كمّثرى
plum	barqūq (m)	برقوق

strawberry (garden ~)	farawla (f)	فراولة
cherry	karaz (m)	كرز
grape	'inab (m)	عنب
raspberry	tūt al 'ullayq al aḥmar (m)	توت العليق الأحمر
blackcurrant	'inab aθ θa'lab al aswad (m)	عنب الثعلب الأسود
redcurrant	kiʃmiʃ aḥmar (m)	كشمش أحمر
gooseberry	'inab aθ θa'lab (m)	عنب الثعلب
cranberry	tūt aḥmar barriy (m)	توت أحمر برّيَ
orange	burtuqāl (m)	برتقال
mandarin	yūsufiy (m)	يوسفي
pineapple	ananās (m)	أناناس
banana	mawz (m)	موز
date	tamr (m)	تمر
lemon	laymūn (m)	ليمون
apricot	miʃmiʃ (f)	مشمش
peach	durrāq (m)	دراق
kiwi	kiwi (m)	كيوي
grapefruit	zinbā' (m)	زنباع
berry	ḥabba (f)	حبّة
berries	ḥabbāt (pl)	حبّات
cowberry	'inab aθ θawr (m)	عنب الثور
wild strawberry	farāwla barriyya (f)	فراولة برّية
bilberry	'inab al aḥrāʒ (m)	عنب الأحراج

190. Flowers. Plants

flower	zahra (f)	زهرة
bouquet (of flowers)	bāqat zuhūr (f)	باقة زهور
rose (flower)	warda (f)	وردة
tulip	tulīb (f)	توليب
carnation	qurumful (m)	قرنفل
gladiolus	dalbūθ (f)	دلبوث
cornflower	turunʃāh (m)	ترنشاه
harebell	ʒarīs (m)	جريس
dandelion	hindibā' (f)	هندباء
camomile	babunʒ (m)	بابونج
aloe	aluwwa (m)	ألوَة
cactus	ṣabbār (m)	صبّار
rubber plant, ficus	tīn (m)	تين
lily	sawsan (m)	سوسن
geranium	ibrat ar rā'i (f)	إبرة الراعي

hyacinth	zanbaq (f)	زنبق
mimosa	mimūza (f)	ميموزا
narcissus	narʒis (f)	نرجس
nasturtium	abu xanʒar (f)	أبو خنجر
orchid	saḥlab (f)	سحلب
peony	fawniya (f)	فاوانيا
violet	banafsaʒ (f)	بنفسج

pansy	banafsaʒ muθallaθ (m)	بنفسج مثلث
forget-me-not	'āðān al fa'r (pl)	آذان الفأر
daisy	uqḥuwān (f)	أقحوان

poppy	xaʃxāʃ (f)	خشخاش
hemp	qinnab (m)	قنب
mint	na'nā' (m)	نعناع

lily of the valley	sawsan al wādi (m)	سوسن الوادي
snowdrop	zahrat al laban (f)	زهرة اللبن
nettle	qarrāṣ (m)	قرّاص
sorrel	ḥammāḍ (m)	حمّاض
water lily	nilūfar (m)	نيلوفر
fern	saraxs (m)	سرخس
lichen	uʃna (f)	أشنة

greenhouse (tropical ~)	dafī'a (f)	دفيئة
lawn	'uʃb (m)	عشب
flowerbed	ʒunaynat zuhūr (f)	جنينة زهور

plant	nabāt (m)	نبات
grass	'uʃb (m)	عشب
blade of grass	'uʃba (f)	عشبة

leaf	waraqa (f)	ورقة
petal	waraqat az zahra (f)	ورقة الزهرة
stem	sāq (f)	ساق
tuber	darnat nabāt (f)	درنة نبات

| young plant (shoot) | nabta saɣīra (f) | نبتة صغيرة |
| thorn | ʃawka (f) | شوكة |

to blossom (vi)	nawwar	نوّر
to fade, to wither	ðabal	ذبل
smell (odor)	rā'iḥa (f)	رائحة
to cut (flowers)	qaṭa'	قطع
to pick (a flower)	qaṭaf	قطف

191. Cereals, grains

| grain | ḥubūb (pl) | حبوب |
| cereal crops | maḥāṣīl al ḥubūb (pl) | محاصيل الحبوب |

ear (of barley, etc.)	sumbula (f)	سنبلة
wheat	qamḥ (m)	قمح
rye	ʒāwdār (m)	جاودار
oats	ʃūfān (m)	شوفان
millet	duχn (m)	دخن
barley	ʃaʕīr (m)	شعير
corn	ðura (f)	ذرَة
rice	urz (m)	أرز
buckwheat	ḥinṭa sawdā' (f)	حنطة سوداء
pea plant	bisilla (f)	بسلّة
kidney bean	faṣūliya (f)	فاصوليا
soy	fūl aṣ ṣūya (m)	فول الصويا
lentil	'adas (m)	عدس
beans (pulse crops)	fūl (m)	فول

REGIONAL GEOGRAPHY

Countries. Nationalities

192. Politics. Government. Part 1

politics	siyāsa (f)	سياسة
political (adj)	siyāsiy	سياسي
politician	siyāsiy (m)	سياسي
state (country)	dawla (f)	دولة
citizen	muwāṭin (m)	مواطن
citizenship	ʒinsiyya (f)	جنسية
national emblem	ʃiʿār waṭaniy (m)	شعار وطني
national anthem	naʃīd waṭaniy (m)	نشيد وطني
government	ḥukūma (f)	حكومة
head of state	ra's ad dawla (m)	رأس الدولة
parliament	barlamān (m)	برلمان
party	ḥizb (m)	حزب
capitalism	ra'smāliyya (f)	رأسمالية
capitalist (adj)	ra'smāliy	رأسمالي
socialism	iʃtirākiyya (f)	إشتراكية
socialist (adj)	iʃtirākiy	إشتراكي
communism	ʃuyūʿiyya (f)	شيوعية
communist (adj)	ʃuyūʿiy	شيوعي
communist (n)	ʃuyūʿiy (m)	شيوعي
democracy	dimuqraṭiyya (f)	ديموقراطية
democrat	dimuqrāṭiy (m)	ديموقراطي
democratic (adj)	dimuqrāṭiy	ديموقراطي
Democratic party	al ḥizb ad dimukrāṭiy (m)	الحزب الديموقراطي
liberal (n)	libirāliy (m)	ليبرالي
liberal (adj)	libirāliy	ليبرالي
conservative (n)	muḥāfiẓ (m)	محافظ
conservative (adj)	muḥāfiẓ	محافظ
republic (n)	ʒumhūriyya (f)	جمهورية
republican (n)	ʒumhūriy (m)	جمهوري
Republican party	al ḥizb al ʒumhūriy (m)	الحزب الجمهوري

elections	intixābāt (pl)	إنتخابات
to elect (vt)	intaxab	إنتخب
elector, voter	nāxib (m)	ناخب
election campaign	ḥamla intixābiyya (f)	حملة إنتخابيَة

voting (n)	taṣwīt (m)	تصويت
to vote (vi)	ṣawwat	صوَت
suffrage, right to vote	ḥaqq al intixāb (m)	حقَ الإنتخاب

candidate	muraʃʃaḥ (m)	مرشَح
to be a candidate	raʃʃaḥ nafsahu	رشَح نفسه
campaign	ḥamla (f)	حملة

| opposition (as adj) | muʻāriḍ | معارض |
| opposition (n) | muʻāraḍa (f) | معارضة |

visit	ziyāra (f)	زيارة
official visit	ziyāra rasmiyya (f)	زيارة رسميَة
international (adj)	duwaliy	دوليَ

| negotiations | mubāḥaθāt (pl) | مباحثات |
| to negotiate (vi) | aʒra mubāḥaθāt | أجرى مباحثات |

193. Politics. Government. Part 2

society	muʒtamaʻ (m)	مجتمع
constitution	dustūr (m)	دستور
power (political control)	sulṭa (f)	سلطة
corruption	fasād (m)	فساد

| law (justice) | qānūn (m) | قانون |
| legal (legitimate) | qānūniy | قانونيَ |

| justice (fairness) | ʻadāla (f) | عدالة |
| just (fair) | ʻādil | عادل |

committee	laʒna (f)	لجنة
bill (draft law)	maʃrūʻ qānūn (m)	مشروع قانون
budget	mīzāniyya (f)	ميزانيَة
policy	siyāsa (f)	سياسة
reform	iṣlāḥ (m)	إصلاح
radical (adj)	radikāliy	راديكاليَ

power (strength, force)	quwwa (f)	قوَة
powerful (adj)	qawiy	قويَ
supporter	muʼayyid (m)	مؤيَد
influence	taʼθīr (m)	تأثير

| regime (e.g., military ~) | niẓām ḥukm (m) | نظام حكم |
| conflict | xilāf (m) | خلاف |

conspiracy (plot)	mu'āmara (f)	مؤامرة
provocation	istifzāz (m)	إستفزاز
to overthrow (regime, etc.)	asqaṭ	أسقط
overthrow (of government)	isqāṭ (m)	إسقاط
revolution	θawra (f)	ثورة
coup d'état	inqilāb (m)	إنقلاب
military coup	inqilāb 'askariy (m)	انقلاب عسكريّ
crisis	azma (f)	أزمة
economic recession	rukūd iqtiṣādiy (m)	ركود إقتصاديّ
demonstrator (protester)	mutaẓāhir (m)	متظاهر
demonstration	muẓāhara (f)	مظاهرة
martial law	al aḥkām al 'urfiyya (pl)	الأحكام العرفيّة
military base	qa'ida 'askariyya (f)	قاعدة عسكريّة
stability	istiqrār (m)	إستقرار
stable (adj)	mustaqirr	مستقرّ
exploitation	istiɣlāl (m)	إستغلال
to exploit (workers)	istaɣall	إستغلّ
racism	'unṣuriyya (f)	عنصريّة
racist	'unṣuriy (m)	عنصريّ
fascism	fāʃiyya (f)	فاشيّة
fascist	fāʃiy (m)	فاشيّ

194. Countries. Miscellaneous

foreigner	aʒnabiy (m)	أجنبيّ
foreign (adj)	aʒnabiy	أجنبيّ
abroad	fil xāriʒ	في الخارج
(in a foreign country)		
emigrant	nāziḥ (m)	نازح
emigration	nuziḥ (m)	نزوح
to emigrate (vi)	nazūḥ	نزح
the West	al ɣarb (m)	الغرب
the East	aʃ ʃarq (m)	الشرق
the Far East	aʃ ʃarq al aqṣa (m)	الشرق الأقصى
civilization	ḥaḍāra (f)	حضارة
humanity (mankind)	al baʃariyya (f)	البشريّة
the world (earth)	al 'ālam (m)	العالم
peace	salām (m)	سلام
worldwide (adj)	'ālamiy	عالميّ
homeland	waṭan (m)	وطن
people (population)	ʃa'b (m)	شعب

population	sukkān (pl)	سكّان
people (a lot of ~)	nās (pl)	ناس
nation (people)	umma (f)	أمّة
generation	ʒīl (m)	جيل
territory (area)	arḍ (f)	أرض
region	mintaqa (f)	منطقة
state (part of a country)	wilāya (f)	ولاية
tradition	taqlīd (m)	تقليد
custom (tradition)	ʿāda (f)	عادة
ecology	ʿilm al bīʿa (m)	علم البيئة
Indian (Native American)	hindiy aḥmar (m)	هنديَ أحمر
Gypsy (masc.)	ɣaʒariy (m)	غجريَ
Gypsy (fem.)	ɣaʒariyya (f)	غجريّة
Gypsy (adj)	ɣaʒariy	غجريَ
empire	imbiraṭuriyya (f)	امبراطوريّة
colony	mustaʿmara (f)	مستعمرة
slavery	ʿubūdiyya (f)	عبوديّة
invasion	ɣazw (m)	غزو
famine	maʒāʿa (f)	مجاعة

195. Major religious groups. Confessions

religion	dīn (m)	دين
religious (adj)	dīniy	دينيَ
faith, belief	ʾīmān (m)	إيمان
to believe (in God)	ʾāman	آمن
believer	muʾmin (m)	مؤمن
atheism	al ilḥād (m)	الإلحاد
atheist	mulḥid (m)	ملحد
Christianity	al masīḥiyya (f)	المسيحيّة
Christian (n)	masīḥiy (m)	مسيحيَ
Christian (adj)	masīḥiy	مسيحيَ
Catholicism	al kaθūlikiyya (f)	الكاثوليكيّة
Catholic (n)	kaθulīkiy (m)	كـاثوليكيَ
Catholic (adj)	kaθulīkiy	كـاثوليكيَ
Protestantism	al brutistantiyya (f)	البروتستانتية
Protestant Church	al kanīsa al brutistantiyya (f)	الكنيسة البروتستانتيَّ
Protestant (n)	brutistantiy (m)	بروتستانتيَ
Orthodoxy	urθuðuksiyya (f)	الأرثوذكسيّة
Orthodox Church	al kanīsa al urθuðuksiyya (f)	الكنيسة الأرثوذكسيّة

Orthodox (n)	urθuðuksiy (m)	أرثوذكسيّ
Presbyterianism	maʃixiyya (f)	المشيخيّة
Presbyterian Church	al kanīsa al maʃixiyya (f)	الكنيسة المشيخيّة
Presbyterian (n)	maʃixiy (m)	مشيخيّ
Lutheranism	al kanīsa al luθiriyya (f)	الكنيسة اللوثريّة
Lutheran (n)	luθiriy (m)	لوثريّ
Baptist Church	al kanīsa al ma'madāniyya (f)	الكنيسة المعمدانيّة
Baptist (n)	ma'madāniy (m)	معمدانيّ
Anglican Church	al kanīsa al anʒlikāniyya (f)	الكنيسة الإنجليكانيّة
Anglican (n)	anʒlikāniy (m)	أنجليكانيّ
Mormonism	al murumūniyya (f)	المورمونيّة
Mormon (n)	masīhiy murmūn (m)	مسيحيّ مرمون
Judaism	al yahūdiyya (f)	اليهودية
Jew (n)	yahūdiy (m)	يهوديّ
Buddhism	al būðiyya (f)	البوذيّة
Buddhist (n)	būðiy (m)	بوذيّ
Hinduism	al hindūsiyya (f)	الهندوسيّة
Hindu (n)	hindūsiy (m)	هندوسيّ
Islam	al islām (m)	الإسلام
Muslim (n)	muslim (m)	مسلم
Muslim (adj)	islāmiy	إسلاميّ
Shiah Islam	al maðhab aʃʃiʕiy (m)	المذهب الشيعيّ
Shiite (n)	ʃiʕiy (m)	شيعيّ
Sunni Islam	al maðhab as sunniy (m)	المذهب السنّيّ
Sunnite (n)	sunniy (m)	سنّيّ

196. Religions. Priests

priest	qissīs (m), kāhin (m)	قسّيس, كاهن
the Pope	al bāba (m)	البابا
monk, friar	rāhib (m)	راهب
nun	rāhiba (f)	راهبة
pastor	qissīs (m)	قسّيس
abbot	ra'īs ad dayr (m)	رئيس الدير
vicar (parish priest)	viqār (m)	فيقار
bishop	usquf (m)	أسقف
cardinal	kardināl (m)	كاردينال
preacher	tabʃīr (m)	تبشير
preaching	xutba (f)	خطبة

parishioners	ra'iyyat al abraʃiyya (f)	رعية الأبرشيّة
believer	mu'min (m)	مؤمن
atheist	mulḥid (m)	ملحد

197. Faith. Christianity. Islam

| Adam | 'ādam (m) | آدم |
| Eve | ḥawā' (f) | حواء |

God	allah (m)	الله
the Lord	ar rabb (m)	الربّ
the Almighty	al qadīr (m)	القدير

sin	ðamb (m)	ذنب
to sin (vi)	aðnab	أذنب
sinner (masc.)	muðnib (m)	مذنب
sinner (fem.)	muðniba (f)	مذنبة

| hell | al ʒaḥīm (f) | الجحيم |
| paradise | al ʒanna (f) | الجنّة |

| Jesus | yasū' (m) | يسوع |
| Jesus Christ | yasū' al masīḥ (m) | يسوع المسيح |

the Holy Spirit	ar rūḥ al qudus (m)	الروح القدس
the Savior	al masīḥ (m)	المسيح
the Virgin Mary	maryam al 'aðrā' (f)	مريم العذراء

the Devil	aʃ ʃayṭān (m)	الشيطان
devil's (adj)	ʃayṭāniy	شيطانيّ
Satan	aʃ ʃayṭān (m)	الشيطان
satanic (adj)	ʃayṭāniy	شيطانيّ

angel	malāk (m)	ملاك
guardian angel	malāk ḥāris (m)	ملاك حارس
angelic (adj)	malā'ikiy	ملائكيّ

apostle	rasūl (m)	رسول
archangel	al malak ar ra'īsiy (m)	الملك الرئيسي
the Antichrist	al masīḥ ad daʒʒāl (m)	المسيح الدجّال

Church	al kanīsa (f)	الكنيسة
Bible	al kitāb al muqaddas (m)	الكتاب المقدّس
biblical (adj)	tawrātiy	توراتيّ

Old Testament	al 'ahd al qadīm (m)	العهد القديم
New Testament	al 'ahd al ʒadīd (m)	العهد الجديد
Gospel	inʒīl (m)	إنجيل
Holy Scripture	al kitāb al muqaddas (m)	الكتاب المقدّس
Heaven	al ʒanna (f)	الجنّة

Commandment	waṣiyya (f)	وصيّة
prophet	nabiy (m)	نبيّ
prophecy	nubū'a (f)	نبوءة

Allah	allah (m)	الله
Mohammed	muḥammad (m)	محمّد
the Koran	al qur'ān (m)	القرآن

mosque	masʒid (m)	مسجد
mullah	mulla (m)	ملّا
prayer	ṣalāt (f)	صلاة
to pray (vi, vt)	ṣalla	صلّى

pilgrimage	haʒʒ (m)	حجّ
pilgrim	ḥāʒʒ (m)	حاجّ
Mecca	makka al mukarrama (f)	مكة المكرّمة

church	kanīsa (f)	كنيسة
temple	ma'bad (m)	معبد
cathedral	katidrā'iyya (f)	كاتدرائيّة
Gothic (adj)	qūṭiy	قوطيّ
synagogue	kanīs ma'bad yahūdiy (m)	كنيس معبد يهوديّ
mosque	masʒid (m)	مسجد

chapel	kanīsa saɣīra (f)	كنيسة صغيرة
abbey	dayr (m)	دير
convent	dayr (m)	دير
monastery	dayr (m)	دير

bell (church ~s)	ʒaras (m)	جرس
bell tower	burʒ al ʒaras (m)	برج الجرس
to ring (ab. bells)	daqq	دقّ

cross	ṣalīb (m)	صليب
cupola (roof)	qubba (f)	قبّة
icon	īkūna (f)	ايقونة

soul	nafs (f)	نفس
fate (destiny)	maṣīr (m)	مصير
evil (n)	ʃarr (m)	شرّ
good (n)	χayr (m)	خير

vampire	maṣṣāṣ dimā' (m)	مصّاص دماء
witch (evil ~)	sāḥira (f)	ساحرة
demon	ʃayṭān (m)	شيطان
spirit	rūḥ (m)	روح

| redemption (giving us ~) | takfīr (m) | تكفير |
| to redeem (vt) | kaffar 'an | كفّر عن |

| church service, mass | qaddās (m) | قدّاس |
| to say mass | alqa χuṭba bil kanīsa | ألقى خطبة بالكنيسة |

confession	i'tirāf (m)	إعتراف
to confess (vi)	i'taraf	إعترف
saint (n)	qiddīs (m)	قدّيس
sacred (holy)	muqaddas (m)	مقدّس
holy water	mā' muqaddas (m)	ماء مقدّس
ritual (n)	ṭuqūs (pl)	طقوس
ritual (adj)	ṭuqūsiy	طقوسيّ
sacrifice	ðabīḥa (f)	ذبيحة
superstition	xurāfa (f)	خرافة
superstitious (adj)	mu'min bil xurāfāt (m)	مؤمن بالخرافات
afterlife	al 'āxira (f)	الآخرة
eternal life	al ḥayāt al abadiyya (f)	الحياة الأبدية

MISCELLANEOUS

198. Various useful words

background (green ~)	χalfiyya (f)	خلفيّة
balance (of situation)	tawāzun (m)	توازن
barrier (obstacle)	ḥāʒiz (m)	حاجز
base (basis)	asās (m)	أساس
beginning	bidāya (f)	بداية
category	fiʾa (f)	فئة
cause (reason)	sabab (m)	سبب
choice	iχtiyār (m)	إختيار
coincidence	ṣudfa (f)	صدفة
comfortable (~ chair)	murīḥ	مريح
comparison	muqārana (f)	مقارنة
compensation	taʿwīḍ (m)	تعويض
degree (extent, amount)	daraʒa (f)	درجة
development	tanmiya (f)	تنمية
difference	farq (m)	فرق
effect (e.g., of drugs)	taʾθīr (m)	تأثير
effort (exertion)	ʒuhd (m)	جهد
element	ʿunṣur (m)	عنصر
end (finish)	nihāya (f)	نهاية
example (illustration)	miθāl (m)	مثال
fact	ḥaqīqa (f)	حقيقة
frequent (adj)	mutakarrir (m)	متكرّر
growth (development)	numuww (m)	نموّ
help	musāʿada (f)	مساعدة
ideal	miθāl (m)	مثال
kind (sort, type)	nawʿ (m)	نوع
labyrinth	tayh (m)	تيه
mistake, error	χaṭaʾ (m)	خطأ
moment	laḥẓa (f)	لحظة
object (thing)	mawḍūʿ (m)	موضوع
obstacle	ʿaqba (f)	عقبة
original (original copy)	aṣl (m)	أصل
part (~ of sth)	ʒuzʾ (m)	جزء
particle, small part	ʒuzʾ (m)	جزء
pause (break)	istirāḥa (f)	إستراحة

position	mawqif (m)	موقف
principle	mabda' (m)	مبدأ
problem	muʃkila (f)	مشكلة

process	'amaliyya (f)	عمليّة
progress	taqaddum (m)	تقدّم
property (quality)	χaṣṣa (f)	خاصّة
reaction	radd fiʻl (m)	ردّ فعل
risk	muχāṭara (f)	مخاطرة

secret	sirr (m)	سرّ
series	silsila (f)	سلسلة
shape (outer form)	ʃakl (m)	شكل
situation	ḥāla (f), waḍʻ (m)	حالة, وضع
solution	ḥall (m)	حلّ

standard (adj)	qiyāsiy	قياسيّ
standard (level of quality)	qiyās (m)	قياس
stop (pause)	istirāḥa (f)	إستراحة
style	uslūb (m)	أسلوب

system	niẓām (m)	نظام
table (chart)	ӡadwal (m)	جدول
tempo, rate	surʻa (f)	سرعة
term (word, expression)	muṣṭalaḥ (m)	مصطلح

thing (object, item)	ʃay' (m)	شيء
truth (e.g., moment of ~)	ḥaqīqa (f)	حقيقة
turn (please wait your ~)	dawr (m)	دور
type (sort, kind)	nawʻ (m)	نوع
urgent (adj)	ʻāӡil	عاجل

urgently (adv)	ʻāӡilan	عاجلًا
utility (usefulness)	manfaʻa (f)	منفعة
variant (alternative)	ʃakl muχtalif (m)	شكل مختلف
way (means, method)	ṭarīqa (f)	طريقة
zone	mintaqa (f)	منطقة

www.ingramcontent.com/pod-product-compliance
Lightning Source LLC
LaVergne TN
LVHW051302080426
835509LV00020B/3112